MARKETING
for the
NONMARKETING EXECUTIVE

An Integrated Resource Management
Guide for the 21st Century

The St. Lucie Press
Library of Executive Excellence Series

MARKETING
for the
NONMARKETING EXECUTIVE

An Integrated Resource Management
Guide for the 21st Century

NORTON PALEY

S^t_L

St. Lucie Press
Boca Raton London New York Washington, D.C.

#44914289

Library of Congress Cataloging-in-Publication Data

Paley, Norton
    Marketing for the nonmarketing executive : an integrated resource management guide
for the 21st century / Norton Paley.
        p. cm.-- (Library of executive excellence)
  Includes index.
  ISBN 1-57444-286-4
  1. Marketing. 2. Marketing--Management. I Title. II. Series.

  HF5415 .P2333 2000
  658.8—dc21

                                       00-062767

© 2001 by Norton Paley
St. Lucie Press is an imprint of CRC Press LLC

No claim to original U.S. Government works
International Standard Book Number 1-57444-286-4
Library of Congress Card Number 00-062767
Printed in the United States of America 1 2 3 4 5 6 7 8 9 0
Printed on acid-free paper

Preface

As a nonmarketing manager, why should you even think about marketing? How would internalizing the fine points of the subject contribute to your effectiveness on the job? What are the competitive consequences of operating as a marketing-oriented company vs. focusing only on cost and production efficiencies? How is marketing practiced today and what significance does it have for your company operating in the Internet Age? Is it a discipline consisting mainly of advertising and selling and shouldn't those activities be left to their respective functions?

This book promises to dispel any misguided notions about marketing and answer the above questions in enough detail to keep you current and fully in tune with contemporary strategies essential to winning over competing organizations. Further, the central outcome of the book is to provide the underpinnings that will help your organization enjoy a bountiful share in the colossal growth promised for the 21st century.

There could hardly be a better time for understanding marketing's prominence in most of the evolving business models. The Internet Age presents vastly different conditions from those that existed during most of the 20th century.

First, 21st-century managers face an increasing number of global competitors shaped by an undiminishing rate of domestic and cross-ocean mergers and acquisitions. The once insignificant rival of yesterday is often the formidable challenger of today.

Second, Internet entrepreneurs and dot-com companies leap into so-called secure markets and whisk away formerly loyal customers with unanticipated frequency and audacious intensity.

Third, mind-boggling new technologies continue to harness innovative products that are individualized to customers' exacting specifications. And new forms of communications connect sellers to waiting customers with astonishing speed.

And that's not all. There are the proliferating effects of changing demographics, shifting life styles, fragmented geographic markets, and emerging cultural influences that demand imaginative marketing strategies.

Here's how the various nonmarketing functions can benefit from a pragmatic knowledge of marketing principles:

- Upper-level executives or business owners can benefit by internalizing the full meaning of the time-tested marketing concepts that shape a company's success. Those concepts are the underpinnings of a customer-driven organization attempting to operate in a dynamic environment of e-business and e-commerce.
- Finance executives will profit from knowing more about marketing methods as they attempt to understand (and perhaps even empathize with) many of the budget requests and expenditures related to the marketing function.

- Production managers are more apt to grasp a comprehensive picture of the total marketing situation and learn why some of the best products are dropped, certain ones retained, and still others replaced just when optimum production efficiencies are in place.
- Accountants will understand the strategic necessity for the intermittent surges in promotional expenses that play havoc with seemingly well-tailored plans.
- Design engineers or R&D scientists will learn that marketers often use similar scientific methods and apply them to marketing issues. Also, they will learn how to garner support from marketers for advanced technology that can quickly and efficiently be translated into differentiated or value-added products.

Consequently, don't view this book as nice-to-know information. Instead, focus on its primary objectives: (1) to induce you to implement positive change within your company by arming you with the best practices from the winning companies of the past few decades and with those that are evolving in today's new economy; (2) to provide pragmatic guidelines to help you develop competitive strategies for the Internet Age; and (3) to encourage you to create a best-in-class operation against those competing organizations that would relish the notion of dislodging your organization from growing markets.

Imbedded in these objectives are two primary considerations: first, internal changes within your organization are needed if you are to respond to volatile market movements; and second, strategies and tactics are needed to implement meaningful changes that would affect your competitive performance in erratic markets.

ORGANIZATION OF THE BOOK

You can use this book in two ways:

1. You can read the book cover to cover and acquire the basic concepts, explanations, and techniques about marketing.
2. You can jump into the book at any chapter that interests you and receive the mental nourishment and stimulation to tackle your business problems with fresh energy and new ideas.

Within each chapter you will find numerous step-by-step guidelines, actual company examples to provide practical assistance for your business, and summary guidelines in the form of best practices. For instance:

Chapter 1: Describes the evolution of marketing by using five actual case examples. Discusses the value of cross-functional teams and the impact of relationship marketing in organizing for change.

Chapter 2: Talks about the world of markets. Reviews the techniques of locating and evaluating viable market segments.

Chapter 3: Digs into the essence of strategy for the 21st century. Pinpoints the approaches to sharpening strategy skills through the use of the marketing mix. Demonstrates the impact of external forces, such as competition, industry, and the environment on business plans.

Chapter 4: Focuses on the predominant influences and techniques of market intelligence to drive decisions, not only for marketing, but for virtually every function of the organization.

Chapter 5: Emphasizes new product and service development as the cornerstone of corporate growth and vitality. Deals with all aspects of product positioning and implementing a product mix strategy.

Chapter 6: Accentuates customer relationship management and how to integrate customer-driven marketing techniques with the Internet Age.

Chapter 7: Underscores supply chain management as the new era in logistics and distribution. Provides guidelines for choosing a distributor and maintaining channel control.

Chapter 8: Deals with the essence of marketing communications. Provides the foundation techniques for integrating advertising, sales promotion, branding, image, and the use of the Internet into a winning strategy.

Chapter 9: Uses the strategic marketing plan as the focal point where all data associated with objectives, strategies, markets, products, and competition come together into one unified document. Details the development of a plan and provides guidelines to assess your own plan.

Chapter 10: Wraps up the book and provides additional insightful guidelines on strategy and benchmarking.

Finally, and most meaningfully, this book promises that you will learn how to *think* and *act* like a marketing strategist. Good luck.

The Author

Norton Paley has over 25 years of corporate experience in general management, marketing management, and product development at McGraw-Hill Inc., John Wiley & Sons, and Alexander-Norton Inc. He is the author of six books:

- *The Strategic Marketing Planner*
- *Action Guide to Marketing Planning and Strategy*
- *The Manager's Guide to Competitive Marketing Strategies,* 2nd edition
- *Pricing Strategies and Practices*
- *Marketing Principles and Tactics Everyone Must Know*
- *How to Develop a Strategic Marketing Plan: A Step-by-Step Guide*

In addition to advising management on competitive strategies and strategic planning, Paley has extensive experience lecturing to managers and technical personnel at such firms as American Express, Cargill (worldwide), Chevron Chemical, Dow Chemical (worldwide), GTE, McDonnell-Douglas, Ralston-Purina, Johnson & Johnson, U.S. Gypsum, Celanese, and Pacific Bell. His international experiences include lecture tours sponsored by the Republic of China and the U.S. Embassy for the Republic of Mexico.

Columns under his byline have appeared in *Management Review* and *Sales & Marketing Management* magazines.

Table of Contents

Chapter 3
Marketing Strategy for the 21st Century

Chapter 4
Market Intelligence: The Cornerstone of Marketing Strategy

Chapter 9
Strategic Marketing Planning: How to Develop
Business-Building Strategies and Action Plans

Chapter 10
Wrap-Up

1 The Marketing-Driven Company in the Internet Age

INTRODUCTION

What is marketing? What does a marketing-driven company stand for in the Internet Age? As a nonmarketing executive, why should you pay any attention to the subject? To begin answering these questions, let's review the practices of one exemplary company and use it as a role model for how a successful 21st-century organization should operate.

Perhaps the fresh insights outlined in the case example can stimulate your interest in the expanded role of marketing in two ways: First, understanding the ideal role of marketing personnel can help you interface with them, sensitize you to their objectives, and generally enhance your own job performance. Second, internalizing the techniques and practices of marketing can assist in powering-up your company to achieve a competitive advantage and sustain long-term growth.

CASE EXAMPLE: CISCO SYSTEMS

Cisco Systems Inc., the developer of technology networks, epitomizes how a marketing-driven company organizes for results, responds quickly to changes in market behavior, and creates marketing strategies that relate to the individual customer's needs. Labeled an outside-in (market-oriented) rather than an inside-out (production-oriented) organization, the San Jose, CA company operates as a flexible, adaptive, customer-driven champion in its industry.

This still-youthful company, founded in 1984 by a group of Stanford University (California) scientists, has mushroomed to annual revenues in excess of $14 billion. Behind such brilliant success are the underpinnings of how a company should operate in this new century. The central ideas behind Cisco's practices include:

Focus on the customer — The ability to translate the outside-in approach into reality means permitting your core customers to decide your strategy. The essential concept is that users know more about what they need than your senior executives do.

Build networks — The new information technology allows links among customers, suppliers, business partners, and employees. As a result, the continuous multidirectional flow of information and all the internal and external activities move in harmony from product concept to delivery of a wanted product to a customer. In turn,

1

all these networks are encased with superior service that resolves problems quickly and efficiently. Effectively applied, informational technology performs as a powerful competitive marketing strategy and effective business model that allows you to be far more virtual with customers and suppliers.

Create alliances — In the current scheme of organizational and marketing strategy, alliances and other forms of partnering are keys to success. To make the connections work, Cisco maintains a seamless network of links by breeding a high level of trust among various managerial levels to achieve agreed-upon short- and long-term goals.

Develop a corporate culture — Indispensable to Cisco's organization is acquiring and maintaining a mind-set and an orientation that is totally customer driven. A company's culture — expressed as values, things, ideas, and behavioral patterns — emerges to form healthy relationships not only with customers and suppliers, but also with an attitude about employees as intellectual assets.

Apply technology — Using the Internet as an integral part of the marketing strategy impacts directly on the traditional functions of the sales force and customer service. For instance, Cisco obtains more than 50% of its revenues from selling complex, expensive equipment over the Net. Further, 7 out of 10 customer requests for technical support are filled electronically — at satisfaction rates that exceed face-to-face contact.

In summing up Cisco's strategy, Chief Executive Officer John T. Chambers believes the new rules of competition demand that organizations be (1) built on change, not stability; (2) organized around networks, not a rigid hierarchy; (3) based on interdependencies of partners, not self-sufficiency; and (4) constructed on technological advantage, not old-fashioned bricks and mortar.

Working with those guidelines, Chambers practices what he preaches by spending as much as 55% of his time with customers.

> **Key point:** The Internet model with fewer capital assets, a direct-to-customer connection, and freedom from the formal management structure offers a significant level of speed and operational efficiency.

COMBINING MARKETING STRATEGY WITH NEW TECHNOLOGY

Picking up on Cisco's practices, the driving force behind the new applications of marketing strategy is your ability to harness information and technology into a powerful competitive weapon. And central to that strategy is the explosive use of the Internet. The Internet model — with the need for fewer capital assets, a direct-to-customer connection, and freedom from the formal management structure — offers a significant level of speed and operational efficiency that is unsurpassed in its ability to foster exceptional levels of customer relationship marketing.

"I don't think there's been anything more important or more widespread in all my years at GE," declared General Electric Chairman John F. Welch. "Where does the Internet rank in priority? It's No. 1, 2, 3, and 4."

As a component of marketing strategy, electronic commerce was only $300 million in 1995. Just 4 years later it reached $111 billion. During the same period, the 177,000 Web site domains skyrocketed to 4.2 million. As of 1999, 24 million users in Asia surfed the Web, along with 63 million in Western Europe, and 81 million in the U.S. By 2003, International Data Corp. expects the number of Asians on-line to climb 230%, with similar dazzling statistics for other parts of the world.

MARKETING SUCCESSES

What effect has this new marketing model had in the competitive marketplace? In many cases, once-mighty organizations have nose-dived in market share, while the aggressive start-ups have skyrocketed in their respective industries. For instance:

- Dell Computer and Gateway together hold 53% of the direct-response market, primarily through the Internet.
- Priceline.com, an electronic bargaining system, allows buyers to name their price for air fares, hotel rooms, and cars — even mortgages.
- Amazon.com started out selling books at 10% discount. Now it sells at up to 50% off cover price, challenging the traditional leaders such as Barnes & Noble. With competitors attempting to copy its every move, Amazon is diversifying fast with other on-line ventures, such as Drugstore.com, LiveBid.com, and HomeGrocer.com.
- Charles Schwab & Co. pioneered electronic trading and outperformed the traditional industry leaders in grabbing market share with its on-line brokerage services.

The above examples — with particular emphasis on Cisco Systems — simply introduce you to the bold achievements of marketing-oriented, technology-driven companies in the Internet Age: their organizations, their people as intellectual properties, the diverse external forces, and the internal activities that shape everyday operations.

MARKETING DEFINED

Consistent with the above examples, here is a formal definition of marketing:

> Marketing is a total system of interacting business activities designed to plan, price, promote, and distribute want-satisfying products and services to consumers and business-to-business users in a competitive environment, at a profit.

It is important to view marketing as a systematic and organized approach to doing business. It is equally important to recognize that marketing requires the interaction of virtually all business functions. This single concept strengthens the proposition that each business function has a dynamic stake in the successful operation of a company and is dependent on every other function to do its part accurately and consistent with the overall direction of the organization.

Recognizing that it is the job of marketers to act in a state of competitive readiness also is consistent with the above definition. The inference is that marketers operate in much the same ways as senior business strategists. That is, effective marketing must be carefully thought out and thoroughly orchestrated as it is being carried out. These points are amply demonstrated in the Cisco case.

Given the above examples and a precise definition of modern marketing, which issues should concern you and your company? What distinguishing features should characterize the marketing function, particularly in your organization, in the 21st century? How should your market-driven, customer-oriented firm be organized?

To a great measure, the issues connected to those formidable questions took shape during the last two decades of the 20th century through a continuous string of momentous events. For instance:

- Intensified competition from developing countries shocked many traditionally minded executives from mainline firms into devising fresh strategies. For survival, they were forced to respond to prices that often ranged from 30 to 40% below prevailing market pricing.
- Changes in market behavior and new, flexible manufacturing techniques convinced even the most skeptical executives about the vast opportunities and competitive advantages of targeting specialized products and services based on age, income, education, occupation, race, ethnic, and cultural characteristics to dissimilar groups.
- Shifting life styles influenced managers to focus on how different groups live, spend, and act — all of which were being highlighted by the media and influenced by diverse political, economic, and social movements.
- Shortened product life cycles due to the proliferation of new products and the continuing flow of dazzling new and affordable technology convinced executives to probe for emerging or previously unserved market segments. In turn, those circumstances triggered even greater efforts to push for faster-cheaper-smaller-better products.
- Continuous pressures on profitability and productivity activated the pervasive movement toward downsizing, reengineering, and outsourcing. The result: a rush by many forward-looking executives to create market-sensitive organizations committed to total customer satisfaction.

Toward the end of the 20th century, a powerful global framework emerged — the Atlantic Economy. Based on such commonalities as escalating technology, advances in flexible manufacturing techniques, skyrocketing progress in Internet commerce, widespread industry deregulation, shared business values, and substantial financial resources, cross-ocean titans such as DaimlerChrysler, BP Amoco, Bertelsmann-America Online, and Bell Atlantic-Vodafone came on the scene.

These new high-powered global firms began setting the standards on how marketing would be practiced in the new millennium and how a market-driven organization should be operated, not only by large conglomerates but by small and mid-size organizations as well.

THE EVOLUTION OF MARKETING

> **Key point:** As corporations reengineered and downsized to create cost-effective, lean, market-driven organizations, middle-level managers were asked to develop viable competitive marketing strategies for their products and services — and take responsibility for results.

To make any sense of marketing practices and to understand where your company fits on a time scale, it is beneficial to gain an historical perspective of the economic, market, and environmental forces that shaped modern marketing.

Although a few U.S. companies had worked out their own systems and procedures as early as the 1920s, coordinated marketing as a formal activity emerged as a subject for serious study only in the early 1950s. Companies such as General Electric, IBM, General Motors, Eastman Kodak, and Procter & Gamble led the way, with the top management of other dominant companies gradually adopting formal marketing structures.

THE 1950s

The 1950s was a period during which the U.S. exerted overwhelming economic influence throughout most of the world. During that time, top-level corporate planning dominated most of the larger U.S. companies.

Consisting primarily of production plans, this type of planning focused on satisfying an insatiable demand for consumer goods within the U.S. It also responded to a demand for specific industrial products to help those countries ravaged by World War II rebuild their economies and redevelop consumer markets.

Ranking officers at the highest organizational levels developed corporate plans while maintaining a dominant financial focus. Rarely did lower-echelon managers participate in those planning sessions.

In contrast, lower-level managers geared their efforts to maximizing productivity for the short-term satisfaction of market demand. Marketing — as a distinct unifying function enveloping product development, marketing research, advertising, sales promotion, and field selling — was just beginning to emerge in only the most forward-looking organizations.

THE 1960s

Strong consumer demand for products characterized the 1960s; yet serious competition still remained limited. Overall, U.S. companies were able to sell all they produced, so there was no urgency to change procedures, other than to keep the production lines moving efficiently. In general, what was produced was consumed. The business environment was marked by intense economic growth in most industrialized countries.

In addition to domestic markets, and developing markets in European industrial-ized countries, third-world countries slowly emerged as customers for products nec-essary to sustain the basic needs of life. Such products included simple machines, some basic types of agricultural equipment, and essential transportation such as buses and bicycles.

Companies began looking for practical organizational models designed to gain active participation from senior executives who represented the core activities of manufacturing, research and development, sales, and distribution. There was a con-scious effort to integrate diverse business functions through a coordinated plan of op-erations. Despite those good intentions, many functions still remained separated. The dominant parts of marketing still relied on the separated activities of advertising, pub-lic relations, market research, and field selling.

A typical sales department of this period is shown in Figure 1.1. When the man-ager needed advertising or marketing research, the sales vice-president usually con-tacted another freestanding department or hired outside vendors.

THE 1970s

This decade triggered a transitional phase in marketing. With the post-war rebuilding process almost completed, its full effect was about to impact the world. European companies burst onto U.S. markets. It was the Japanese companies, however, that generated the most aggressive and penetrating competition. The full thrust of their competitive assault hit virtually every major industry from machine tools and con-

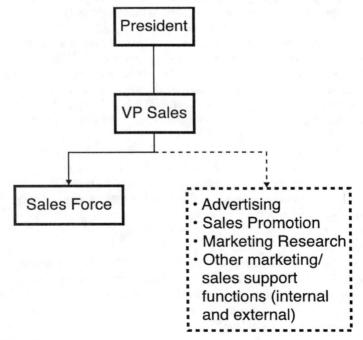

FIGURE 1.1 Sales department.

sumer electronics to automobiles and steel. The new competitive situation ignited a surging movement to group the various independent activities into a unified marketing function.

The 1970s also signaled the start of a period of identifying new and emerging global markets for growth and expansion. In the U.S., customers demanded more varied products and services and they were willing to pay for them. Responding to the continuing population shift out of the cities, businesses followed increasingly affluent customers into the expanding suburban shopping malls.

Executives reshaped their organizations and merged scattered activities of advertising, marketing research, marketing planning, and field selling into a workable organizational structure that would move more efficiently to identify and satisfy changing market demands. Two forms of organizations showed up prominently during this period: the functional organization (Figure 1.2) and the product management organization (Figure 1.3).

Functional Organization

A functional organization assigns responsibilities and creates positions related to the various functions to be performed, thereby permitting a horizontal division of labor that, in turn, results in specialization. The basic advantage of this approach lies in assigning the ultimate responsibility for the marketing function to a single individual. A functional organization is the only setup in which there is no duplication or paralleling of functions. Within that framework, the responsibility of each manager extends to the entire product and market mix.

As the number of functions for separate managers increases, however, the marketing vice-president's span of control may become too broad for a direct reporting relationship. In such a case, subgrouping of the existing functions into a line and staff format could prove helpful.

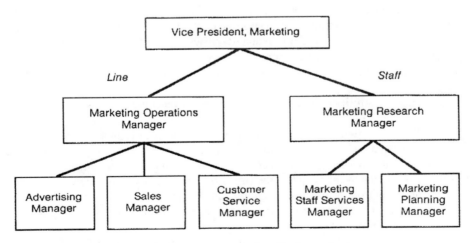

FIGURE 1.2 Functional organization with line and staff subgroupings.

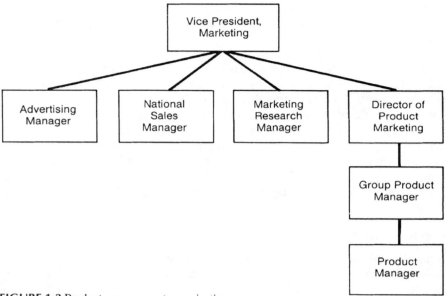

FIGURE 1.3 Product management organization.

Product Management Organization

An alternative approach that larger firms used successfully was a product management organization (Figure 1.3). Created in the late 1920s by Procter & Gamble, this arrangement employs both functional managers who act as resource managers, and product managers who serve as program managers. This form is called a matrix organization because each resource manager interacts with each program manager. Entered graphically in a matrix, the functions represent rows, while the products appear in columns.

Product management becomes necessary when the complexity of the product mix threatens to overtax the functional system, resulting in a dilution of effort that leaves many products virtually unattended. The advent of product management brings order and focus to this disarray by clearly lodging responsibility for the fate of a specific product or product line with a single individual, ensuring it the attention it requires.

The responsibilities of a product manager are far reaching. He or she must:

- Provide a continuing series of programs and projects designed to improve a product line's market position and profitability.
- Mold the marketing effort according to changing consumer demands.
- Coordinate the activities of the firm's functional units with a view toward achieving short- and long-range product objectives.
- Act as an intelligence center for all relevant information concerning the product line.
- Analyze market potential and develop marketing strategies.

- Generate communications campaigns.
- Stimulate interest in and support of the product line among the sales force and distributor network.
- Establish a viable e-commerce strategy (new).

During the 1960s and 1970s, marketing as an independent business discipline expanded rapidly into undergraduate and graduate degree programs at state and private universities. The focus emphasized understanding customer needs and developing comprehensive programs to satisfy the wants of different market segments.

Further, the movement toward a total system of interacting business activities called for the further integration of various business activities such as manufacturing, research and development, and distribution. Doing so justified the use of strategy teams consisting of individuals from each of those functions.

Then, during the late 1970s Strategic Planning took hold. Strategic Planning aimed to build onto the long-term, financially oriented corporate plans of the 1960s by adding a strategic focus to the process. More precisely:

Strategic planning is the managerial process of developing and maintaining a strategic fit between the organization and its changing market opportunities. It relies on developing (1) a mission or strategic direction, (2) objectives and goals, (3) growth strategies, and (4) a business portfolio consisting of markets and products.

No longer could top-down 1950s-style corporate planning driven by a production orientated model suffice. The competitive international marketplace of the 1970s required a more precise orientation satisfied by strategic planning and marketing planning.

THE 1980s

The 1980s spurred the next stage of marketing that emphasized the use of strategic marketing plans which merged two planning formats: the long-term strategic plan and the short-term marketing plan. There are several reasons why the Strategic Marketing Plan (SMP) evolved at this stage of the planning cycle:

1. Although strategic planning permitted managers to create a long-term vision of how the organization could grow, for the most part it lacked implementation. A survey conducted by Deloitte & Touche, the large consulting firm, indicated that while 97% of the Fortune 500 companies wrote strategic plans, only 15% ever implemented anything that came out of the plan.
2. Marketing planning incorporated the various activities associated with the marketing function into an action-oriented plan. The planning period, however, was usually one year. No formalized planning process existed to link the longer-term strategic plan that needed an implementation phase with the shorter-term marketing plan that required a strategic vision.
3. Typically, each plan developed independently within the organization. No

procedure unified planning efforts consistent with the marketing definition of "a total system of interacting activities designed to plan, price, promote, and distribute want-satisfying products to organizational and household users in a competitive environment."

4. The U.S. marketplace experienced turbulent upheavals during the 1980s: a slowing of real growth, changing demographics, changing life styles, fragmented markets, deregulation of major industries, global competition, rapid technological change, shortened product life cycles, and accelerated product innovations.

Under those mind-boggling conditions, the SMP evolved, creating a linkage of the strategic plan with the marketing plan. It linked the internal functions of the organization with the external and volatile changes of a competitive global environment. (The Strategic Marketing Plan is discussed in greater detail in Chapter 9.)

THE 1990s

As corporations of the 1980s and 1990s reengineered and downsized to create cost-effective, lean, market-driven organizations, a further innovation evolved. Middle-level managers were asked to develop viable competitive marketing strategies for their products and services — and take responsibility for results.

The SMP became a hands-on format that managers could use to conceptualize a product with a long-term strategic direction that focused on future customer and market needs. They could project what changes would take place in a framework of industry, consumer, competitive, and environmental areas and identify ways in which technologies would change business practices.

Figure 1.4 graphically shows an organization chart that characterizes the modern marketing operation. Figure 1.4 defines the workings of the company. It is within that unique structure that business life exists and where the relationships with those of the same level, with superiors, or subordinates interact. It is within the organizational unit that product, promotion, pricing, and distribution strategies emerge. It is where leadership is exercised, which, in turn, influences the individual attitudes and collective morale of individuals within the group.

THE 2000s

For the foreseeable future, the marketing-driven organization will continue to hone skills dedicated to sharpening customer-driven practices — again, using the shining example of Cisco Systems as the benchmark for the market-driven organization. Such a dedicated customer orientation will be sustained by the continuing globalization of markets. And the mere attempt at gaining a foothold in emerging markets will employ acquisition, joint venture, or other forms of strategic alliances.

The big growth engines of the U.S., the consolidated efforts of a unified Europe, and an upsurge of economic power along the Pacific Rim will drive growth in numerous markets on both sides of the Atlantic and Pacific. In turn, that means more intense competition; rapid technology advancement; continuing product innovation; and the ongoing search for emerging, neglected, and poorly served markets.

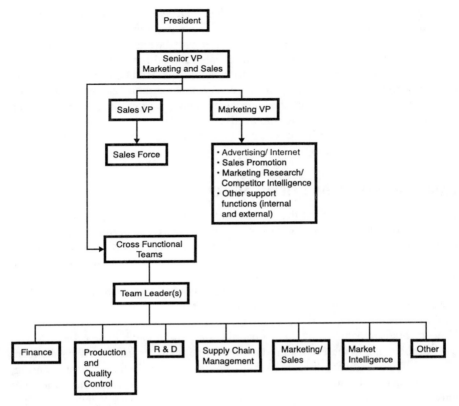

FIGURE 1.4 Modern marketing operation.

Europe's movement toward a single currency, the euro, has resulted in a consolidation of the currency of 11 different countries. With the euro, Europe's 9100 public corporations come close to America's 9900, creating massive NAFTA and euro trading bloc zones. Thus, new markets will rise; others will decline. Countries once dormant will awaken; others, once supreme, will fade. The entire movement will be enveloped by the overriding pursuit for customer satisfaction through relationship marketing.

Then, two additional actions will gain momentum and become entrenched in corporate practices: the use of cross-functional teams and relationship marketing.

CROSS-FUNCTIONAL TEAMS

Key point: The strategy team is one of the most successful organizational formats for conceiving and delivering innovative and entrepreneurial thinking to your organization.

The interactions of people are the key ingredients in implementing the definition of marketing as a *total system of interacting business activities designed to plan, price,*

promote, and distribute want-satisfying products and services to consumer and busi-
ness-to-business users in a competitive environment at a profit.

You can effectively blend people interaction with the marketing concept through cross-functional teams consisting of individuals from all functional areas of the organization such as manufacturing, product development, R&D, finance, distribution, and sales/marketing. These functions may vary in some organizations. But the key idea is that representation from the major interacting functions must be present on a team if it is to fulfill the long-term objectives of the business — as well as manage the day-to-day marketing objectives within a hotly contested competitive environment.

CASE EXAMPLE: DOW CHEMICAL CO.

Dow Chemical Co. is one of the most notable users of cross-functional teams. For over 20 years it has employed an organizational structure that permits teams to operate for individual products, product lines, markets, and industries. Teams function at various levels throughout its worldwide operations. At any given time there may be as many as 40 teams at work within Dow.

These teams have the various designations of Product Management Team (PMT), operating at a product manager level for a product line; Business Management Team (BMT) at the next higher level, dealing with a business unit or major market; and Industry Management Team (IMT), operating on a still broader dimension.

For example, in the PMT a product/marketing manager usually chairs the team and is staffed by individuals representing such functional activities as manufacturing, logistics, finance, technical management, marketing, and sales. This arrangement not only allows for the favorable dynamics of team members working together, but often defuses any adversarial relationships that might exist, e.g., between marketing and manufacturing. There is a growing trend, however, toward the leaderless team, with individuals emerging as particular needs arise or as problems shift toward those with special levels of expertise.

Now, with the pervasive use of the Internet, companies can share information horizontally rather than be channeling it up to the CEO's office and back down again. One of the key points related to the team and the use of the Internet is that decisions can be made rapidly by the people best equipped to make them.

Then there is the use of the team approach within the new reality, where the market landscape changes daily. Here, it is crucial to react fast — something conventional top-down, bureaucratic organizations don't do well. Many companies are adopting teams as a permanent organizational format. In 1987, 28% of the largest 1000 companies had formed at least some teams. By 1996, 78% had some. And the trend will intensify as a generation of team-oriented managers climb higher into executive positions.

Team members may change from time to time and the frequency of meetings may vary with teams. But the key element is the permanency of the team as part of the organizational structure, so that it can be called into action at any time.

The strategy team, business management team, or product management team —

whichever designation you select — is one of the most successful organizational formats for conceiving and delivering innovative and entrepreneurial thinking to your organization. Such a team should be initiated at every operational level by adopting *role* and *responsibility* guidelines.

For our purposes in installing a team or improving the performance of an existing team, let's designate it as a Business Management Team (BMT).

ROLES

The BMT serves as a significant functional contributor, with leadership roles in:

- Defining the business or product strategic direction (mission).
- Analyzing the environmental, industry, customer, and competitor situations.
- Developing long- and short-term objectives and strategies.
- Defining product, market, distribution, and quality plans to implement competitive strategies.

RESPONSIBILITIES

- Creating and recommending new or additional products.
- Approving all product alterations or modifications of a major nature.
- Acting as a formal communications channel for field product needs.
- Planning and implementing strategies throughout the product life cycle.
- Developing e-business and e-commerce programs to improve market position and profitability.
- Identifying market or product opportunities in light of changing consumer and business-to-business demands.
- Coordinating efforts with various internal corporate functions and along the entire supply chain to achieve short- and long-term objectives.
- Coordinating efforts for the interdivisional exchanges of new market or product opportunities.
- Developing a strategic marketing plan.

The following example illustrates a creative variation of the team approach where a company mobilized its nonmarketing people to help activate its competitive marketing strategies.

CASE EXAMPLE: JOHN DEERE

John Deere & Co., producers of farm equipment, taps the expertise of its managerial and hourly work force to implement its marketing and sales strategies. Deere's resourcefulness in capitalizing on its employees' skills has contributed to a sharp increase in net income, along with sizable jumps in sales and market share. Industry analysts have predicted that Deere could join the ranks of Chrysler and Motorola as exemplary prototypes in the revival of U.S. manufacturing.

DEERE'S STRATEGY

Teams of assembly-line workers crisscrossed North America and talked to dealers and farmers about Deere equipment. They traveled singly or in small groups and pitched their sales stories to farmers at regional trade exhibits. Workers in various job functions routinely made unscheduled visits to local farmers to discuss their problems and needs.

In most places the "new" sales reps were accepted as friendly, non-threatening individuals who had no ulterior motive other than to present an honest, grass-roots account of what goes into making a quality Deere product. Enlisting the work force for marketing duties was triggered by the weakening of demand for farm equipment during a recession period, and the aggressive actions of competition — in particular from Deere's chief rival, Caterpillar Inc.

Underlying the work force strategy is Deere's view of the marketing-centered concept: All employees are valuable resources to serve the needs of customers. (A similar viewpoint was expressed by Cisco Systems.) Further, many of the workers supporting the marketing effort had over 15 years experience with the Moline, IL company. They were trained in advanced manufacturing methods, total quality programs, and teamwork. According to Deere's management, harnessing that expertise demonstrates to customers that, as makers of the products, they are the company's best spokespeople.

Noteworthy benefits of Deere's strategy are

- *Early identification of customers' problems.* Equipment performance or maintenance problems are quickly identified, with some handled on the spot by the Deere workers. Other problems are addressed back at the plant by cross-functional teams.
- *Early detection of competition and new benefits and values for customers.* As the Deere workers hustle it in the sales territories, they experience real-world training that sensitizes them to the issues of product quality, technical assistance, on-time delivery, cost reduction, customer relationships, and the potential threats of competition.
- *Mobilization of the work force to support the marketing effort.* This fits the broad strategy of marketing the whole company — the sum of its competencies, products and services, and value systems — in a form that makes customers want to do business with Deere.
- *Building a subtle, yet powerful image of management-labor harmony.* The marketing implication of this strategy is that with unity of effort comes continuous product improvement and speedy resolution of customers' problems.
- *Strengthening customer relationships.* Customers develop a stronger affinity for the company through their meetings with workers from functions

other than sales and marketing. This form of bonding breaks down sales resistance.

GUIDELINES

What can be learned from the Deere case? If you decide to establish a cross-functional strategy team or attempt to increase the output of an ongoing one, empower the team members with specific duties and responsibilities that culminate in a strategic marketing plan. Deere's list of responsibilities differ only slightly from those already listed in this chapter:

1. Recommend new or value-added products and services that resolve customers' problems.
2. Support product modifications that would result in a competitive advantage.
3. Develop strategies that could be phased in at various stages of the product's life — from introduction, through growth, into maturity, and decline.
4. Identify market/product opportunities based on changing technologies.
5. Coordinate efforts to foster sound customer relationships.
6. Initiate reliable communications from the field back to product design and manufacturing personnel.
7. Deliver a plan to management that assures ongoing funding for the team's product or service recommendations.

RELATIONSHIP MARKETING

> **Key point:** Require a customer-relationship plan that details the objectives, actions, and necessary resources to implement a program.

The second action, one that is central to the new wave of business practices for the 2000s, is relationship marketing.

Relationship marketing is the practice of building long-term satisfying relations with key parties — customers, suppliers, distributors — in order to retain their long-term preference and business.

The intent is to deliver high-quality, distinctive service and competitive prices to customers. The pledge is to cut down on activity costs and time. Again, Cisco Systems and John Deere are prime examples of companies that are standout models for relationship marketing.

Relationships can run the gamut from being an almost nonexistent one of a salesperson simply selling a product, to that of a flourishing association where partnering means working consistently with a customer to discover ways to generate customer savings. Or it can mean helping the customer design a product for *its* customers. In some instances relationships can include placing an individual on the customer's premises to assist in a variety of tasks from inventory control to providing technical assistance.

Thus, the movement is to evolve from transaction marketing to relationship marketing. To implement the changeover, track your customers and determine which ones are worthy of the full services provided by relationship marketing. Therefore:

- Identify the key customers that warrant relationship marketing.
- Train the salesperson or other contact individual to deal with the customer.
- Require a customer-relationship plan that details the objectives, actions, and required resources to implement the program.
- Make the Internet and related technology an integral part of the relationship-marketing plan.

CASE EXAMPLE: OFFICE DEPOT

Office Depot demonstrates the tangible cost advantages and additional customer support for its office supply business as it fulfills the aims of relationship marketing by including the Internet into the plan. For instance, Office Depot reports the following:

- The Internet cuts in half the cost of processing an order. Typically, it costs about $2 to process a phone order, but over the Web that drops to less than $1.
- Office Depot wins new customers who aren't close to its stores and now use the company's Web site to order goods.
- The company is able to hold on to its customers. Those that might have departed to on-line competitors now stay with Office Depot.
- Customers benefit by reducing the cost of purchasing office products. On average, corporations spend $75 to $175 to issue a purchase order for an item and then pay for it. The Net cuts that to between $15 and $25.
- Business people can place orders from their desks and reduce phone calls to the purchasing department.
- Customers can get an up-to-the-minute review of Office Depot's extensive inventory and order what they want and when they want delivery, thereby doing away or reducing the amount of supplies they maintain on their own premises.

CULTURAL DIVERSITY

There is yet another and more subtle dimension to relationship marketing: *cultural diversity*. The topic is gaining increasingly more attention in managers' thinking. And with good reason, as revealed by the Hudson Institute's *Workforce 2000* study of the work force of the future.

Some of the findings reveal that of the more than 25 million people who joined the workplace between 1985 and 2000, 85% were minorities and women, while white males accounted for only 15%. White females, immigrants, and minorities of various black, Hispanic, and Asian origins comprised the 85% group. While the percentages may vary in some areas, the findings easily underscore the need to take into account an increasingly diverse work force.

Coming to grips with cultural diversity now takes center stage as the new down-sized, reengineered, and compact organization moves to implement the strategy of getting closer to the customer. As a result, managing diversity means creating an organizational culture that welcomes multiple perspectives by tapping into the talents and contributions of all employees and customers.

To fully benefit from diversity through the vantage point of relationship marketing, you must grasp its essence from two points of view: your organization's culture and your customer's culture.

ORGANIZATION CULTURE

Use the following guidelines:

- Tune in to the variety of values and assumptions held by diverse groups or individuals in your firm.
- Develop a core set of shared values that can be communicated within your group. Those core values help determine the boundaries of cultural change.
- Begin the process by involving employees with diverse backgrounds in decision making as a means for welcoming their contributions. Again, use the cross-functional strategy team as your organizational format.

MARKET CULTURE

The second dimension to cultural diversity is more comprehensive and one that bears directly on relationship marketing. Use the following guidelines:

- Cultural values come and go. The three basic components of culture — things, ideas, and behavior patterns — undergo additions, deletions, or modifications on a continuing cycle. Some components die out, new ones are accepted, and existing ones can be changed in some observable way. Although the pace of change varies from society to society when viewing cultures over time, there is nothing as constant as change. Any cultural environment today is not exactly the same as it was last year nor will it be the same one year hence. The cultural environment, therefore, needs constant monitoring.*

---

* Adapted from Ferraro, G., *The Cultural Dimension of International Business*, Prentice-Hall, Upper Saddle River, NJ, 1998.

- Society holds a variety of values. Some are classified as primary beliefs and values and tend to be long lasting. These values relate to work, marriage, charity, and honesty. They are usually passed on from parents to children and are reinforced within the institutions of schools, churches, businesses, and government.
- A range of secondary beliefs also exist and are within the marketer's ability to influence through educational advertising and the types of products and services purchased. Such beliefs can range from when individuals should marry and how much debt should be carried.
- Subcultures rise and fall, from the rebellious youths of the 1960s to the variety of current religious cults, all with different beliefs, preferences, and behaviors. Each has a major impact on hairstyles, clothing, sexual norms, and categories of products.

LOOKING AHEAD

> **Key point:** Coordinating activities among upper- and middle-level managers produces substantive marketing plans that integrate the core strengths of the firm into innovative strategies, and guards against embellishing and replaying last year's strategies.

With the myriad of competitive changes presented in this chapter, your current organization setup, market orientation, and people involvement may have been appropriate when initially established, but now may have outlived its service. The product-market mix of your firm, as well as the competitive situation in the marketplace, has changed dramatically over the years. Whatever the present structure, it probably warrants a review of its resourcefulness, flexibility, efficiency, and ability to compete in a global environment.

CHOOSING THE RIGHT SETUP

Given such a wide range of choices, it is not easy to decide on the optimum solution for your firm. The following guidelines should prove helpful.

- While a company with a small number of product lines can do well with a functional organization, a wide range of lines requires product management.
- If your product mix is fairly homogeneous you can rely on a functional organization, whereas a varied collection of products warrants product management.
- Highly technical and complex products require product expertise, which is the cornerstone of the product management system.
- Mostly homogeneous markets can be served by a functional or product setup, while heterogeneous markets demand a market organization that re-

sponds to their unique needs and buying patterns. An example of the latter situation is a single division of the food-marketing business serving both grocery and institutional markets.

- The size of your firm is another factor. If it is small or medium in size, a functional organization is likely to work well for you. The geographic dispersion of your markets should also be considered. If they are regional, or otherwise fairly concentrated, a product or market setup is a good choice. But if they are dispersed over a large area, you should look into the advantages of a geographic setup.

Answering some of the following questions will also assist you in determining the adequacy of your marketing organization:

- Is it efficient? That is, does work get done with a minimum of waste, and does your setup respond swiftly to changes in the marketplace?
- Are all jobs clearly delineated as precise responsibilities and areas of authority?
- Is your structure internally consistent or the result of historic accidents?
- Is it up to date and compatible with the company's current and expected future situation?
- Is it streamlined, with no unnecessary management layers to impede the flow of information from the field to the main office?
- Finally, does it represent the optimum use of the firm's talent pool?

Negative responses will pinpoint the need for a change.

To illustrate the above concepts, the following case illustrates how managers from diverse company functions cooperate to improve the quality of the company's marketing efforts and strategies.

CASE EXAMPLE: ROCKWELL INTERNATIONAL

Rockwell International Corp. demonstrates remarkable adeptness in encouraging its managers to pursue interdivisional and cross-functional cooperation for market advantage. In Rockwell's situation, cooperation doesn't mean just acting the good corporate citizen.

Here's how cooperation works at Rockwell. To the casual observer, the Seal Beach, CA company looks like a 1970s-style conglomerate consisting of dissimilar companies and products merged under a corporate umbrella. An in-depth examination reveals quite another scene.

First, Rockwell managers freely coordinate with their counterparts in other business units to tap each other's core skills, technologies, and competencies and then integrate them into new products. To illustrate: one Rockwell division bends, welds, and fuses metals into components for cars, trucks, and aircraft fuselages. A second division serves the telecommunications and industrial automation markets with innovative product systems that use the latest technology. By implanting the distinctive technology from telecommunications into the commodity-type products from the metals operation, engineers can, for example, digitize an existing product for a new application. The payoff is that Rockwell's vehicle division doesn't sell just metal. It combines high-tech with old-tech and produces such new-wave products as autonavigation devices and innovative power-window regulators, as well as other parts that join metal with electronics.

Second, marketing and sales personnel benefit from the coordinated approach with a continuing flow of innovative new products. They also gain by offering modified products to existing markets, thereby profiting from the extended sales cycles. The result is Rockwell divisions enjoy a number of market successes based on coordination and cooperation. For example, most Japanese fax machines use Rockwell chips, thereby bestowing upon its telecommunications unit an overwhelming 80% of the market for fax and modem chips. Two out of three U.S. daily newspapers use Rockwell's printing presses. About 65% of the trucks built in North America use Rockwell axles. And almost 75% of U.S. space flights were launched with Rockwell rocket engines.

Third, cooperation and coordination, particularly among upper- and middle-level managers, produce substantive marketing plans that integrate the core strengths of the firm into innovative strategies, and guard against embellishing and replaying last year's strategies.

GUIDELINES

What can be learned from the Rockwell case? Achieving organizational cooperation and coordination requires an internal selling job. As one executive states, "The first place to sell marketing is on the inside — and that's the hardest of all."

Admittedly, it's a tough task. However, there are a few things going for you. For example:

- *Organizational downsizing* and the extensive use of communication devices (computers, faxes, electronic mail) create fertile opportunities for cooperative networking among divisions and business units.
- *Widening interest among executives* in forming cross-functional teams results in the capacity to coordinate diverse levels of expertise and apply them to new product and market development.
- *New organizational designs*, including team structures concentrated around core business processes, foster cooperative efforts and in due time lead to the breaking down of departmental barriers.
- *Increasing responsiveness to such initiatives as customer relationship management* tempts marketing and sales managers with the prize of single-source contracts or a preferred supplier status. Those agreements encourage still further supply-chain cooperation through long-term supplier-customer bonding. An example of such bonding is the value-added practice of placing supplier's personnel at a customer's disposal and using

electronic gadgetry to transfer technical information and maintain inventory control.

The successful blending of skills and beliefs to foster cooperation, results in lessening the effects of self-interest, turf protection, and entrenched biases exhibited by various functional managers with whom you have to cooperate. Table 1.1 shows the primary differences between key corporate functions and marketing that need attention before you can make the internal "sale" that leads to cooperation.

TABLE 1.1
Differences between Key Corporate Functions and Marketing

Function	Their Focus	Marketing Focus
R&D	Basic research	Applied research
	Functional features	Marketable features
Engineering	Standard designs and components	Custom models and components
	Few models	Numerous models
Manufacturing	Long production runs	Short runs, custom orders
	Infrequent model changes	Frequent model changes
Finance	Rigid budgets	Flexible budgets
	Cost justification for all product innovations	Opportunistic investments for market development

BEST PRACTICES

1. Indispensable to an organization's growth and prosperity is acquiring and maintaining a mind-set that is totally customer driven.
2. The Internet model — with fewer assets, a direct-to-customer connection, and freedom from the formal management structure — offers speed and efficiency that is unsurpassed in its ability to foster exceptional levels of customer relationship marketing.
3. Look at marketing as a systematic and organized approach to doing business that requires interacting business activities. Each business function has a vital stake in the successful operation of the company and depends on every other function to do its part accurately and consistently with the overall direction of the organization.
4. Continuing pressures on profitability and productivity activated the pervasive movement toward downsizing, reengineering, and outsourcing. The result: A rush by many forward-looking executives to create market-sensitive organizations committed to total customer satisfaction.
5. The cross-functional team is one of the most successful organizational formats for conceiving and delivering innovative and entrepreneurial thinking to your organization.
6. Central to the new-wave business practice for the 21st century is relationship marketing.

2 The World of Markets

INTRODUCTION

The world of markets is as large or as small as you want it to be. You can think of this decade as the Atlantic Century, looking east to the U.K. and beyond to continental Europe with its burgeoning economy of euro zones. You can look further east to the gathering momentum of Eastern Bloc countries that are emerging and accelerating into the world market of competition.

You can reverse direction to the Pacific Rim and look at fully industrialized Japan. Also, there's the monumental potential of China that promises to develop as a world-class market, as well as numerous other markets climbing out of the Asian crisis of the late 1990s.

Or, you can look south to Latin America and its conglomerate of countries, with some still emerging, others developing, and a few flourishing. These markets within markets are the opportunities called segments that beckon those insightful executives who are knowledgeable and bold enough to select, target, and position his or her company for growth and prosperity.

Thus, the reality, and perhaps the urgency, is that every nonmarketing manager should demonstrate above-average knowledge of modern strategic marketing and be able to interact astutely with marketers and other strategy planners. This means becoming proactive in contributing to the survival and growth of your organization.

To immerse yourself into the realities of the competitive world of markets, the following actual case is designed to give a hands-on approach to strategic marketing and how to make it applicable to the everyday work of dealing with existing markets, new markets, and product applications.

As you review the PPG Industries case example below, act as if you are attending the company's strategy meeting and discussing a major business problem with other managers. Then, think how you would have contributed to the decision-making process that resulted in the successful solution. What questions would you have asked? What information would you have needed to make an intelligent evaluation of the suggestions made by others sitting in on the session? Overall, what meaningful contribution could you have made?

Following the case example are the relevant guidelines containing information that would have equipped you to have participated actively and intelligently in the session. You will acquire knowledge you can use in your own company's strategy meetings, should a similar problem surface.

CASE EXAMPLE: PPG INDUSTRIES

PROBLEM

How do we cope with a condition of erratic marketing and loss of sales momentum?

SITUATION

PPG Industries, Inc., a glass, paint, and chemical company, has operated successfully for most of its 112 years. However, during one period, telltale signs indicated the company was faltering in some of its product development and marketing efforts. For example, after several years of intense work, PPG engineers developed a bluish-tinted windshield that would admit filtered sunlight but block the heat.

Market: all automakers.

Result: no interest. Automakers didn't like the color or the price. Further, overall sales languished during the same period. These conditions spurred PPG management to take remedial action before its problems started festering.

PPG's STRATEGIES

- Managers reasoned they should explore higher-growth market segments, such as sunglasses, by using its unique technology for lenses that would lighten or darken automatically in response to light levels.
- They considered initiating innovative programs to run auto paint operations for such companies as Chrysler, with the opportunity to grab a larger share of the coatings and chemicals business.
- Marketing and sales looked at establishing an insurance claims network that steered window replacement business to PPG distributors.
- Marketing and engineering, working cooperatively, saw the advantages of penetrating new segments where its products could displace other materials. In one such segment they looked into using glass instead of aluminum for computer hard disks.
- PPG agreed to push abroad into China and South America by setting up production facilities and initiating segmentation strategies similar to those used in its domestic markets.

GUIDELINES

> **Key point:** Subdividing the market helps identify and satisfy the specific needs of individuals within your chosen segments, thereby strengthening your market position.

If you had been asked to make meaningful contributions at PPG's strategy meeting, the following guidelines and information would have been helpful.

The central strategy underlying PPG's actions focused on segmenting markets for new products and product applications. You could have raised the point that the specialized marketing skills needed to implement segmentation strategies are quite different from those honed after many years of treating PPG's numerous product lines as mere commodities. You could have pinpointed your questions based on the criteria for selecting segments. Then, you could have helped the team decide upon a viable choice worth the expenditure of resources. Specifically, if you had sat in on the PPG strategy session (or your own), the following guidelines for selecting segments would have been useful.

Define segment size and growth — Determine if an existing segment is worth occupying and holding. That is, does it have enough growth potential to warrant a commitment for the long pull? To assist in finding answers, there are substantial quantities of reliable information at federal and state government agencies. Other useful sources include trade associations, trade periodicals, and suppliers of marketing research data, such as Frost & Sullivan and Stanford Research Institute. In particular, many associations and business publications now permit easy access to their archives over the Internet.

Look at segment structure — All segments have a definable structure consisting of:

- *Market characteristics.* Determine the segment structure by looking at where you would fit within the maze of suppliers, existing competitors, emerging competitors, alternative product and service offerings, and assorted groups of customers. (PPG focused on the latter two segments by substituting glass for aluminum computer disks and running paint operations for Chrysler.) Next, understand the complexities of the distribution channel. Is there sufficient room for your product in the existing channel or would you have to pioneer a new pathway to your customer?
- *Buyer behavior.* Look at the innumerable market developments that are undoubtedly reshaping buyer behavior. They include: intensifying global competition, increasing service demands from customers, dazzling new technology, and numerous lean organizations resolutely committed to product quality and total customer satisfaction. Then ask, segment by segment, what fresh strategies would you initiate to deal with those developments?

But that's not all you need to know about segmentation. Let's take a more detailed view of how you can help apply this strategy and thereby strengthen your product's market position as you push your company to further growth.

MARKET AND PRODUCT SEGMENTS

Key point: Selecting, targeting, and positioning a segment is the essence of a competitive strategy. It optimizes your resources and concentrates them at the point of impact.

Segmentation means splitting the overall market into smaller submarkets or segments that have more in common with one another than with the total market. Subdividing the market helps you identify and satisfy the specific needs of individuals within your chosen segments and thereby strengthen your market position. Further, segmentation also allows you to concentrate your strength against the weaknesses of your competitors and improve your competitive ranking.

In practice, segments are moving targets subject to changing buyer preferences driven by the dynamics of political, social, and environmental influences within groups. Numerous examples exist of companies concentrating on segments.

Starting in the mid-1980s, big companies such as AT&T, Sears Roebuck, and Coca-Cola learned to target distinct ethnic and demographic segments. They understood that heavily diverse communities of Americans don't necessarily respond to mass-market messages. However, some branded products that had prospered in the 1980s by predicting (and sometimes shaping) popular trends ran into some difficulties during the 1990s. Their products weren't firing up the same excitement with today's kids as with their baby boomer parents.

Companies also found to their dismay that succeeding generations needed new targeting and positioning strategies. For instance, a formidable brand such as PepsiCo Inc. struggled to build loyalty among teens. Nike Inc.'s sneaker sales tumbled among teens toward the end of the 1990s. And Levi-Strauss & Co. continues to fight valiantly to halt market share erosion as it moves forward to assume its "hot-brand" position.

Then, managers began looking at opportunities uncovered through market research that revealed a range of behaviors displayed by diverse segments of the population. For instance, Hispanics eat more fast food than other groups. African Americans spend more money and time on their hair. Older populations purchase a lot of luxury travel plans. And gays and lesbians drink more imported beer than other groups in the U.S.

Even a small organization can see the enormous potential of segmentation. Boreal Ski Area, a resort near Lake Tahoe, wanted to boost its business. Using research and a bit of intuition, the resort management reached out to San Francisco's large Chinese population. Additional research showed that Chinese people value family activities. Further, they have the highest average household income ($56,547) as well as the fastest population growth (3.81%). Also, Chinese immigrant parents perceive skiing as an activity to help their children assimilate. Armed with such favorable information, the resort moved to run ads in four local Chinese-language newspapers and advertised on a Chinese TV station. Its Asian customer base increased by about 10% in a relatively short time.

CHOOSING MARKET SEGMENTS

As illustrated by the above examples, look at segmentation as an essential part of how to survey a market, and in particular how to relate to specific groups and even individuals within a group. Selecting, targeting, and positioning a segment is the essence of a competitive strategy.

The proper application of segmentation optimizes resources and concentrates them at the point of greatest impact. Therefore, in providing input to a segment analysis, you should know which criteria to use in choosing market segments, what factors to use in identifying a market segment, and how to develop a segmentation analysis. Use the following criteria to guide you in selecting market segments.

- *Measurable.* Can you quantify the segment? For example, you should be able to assign a number to how many factories, how many farm acres, or how many people are within the market segment.
- *Accessible.* Do you have access to the market through a dedicated sales force, distributors, transportation, or warehousing?
- *Substantial.* Is the segment of sufficient size to warrant attention as a segment? Further, is the segment declining, maturing, or growing?
- *Profitable.* Does concentrating on the segment provide sufficient profitability to make it worthwhile? Use your organization's standard measurements for profitability, such as return on investment, gross margin, or profits.
- *Compatible with competition.* To what extent do your major competitors have an interest in the segment? Is it of active interest or of negligible concern to your competitors?
- *Effectiveness.* Does your organization have sufficient skills and resources to serve the segment effectively?
- *Defendable.* Does your firm have the capabilities to defend itself against the attack of a major competitor?

Answering those questions will help you select a market segment with above-average potential for concentrating your resources and with concrete information for further analysis of buyer behavior. These criteria can also be used as ongoing tests for the viability of a market segment once you have chosen it. But how do you select one? Begin by understanding the categories for segmenting markets.

CATEGORIES FOR SEGMENTING MARKETS

The four most common ways to segment a market is by *demographic, geographic, psychographic (behavioral)*, and *product attributes*. Each of these factors, particularly when used in combination with the others, represents an opportunity or identifies a need that can be satisfied with a product. Table 2.1 defines each of the categories.

Let's examine these segmentation categories in greater detail.

Geographic Segmentation

Key point: There are numerous cultural differences in many markets that share several related traits and characteristics, known as *cultural universals*.

TABLE 2.1
Categories for Segmenting Markets

Geographic
    Region, City, or Metro size; Population density, climate
Demographic
    Age, Family size, Gender, Income, Occupation, Education, Religion,
        Race, Nationality, Social class
Psychographic
    Life styles, Personality, Self-image, Cultural influence
Product Attributes
    Benefits preferred, Buying-readiness status, Usage rate, Loyalty ranking,
        Attitudes toward product or service

Geographic segmentation is relatively easy to perform because the individual segments can be clearly delineated on a map. It is a sensible strategy to employ when
there are distinct differences in climatic conditions or cultural patterns.

Internationally, blocks or clusters of countries can be approached in a similar
fashion, particularly if they share the same language and cultural heritage. For instance, in most of Latin America the same advertising media are often appropriate for
several countries.

While there are numerous cultural differences in many of those countries — as
well as in other parts of the world — there are common problems that share several
related features, known as *cultural universals*. These include economic systems, marriage and family systems, educational systems, social control systems, and supernat-
ural belief systems.

Case Example — The recent economic boom in Latin America illustrates how
segmentation can work for enterprising managers. This vast region is experiencing
explosive growth resulting from a variety of dramatic changes, such as lowering of
trade barriers, declining inflation and steadier prices, economic recovery and rising
incomes, democratic freedom and freer expression, and the profusion of dazzling
new communications technologies. Influenced by those dynamic changes, enterprising managers continue to discover attractive opportunities by segmenting markets
and then targeting the identified groups. For example:

- Demographics reveal that of Latin America's nearly half-billion people,
  almost half the population is younger than 20. Hooked on new technology
  and yearning to follow the leading trends in world markets, these new consumers hunger for every enticement from fast foods to PC banking.
- With an estimated 35% of women in the work force, this emerging growth
  segment is creating a strong demand for new products and services tailored
  to their individual needs.
- Upgraded telephone lines, the result of privatizing state-run telecom services, have exposed large groups of individuals to the use of the Internet

— with the corresponding skyrocketing sales in high-tech products and services.

- With working-class Latins grabbing the latest electronic products and with telephone rates and cellular phone prices dropping dramatically, cell phones are multiplying at triple digit levels, thereby exposing a dynamic and previously overlooked segment.

- Steadier currencies are making it possible for banks to latch on to another emerging segment by offering consumers home mortgages, life insurance, and private pension funds.

- There is a new sensitivity to otherwise poorly served groups, such as the millions of Afro-Latins, whose buying power is also rising. Seeing the segment as an opportunity, beauty products companies are launching lines of cosmetics to reach this flourishing market. And new magazines are directing editorial attention to meeting their particular cultural and cosmetic desires.

Domestically, segmentation can be applied by city, county, region, or state size; by population density; or by other geopolitical criteria. However, such segmentation is effective only if it reflects differences in need and motivation patterns. Many firms, for example, adjust their advertising efforts to an area as small as a county.

Demographic Segmentation

Besides geographic information, demographic variables are also important segmentation factors. They owe their popularity to two facts: (1) they are easier to observe and/or measure than most other characteristics, and (2) their breakdown is often closely linked to differences in behavioral patterns. Demographic factors include age, sex, family size, stage in the family life cycle, income, occupation, education, religion, race, nationality, and social class. The following example illustrates the current designation of a market labeled Generation Y.

Generation Y

Generation Y, estimated at 60 million strong, is known by several names: Echo Boomers, or the Millennium Generation. They are the children of baby boomers, have a huge buying clout, and are a group that big companies want to envelop with a huge array of products and services. Marketers yearn to reach these kids, born between 1979 and 1994, as they begin to converge on the shopping malls. (In contrast, the once-sought-after baby boomers numbered just 17 million.)

Consequently, Generation Y is a segmented, identifiable, and reachable market. That's the good news; they are a viable target for those companies that can create the fashion, entertainment, and games those kids can embrace. It's also a moneymaking opportunity for firms that supply the brand marketers with raw materials, equipment, and related services.

The tough news, however, is the immense difficulty in winning the attention and hearts of a segment so diverse in its demographic profile. For instance, one in three is not Caucasian. One in four lives in a single-parent household. Three in four have working mothers. While the baby boomers are still learning Microsoft Windows, their kids are playing at computers in kindergarten. Indeed, such a monumental task takes all the brains and brawn of marketers and nonmarketers working in harmony to understand and interpret the teenagers' values, tastes, and motivations, then translate them into brands they will buy.

The following case shows how one savvy marketing company used demographic and buying behavior segmentation in an industry loaded with look-alike products.

CASE EXAMPLE: PAGING NETWORK

Paging Network, a relatively small developer of paging systems, is doing a remarkable job of outflanking such major competitors as the paging subsidiaries of Southwestern Bell Corp. and Pacific Telesis Group. PageNet, as it's known, climbed to the number one position in the paging industry. During the past few years, it posted impressive performance by adding new customers at the rate of about 50% annually. In contrast, Southwestern Bell, in the number two position, has grown at around 10% a year.

PAGENET'S STRATEGIES

Any successful application of strategies usually owes credit to the process behind the achievement. In PageNet's case, that process turned out to be segmentation. Its use of segmentation is impressive even though the company did not have a unique technology. In effect, PageNet was one of the pack, operating in an undifferentiated industry where all competitors with look-alike products were scrambling for customers. PageNet attacked its market with the following strategies:

- Armed with a user profile and a foothold into a large number of geographic segments, the segmentation process moved to the next step: market penetration. With geographic coverage of 45% achieved by the mid-1990s, management set an ambitious goal of 75% market coverage. To reach that objective, they turned to demographic and life-style segmentation to target new customer segments for paging services. For example, new parents leaving a child with a babysitter, teenagers beginning to date, and elderly people living alone.
- As an outcome of its segmentation approach and competitor analysis, PageNet decided on aggressive pricing as its prime strategy and selected an average price differential about 20% below that of its competitors. The decision to make pricing one of the driving forces came after managers observed a significant number of small competitors serving the industry with outmoded equipment and inefficient methods of operation, resulting in high costs and low profits. PageNet supported its aggressive pricing strategy by strengthening internal operations and establishing cost-cutting efficiencies. Result: its costs came in at 33% lower than the industry average.
- Successful implementation of market segmentation depends upon distrib-

ution. PageNet selected the electronics departments of Kmart, Wal-Mart, and Home Depot to reach diverse consumer audiences. Again, relying on aggressive pricing, it gave those outlets extremely attractive prices at or below wholesale cost. In return, PageNet keeps the revenue from the monthly service charge, with an initial forecast of 80,000 new users when first introduced.

PSYCHOGRAPHIC SEGMENTATION

The most exciting form of segmentation results from the application of psychographic variables, such as *life style, personality, user status, usage rate, spending behavior*, and *marketing-factor sensitivity*. Banks, car manufacturers, and liquor producers, to name a few, avail themselves to the advantages of psychographic segmentation. It is a branch of market segmentation that is still evolving and promises great vitality in the future. Department stores use *life style* departments that vary according to neighborhood.

Personality is somewhat of an isolated psychographic variable. Although attractive to marketers, it still requires developmental work before it can prove to be a valid criterion for segmentation.

User status refers to a breakdown according to nonuser, ex-user, potential user, first-time user, and regular user groups that might respond favorably to different kinds of stimulation. Consequently, companies with high market share are especially eager to attract potential users, while smaller competitors with lower market share are better off trying to convert existing users.

Usage rate is of practical importance in segment marketing. Typically, nonusers are distinguished from light, medium, and heavy users of their product; heavy users often represent a relatively small share of total households or industrial buying yet account for the major portion of the sales volume in the market. For example, with regard to beer consumption, 17% of the households in the U.S. account for 50% of the users and 88% of the beer consumed. In contrast, the usage of toilet tissue is far less concentrated; 50% of the households account for 75% of the total consumption.

The term *spending behavior* covers a variety of patterns from emotional to practical, from brand loyalty to price- and deal-consciousness.

Market-factor sensitivity refers to the responsiveness of buyers to the various elements of the marketing mix: quality, price, service, advertising, product design, sales promotion, and channel availability.

VALS (Values and Life Styles)

With cultures, values, and life styles taking on greater importance in product creation and market development, you should be armed with information that grasps how groups live, spend, and behave. In particular, VALS is a useful form of life style segmentation that explores activities people are involved with, interests they pursue, and opinions they hold.

The method divides life styles into nine categories consisting of: *survivors, sus-*

tainers, belongers, emulators, achievers, I-am-me, experiencers, societally conscious, and *integrateds.* Figure 2.1 describes the VALS framework based on the Standard Research Institute's analysis of answers from 20,713 respondents to over 800 questions.

Using VALS or other forms of psychographic segmentation is not a do-it-yourself exercise. Effective application requires the specialized assistance of professionals, usually trained in some sphere of the social sciences. However, PageNet was able to use a simple form of life-style segmentation by observing new groups for its paging services beyond just demographic profiling: new parents leaving a child with a babysitter, teenagers beginning to date, and elderly people living alone.

Categories	%	Life Styles
Survivors	4%	Disadvantaged people who tend to be despairing, depressed, and withdrawn.
Sustainers	7%	Disadvantaged people who are struggling to get out of poverty.
Belongers	33%	People who are conventional, conservative, nostalgic, and unexperimental, and who would rather fit in than stand out.
Emulators	10%	People who are ambitious, upwardly mobile, and status conscious; they want to "make it big."
Achievers	23%	The nation's leaders, who make things happen, work with the system, and enjoy the good life.
I-am-me	5%	People who are typically young, self engrossed, and given to whim.
Experiencers	7%	People who pursue a rich inner life and want to experience directly what life has to offer.
Societally conscious	9%	People who have a high sense of social responsibility and want to improve conditions in society.
Integrateds	2%	People who have fully matured psychologically and combine the best elements of inner and outer directedness.

FIGURE 2.1 The VALS framework.

GEODEMOGRAPHIC SEGMENTATION

Another technique for segmenting a market is known as geodemography. It combines many of the advantages of geographic and demographic segmentation. It is based on census data obtained from the 256,000 census "block" groups or neighborhoods in the U.S. People having similar life styles tend to cluster in neighborhoods. Some market analysts believe that geodemography can give businesses more precise information about their target markets and how best to reach them.

For example, consider a block group with a high concentration of families having annual incomes over $80,000 and made up of business managers and professionals who are college educated and over age 50. This group likes to watch television programs similar to the popular *60 Minutes* and also consumes four times the nation's average usage of vodka.

Another block group is categorized by watching *Seinfeld,* a television situation comedy popular during the 1990s, and drinks almost no vodka. Members of this group tend to cut across a variety of demographic, geographic, and psychographic sectors. It is obvious, then, that individual approaches would be required for two such differing targets.

Potential users of geodemography are banks that need to determine where to install automatic teller machines, and baby food manufacturers that want to test-market a new product at clusters with large numbers of first-time mothers. The technique also is of particular interest to catalogers, credit card companies, and other businesses that have large direct-mail programs.

LOCATING A VIABLE SEGMENT

> **Key point:** When deciding on a potential segment, free your mind of biases. You are attempting to capture precise, uncluttered, and objective characteristics of a segment.

How do you begin implementing a segmentation strategy? Follow these guidelines:

1. If your business is primarily local or regional, think about the predominant groups in your area. Is there a substantial industrial base? What type of industry is dominant? How would you describe the demographic profile? Then, match that information against your customer base as well as to your own company's capabilities.
2. You could hire the professional help of an advertising agency or market research firm. If the cost is beyond your budget, do your own observations. Assemble a focus group (discussed in detail in Chapter 4) and invite guests from the target community. You can gauge the viability of a segment by participating in an event, such as a trade show. The event can be either local, regional, or national.
3. At another level, you can take out an ad in a local publication or use a highly targeted mailing list at relatively low rates to test for response. (The example cited earlier of the Boreal Ski Area described how the company successfully focused on San Francisco's large Chinese population.)
4. Or you can find a segment by using a systematic approach of walking around and employing the following techniques:

   - Define the physical dimension of the segment that you have singled out for targeting. Describe the segment in nonjudgmental terms. Use facts built around the physical layout of factories, stores, warehouses, roads, and other transportation hubs, as well as consumers' locations within specific and well-defined geographic areas. For the most part, the activity requires you to observe closely, yet guard against being hindered by biases and preconceptions such as, "We've looked at that market before."
   - Keep your observations as objective as possible. The so-called objective business terms used to define the characteristics of a segment may be laced with false or misleading assumptions that could distort the actual behavioral patterns of the group. One remedy is to create your own descriptive language. That is, use terms, descriptions, or vocabulary borrowed from a neutral field that does not distort or create false

assumptions, such as military, sports, or agricultural terms. The intent is to free your mind of biases. You are attempting to capture accurate, unadorned, and objective characteristics of a segment.

- Try to interpret meaningful gestures or body language while observing the purchasing process at a distance. Of course, not all gestures are readily interpreted, unless you have an intimate knowledge of the group. Until sufficient experience is accumulated, you will have to gain expertise through continuous observation and by asking knowledgeable individuals who understand the gestures to decode them for you.
- Observe the types of behavior associated with an event, such as a purchase of a consumer product or a lengthy negotiation for the purchase of capital equipment or a computer. Look for any signs of a "ritual" that seems to be tied to the event and thereby defines the culture of the group or organization.

The purpose of this entire four-step process is to add greater precision to your strategic thinking and thereby make meaningful contributions to your company's market-driven objectives. Also, with resources often limited, competition more intense, and viable segments harder to locate, you now have an additional evaluation tool to aid your decision making.

EVALUATING A MARKET SEGMENT

> **Key point:** Portfolio analysis is an excellent quantitative tool for use by firms of any size to make investment decisions on a market-by-market or product-by-product basis.

The final step after selecting a market segment is to expose it to a screening analysis to determine if it has a long-term potential and will provide an adequate pay-out for the investment of time, manpower, and resources.

The evaluation process is known as *portfolio analysis* and consists of formal models that use a variety of criteria to rate the attractiveness of markets. In practice, portfolio analysis is an excellent quantitative tool for use by all size firms to make investment decisions on a market-by-market or product-by-product basis.

Therefore, if attending a strategy meeting, your job is to participate in selecting the portfolio model that best suits your business. The results can provide immeasurable help in systematically selecting a market segment, analyzing your competitive situation, developing marketing strategies, and even influencing the priorities of your job. The following case introduces you to the practical application of portfolio analysis.

CASE EXAMPLE: IMPERIAL CHEMICAL INDUSTRIES

Imperial Chemical Industries (ICI) has traditionally served the bulk chemicals market. However, for the last few years that market has suffered from intense competition, a downturn in industry consumption, and the fall of commodity prices. In turn, those issues caused a depressing effect on ICI's profits. The alarming situation has even threatened the London-based company's independence, as acquisition-hungry suitors tried to take over the company and possibly erase a venerable British industrial name. Looking for business-building approaches to retain its autonomy and set a course of self-reliance for the long term, ICI activated the following bold strategies.

ICI's STRATEGIES

- Spend heavily on strengthening its line of specialty items such as flavors and fragrances, industrial adhesives, and paints through internal product development and by acquisitions in both Europe and North America. For acquisitions, two leading U.S.-based companies fit ICI's criteria: National Starch & Chemical Co., a leader in supplying adhesives used by companies such as Intel Corp. in assembling packages of chips, and the other, Quest, that produces fragrances and is involved in the profitable business of creating new flavors and textures for foods.
- Sell off significant portions of its bulk chemical businesses including pigments, explosives, and fertilizers. ICI management concluded after studying the situation that it no longer had the marketing power to compete with the industry leaders in bulk chemicals.
- Shift sales from Britain to Continental Europe and North America. By acquiring strong companies both in the U.S. and on the Continent, ICI has an immediate presence in those lucrative segments.

In implementing these strategies, ICI management exercised meticulous judgment in designating which companies to buy and sell and which markets to build, maintain, or exit on a segment-by-segment evaluation.

The following section describes three of the more popular models of portfolio analysis used in assessing markets and products, all of which can apply to your business, and about which you should have some familiarity: *BCG Growth-Share Matrix*, *General Electric Business Screen*, and the *Arthur D. Little Matrix*.

BCG GROWTH-SHARE MATRIX

A technique developed by the Boston Consulting Group, this classic model can prove highly useful in assessing a portfolio of businesses or products. BCG Growth-Share Matrix (Figure 2.2) graphically shows that some products may enjoy a strong position relative to those of competitors, while other products languish in a weaker position.

As such, each product benefits from a distinct strategy depending on its position in the matrix. The various circles represent a product. From the positioning of these circles, management can determine the following information:

- Dollar sales, represented by the area of the circle.
- Market share, relative to the firm's largest competitor, as shown by the horizontal position.

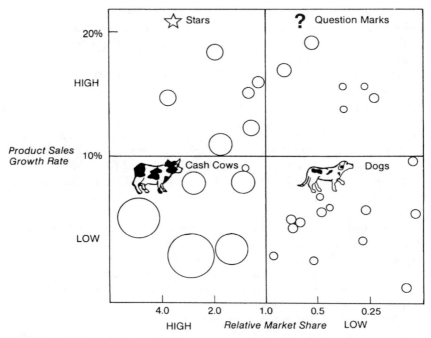

FIGURE 2.2 BCG growth-share matrix.

- Growth rate, relative to the market in which the product competes, as shown by the vertical position.

In addition, the quadrants of the matrix arrange products into four groups:

1. *Stars*: products that have high market growth and high market share. These products need constant attention to maintain or increase share through active promotion, effective distribution coverage, product improvement, and careful pricing strategies.
2. *Cash cows*: products that have low market growth and high market share. Such products usually hold market dominance and generate strong cash flow. The object: retain a strong market presence without large expenditures for promotion and with minimal outlay for R&D. The central idea behind the cash cow is that businesses with a large share of market are more profitable than their smaller-share competitors.
3. *Question marks* (also known as problem children or wildcats): products with potential for high growth in a fast-moving market but with low market share. They absorb large amounts of cash (usually taken from the cash cows) and are expected to eventually reach the status of a star.
4. *Dogs*: products with low market growth and low market share, reflecting the worst of all situations. A number of alternatives are possible: maintain the product in the line and support the image of a full-line supplier and

thereby deny access to the market through which an eager competitor could enter, quickly eliminate the product from the line, or harvest the product through a slow phase out.

As you review the growth-share matrix, note on the vertical axis how product sales are separated into high and low quadrants. The 10% growth line is simply an arbitrary rate of growth and represents a middle level. For your particular industry the number could be 5, 12, or 15%.

Similarly, on the horizontal axis there is a dividing line of relative market share of 1.0 so that positioning your product in the lower left-hand quadrant would indicate high market leadership, and in the lower right-hand quadrant low market leadership.

The significant interpretations of the matrix are as follows:

- The amount of cash generated increases with relative market share.
- The amount of sales growth requires proportional cash input to finance the added capacity for market development. If market share is maintained, then cash requirements increase only relative to market growth rate.
- Increases in market share usually require cash to support advertising and sales promotion expenditures, lower prices, and other share-building tactics. On the other hand, a decrease in market share may provide cash for use in other product areas.
- Where a product moves toward maturity, it is possible to use just enough funds to maintain market position and use surplus funds to reinvest in other products that are still growing.

In summary, the BCG Growth-Share Matrix permits you to evaluate where your products and markets are relative to competitors. It also helps you calculate what investments are needed to support such basic strategies as expanding into emerging market segments, building share for your product in existing markets, harvesting products, or withdrawing from the market.

GENERAL ELECTRIC BUSINESS SCREEN

The BCG Growth-Share Matrix focuses on cash flow and uses only two variables: growth and market share. On the other hand, the General Electric Business Screen (Figure 2.3), also known as multifactor analysis, is a more comprehensive analysis that provides a graphic display of where an existing product fits competitively in relation to a variety of criteria. It also aids in projecting the chances for a new product's success.

The key points in using the GE Business Screen are the following:

1. *Industry attractiveness* is shown on the vertical axis of the matrix. It is based on rating such factors as market size, market growth rate, profit margin, competitive intensity, cyclicality, seasonality, and scale of economies. Each factor is then given a weight of high, medium, or low in overall attractiveness to classify an industry, market segment, or product.

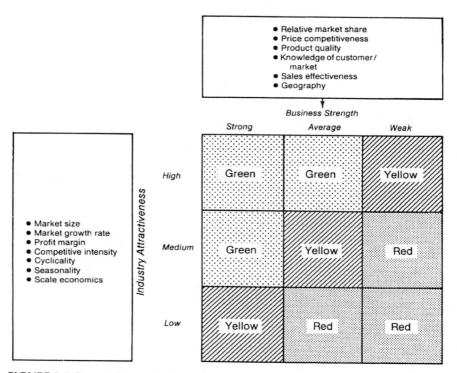

FIGURE 2.3 General Electric Business Screen.

2. *Business strength* is shown on the horizontal axis. A weighted rating is made for such factors as relative market share, price competitiveness, product quality, knowledge of customer and market, sales effectiveness, and geography. The results would show your ability to compete and, in turn, provide insight into developing strategies in relation to competitors.

3. The matrix is divided into three color sectors: green, yellow, and red. The green sector has three cells at the upper left and indicates those markets that are favorable in industry attractiveness and business strength. These markets have a "green light" to move in aggressively. The yellow sector includes the diagonal cells stretching from the lower left to upper right. This sector indicates a medium level in overall attractiveness. The red sector covers the three cells in the lower right. This sector indicates those markets that are low in overall attractiveness.

A more comprehensive view of the factors contributing to industry attractiveness and business strength is given in Table 2.2. The variety of factors is not meant to overwhelm, but to provide for the practical application of any factors that could possibly contribute to a more meaningful analysis. For personal use, you can add or delete factors to suit your business and industry.

TABLE 2.2
Factors Contributing to Market Attractiveness and Business Strength

Market Attractiveness	Function
Market size	Measures size of key segments, your share of each segment relative to closest competitors
Market growth rate	Identifies annual rate of growth projected over a 3- to 5-year period
Profit margins	Indicates your margins and relationship of margins to your company's financial criteria
Competitive intensity	Compares types of competitors in terms of products, pricing, distribution, promotion, personnel, marketing capability, market share by segment and competitor
Cyclicality, seasonality	Determines effects of economic, industry, technology, or seasonality cycles on segment entry and growth rate
Scale economics	Measures effects of economies of scale and experience related to productivity and profitability

Business Strength	Function
Relative market share	Compares competitors within an overall market, individual segments, product applications, and against top three competitors
Price competitiveness	Evaluates sensitivity to price, value-added services, offerings of competitors, and external market factors
Product quality	Measures customer perceptions of quality, price/value relationships, comparisons with competitors' offerings
Knowledge of customer/market	Indicates level of market intelligence related to how business will change in 3 to 5 years; Customer functions to be satisfied as market evolves; Technologies needed to satisfy customer/market needs; Changes anticipated in buyer behavior, competition, environment, culture, and the economy
Sales effectiveness	Evaluates efficiency of sales force, advertising, sales promotion; Weighs impact of the Internet on sales force functions and distribution channels
Geography	Assesses movement of key customers, changes in location of selected segments, ability to provide adequate market coverage and service

Finally, to show an even more practical application of the GE Business Screen, Figure 2.4 illustrates the strategy options for each of the nine cells of the matrix.

ARTHUR D. LITTLE MATRIX

Another time-tested portfolio analysis approach is associated with the consulting organization, Arthur D. Little, Inc. In one actual application, a major manufacturer in the health care industry used this approach to analyze how its various products stacked up in market share.

In Figure 2.5, some of the company's products are used to demonstrate the function of this matrix. First, note the similarities of this format to the other portfolio analysis approaches already discussed. The competitive positions of various products

Business Strength

Strong	Average	Weak
Invest for Growth	Select Areas for Maximum	Judiciously Invest for Earnings
Budget for maximum	Investment	Defend profitable market
investment	Invest to expand existing	segments
Search for global	segments	Review industry outlook for
opportunities	Search for high-potential	its long-term potential
Minimize short-term	segments that are emerging,	Identify joint-venture
profit expectations	neglected, or poorly served	opportunities
Go for maximum market share	Search for acquisitions and	
	partnering opportunities	
Invest for Growth	Invest for Earnings	Harvest or Divest
Build prudently on market and	Concentrate on selected	Avoid unnecessary invest
distribution strengths	segments	ments or commitments
Fill gaps in product line	Monitor segments and make	Move to the most profitable
Evaluate strengths and	contingency plans	segments
strategies of competitors		Position for divestiture of least
		profitable segments or
		products
Invest for Earnings	Conserve or Raise Cash Flow	Withdraw
Maintain market position	Conduct product audit and	Exit market
Look for specialized market	delete unprofitable products	Develop best market position
niches	Minimize investments	to optimize terms of sale
Search for partnering	Search for potential	
opportunities	opportunities	
Invest to support current		
market share		

FIGURE 2.4 Strategy options based on the GE Business Screen.

are plotted on the vertical axis according to such factors as *leading*, *strong*, *favorable*, *tenable*, *weak*, and *nonviable*. On the horizontal axis, the maturity levels for the products are designated *embryonic*, *growth*, *mature*, and *aging*.

The key interpretations for this matrix are as follows:

1. **Nonviable**: indicates the lowest possible level of competitive position.
2. **Weak**: designates unsatisfactory financial performance but with some opportunity for improvement.
3. **Tenable**: shows a competitive product position where financial performance is barely satisfactory. These products have a less than average opportunity to improve competitive position.
4. **Favorable**: displays a competitive position that is better than the survival rate. These products also have a limited range of opportunities for improvement.

5. **Strong**: suggests an ability to defend market share against competing moves without the sacrifice of acceptable financial performance.
6. **Leading**: reveals the widest range of strategic options because of the competitive distance between the given products and the competitors' products.

An examination of the four products shows how this matrix worked during a particular period in those products' life cycle:

Automated radioimmunoassay (a sophisticated diagnostic product used in laboratories) was considered in its embryonic stage with a favorable competitive position at the time the analysis was prepared. This favorable position offered the manager a range of strategy options, as long as the decisions related to the overall corporate strategy.

Single-use hypodermic needles and syringes had a strong competitive position in a growth industry. Here, too, strategy options were fairly flexible and depended on competitive moves as well as on how quickly increases in market share were desired.

Blood collection system products (Vacutainers) had a leading competitive position in a mature industry. To hold existing market share, the company's strategy centered on product differentiation.

Mercury/glass hospital thermometers had a strong competitive position in a

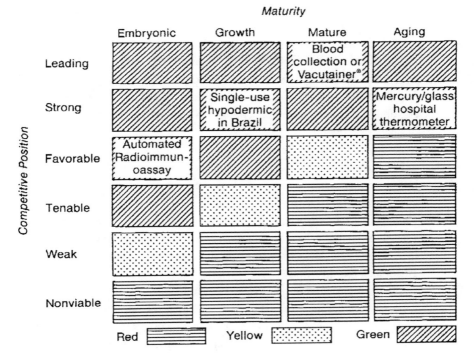

FIGURE 2.5 Arthur D. Little Matrix applied to products.

declining industry. This product had less price flexibility. However, by using service, repackaging, and distribution innovations, the company attempted to maintain its strong position before giving in to price reductions.

As in the GE Business Screen, a green-yellow-red system is used to indicate strategic options. Green indicates a wide range of options; yellow indicates caution for a limited range of options for selected development; and red is a warning of peril with options narrowed to those of withdrawal, divestiture, and liquidation.

The three major screening tools described above can add greater precision to your decisions and aid in allocating resources to market segments and products for the greatest return.

BEST PRACTICES

The following categories contain ideas that could impact the buying process and consequently your decision on selecting segments:

1. *Responsiveness*. Often tied to just-in-time delivery, responsiveness relates to the goal of zero inventory for customers, or to assistance in helping to avoid inventory buildup. Are you prepared to deliver on time and save the customer inventory costs?
2. *Quality control*. You will achieve maximum cost savings if the buyer receives trouble-free products without the need for further inspection. For you, time is saved and complaints are reduced. For your customers, improved quality helps them achieve a higher level of satisfaction from *their* customers. Are there sufficient control systems in place to assure delivery of quality products?
3. *Nearness to customer*. In situations where frequent service calls are required, proximity to customers and the need for a speedy response are factors in segment selection. How close are your service personnel to key customers?
4. *Communications*. New technology constantly transforms ordering and fulfillment systems. Where do you rank, relative to your competitors, in utilizing the new and expanding forms of communications to meet customers' requirements?
5. *Dependable production schedules*. As customers begin to make their sales forecasts and production schedules available, an opportunity arises to develop a stable production capability to meet customers' rigid schedules. What commitments do you need from your production people to satisfy such buyer behavior?

3 Marketing Strategy for the 21st Century

Strategy is the art of coordinating the means (money, human resources, and materials) to achieve the ends (profit, customer satisfaction, and company growth) as defined by company policy and objectives.

INTRODUCTION

As an extension of the above formal definition, there is a more straightforward and pragmatic definition to keep in mind: *Strategies are actions to achieve objectives.* The notion here is that unless there is an action component to strategies, they are merely wishful thoughts.

To grasp the full meaning of both definitions, let's examine how one company applied strategy to solve its problem. As in the preceeding chapter, review the actual case and act as if you were sitting in at the company's strategy meeting and asked to make a meaningful contribution. Think how you would have participated in the session. What questions would you have raised? How would you have evaluated the recommendations made by others at the meeting?

After you review the case you will find relevant information and guidelines that would have prepared you to furnish advice leading to positive action.

CASE EXAMPLE: EMC CORP.

PROBLEM

How do we energize a product line plagued by missed opportunities, poor product quality, sluggish sales, and dismal profits?

SITUATION

EMC Corp., developers of computer storage equipment, faced extinction in 1988. Markets for the company were changing. A well-known competitor held the dominant market position. Customers were fed up with EMC's dismal product performance. Internally, the company was reeling from quality control problems, and numerous other competitors were chipping away at its market share.

In particular, EMC was plagued with equipment problems that reached crisis pro-

portions. Every piece of equipment the company sold during that period was crash-
ing because EMC engineers failed to detect faulty disk drives supplied by NEC Corp.

Galvanized by a hard-driving new executive, Michael C. Ruettgers, EMC managers at all levels bore down on the following areas with bold steps to cope with the
desperate situation:

EMC's STRATEGIES

1. *Satisfy each customer*. Ruettgers drove forward with the fundamental
   belief that to stay solvent for the future customer satisfaction must take
   first priority. To appease distraught customers, Ruettgers offered to replace
   the faulty parts or buy whole new systems. In less than a year, EMC spent
   $100 million on the remedial action.
2. *Fix EMC's products*. Engineering specialists were hired to locate the product problems. Ruettgers organized new quality control procedures, inves-
   tigated and tested every batch of parts, and scrutinized all finished systems
   developed by the company.
3. *Concentrate full efforts on a single competitor*. The bold decision was to
   target one competitor: the formidable IBM. The daring strategy meant canceling virtually all-new projects related to providing storage systems to
   minicomputer companies such as Digital Equipment, Wang, and Unisys.
   Instead EMC would focus all product development and marketing efforts
   to unseat IBM from its leadership position.
4. *Employ an innovative product strategy*. EMC's product strategy called for
   delivering a superfast, world-class storage system that companies could
   use to instantly access their most important information. It did so with an
   ingenious system that replaced giant memory devices with a host of inexpensive disk drives linked together. In an amazingly short period of six
   months, IBM mainframe customers began switching over to EMC systems
   so rapidly that revenues from discarded projects had no effect on the bottom line.
5. *Buy market share with a lower price*. The issues of product quality and
   product performance are summed up by one customer who described
   EMC's units as "faster, more reliable, and about 30% cheaper than our
   other stuff." Thus, using an aggressive pricing strategy of undercutting
   IBM's prices was successful, but only as long as quality problems were
   solved and EMC continued to demonstrate superior product attributes.
6. *Anticipate market direction, employ strategic long-term thinking, and execute strategies with speed*. Again EMC acted boldly and bet its R&D
   money and talent on innovative, but yet unproven, software for connecting different types of computers to a single storage system. The idea for
   the new system originated through direct contact with customers and lis-
   tening to their mind-boggling problems of trying to recover lost data from
   a variety of incompatible computers. Moving rapidly to solve the problem,

EMC beat out competitors by two years and grabbed the top tier of customers with its innovative system, leaving competitors in its wake. Consequently, maintaining a customer-driven orientation and resolving their problems became the unbounded driver of product development.

7. *Motivate the sales force.* Through a combination of forceful verbal pushes, salespeople (most of whom were college athletes and used to running hard and fast to reach a goal) are prodded to reach sales objectives beyond their normal quotas. Backing up the motivation, EMC rewards them with a combination of stock options, commissions, and bonuses that can drive paychecks over $1 million.

Thus, EMC came back from the brink, built a powerful high-tech enterprise, and created one of the most successful business cultures of the 1990s.

> **Key point:** Maintaining a customer-driven orientation and resolving their problems should be the backbone of product development.

NEED TO KNOW

Had you participated in EMC's strategy meeting, here is tangible information you would have found relevant. The various elements contributing to EMC's remarkable success can be categorized into two parts: the *marketing mix* as a practical structure to develop marketing strategies; and the *external forces* consisting of customers, competitors, industry, and environment that are common to most businesses.

Let's begin with the marketing mix.

MARKETING MIX

The structure for developing a multifaceted marketing strategy as demonstrated by the EMC study consists of the product, price, promotion, and distribution. These four components are universally referred to as the marketing mix. It serves as one of the most pragmatic and organized techniques for developing (or screening) competitive marketing strategies.

Table 3.1 below illustrates the framework. Each of the four primary components that comprise the marketing mix signifies a potential driver of strategy. In turn, under each of the four listings you can choose items that suggest strategy possibilities. In selecting which parts of the marketing mix should spearhead a strategy, do the following:

- Compare your company's performance to that of competitors for each of the selected parts and decide if you have a clear-cut competitive advantage.
- Check that the items you picked represent your customers' primary needs or wants, and the reasons why they will buy your product rather than a competitive offering.

TABLE 3.1
Creating Strategies Out of the Marketing Mix

Product	Price	Promotion	Distribution
Quality	List price	Advertising:	Channels:
Features	Discounts	Customer and	Direct sales force
Options	Allowances	Trade	Distribution
Style	Payment period	Personal selling:	Dealers
Brand name	Credit terms	Incentives	Market coverage
Packaging		Sales aids	Warehouse
Sizes		Samples	locations
Services		Training	Inventory control
Warranties		Sales Promotion:	systems
Returns		Demonstrations	Physical distribution
Versatility		Contests	
Uniqueness		Premiums	
Utility		Coupons	
Reliability		Manuals	
Durability		Telemarketing	
Patent protection		Internet	
Guarantees		Publicity	

> **Key point:** The four components of the marketing mix — product, price, promotion, and distribution — represent potential drivers of your strategy.

APPLICATIONS

In applying the marketing mix, your entire purpose is to single out areas that would help build strategies and tactics. If they are implemented with skill they could represent a distinctive competitive advantage.

The following guidelines show the use of some components of the marketing mix along with accompanying actions. (Many of these actions were expertly performed by EMC.) You will find them useful for evaluating recommendations made by others or as suggestions made by you.

GUIDELINES

1. Select a feature of your product, such as quality, packaging, options, or features that could represent a competitive advantage and that larger competitors cannot match. Use either formal market research or personal observation to identify possibilities for differentiating your product or service.

2. Commit to quality and service as an organizational priority. That translates to initiating programs and systems that encourage individuals in various functions to strive for quality. (Initially, EMC focused on this area to climb

out of its dismal predicament.)

3. Focus on specialty products that command premium prices. Leave the commodity price segment to others, unless you are the low-cost producer. As discussed in the previous chapter, that means segmenting your market for specific product applications.

4. Establish long-term alliances with customers to grow with them and to build technology and product relationships. Recommend ways to encourage trust with customers and suppliers so that sensitive information can be shared for mutual interests. If possible, encourage others to design product features, propose product options, or identify viable new services.

5. Maintain a market-driven orientation throughout the organization — within all functions — that leads to closer relationships with customers. Organize strategy teams made up of functional managers (discussed in Chapter 1). Then, use the teams' strategic marketing plans as lines of communication to respond rapidly to market opportunities. (Strategic marketing planning is detailed in Chapter 9.)

6. Investigate opportunities that complement your long-term objectives. Seek joint ventures, licensing, or exporting situations that can expand your presence in existing markets and help extend into new or undeveloped markets.

7. Partner salespeople with customers to provide product solutions to customers' problems. Suggest going beyond traditional forms of sales training. Instead, teach salespeople how to think like strategists, so they can help their customers achieve a competitive advantage.

8. Identify market niches that are emerging, neglected, or poorly served. Reassess how you segment your markets. Search for additional approaches beyond the usual criteria of customer size, frequency of purchase, and geographic location. Look for potential niches related to just-in-time delivery, performance, application, quality, or technical assistance. Or use any other strategy area from Table 3.1 that builds a unique competitive advantage for your company.

EXTERNAL FORCES

The second part that highlights EMC's superb performance deals with the *external forces* that are common to most businesses: customers, competitors, industry, and environment. As noted in Figure 3.1, the customer is at the center of the forces.

Let's see how each contributes to shaping competitive marketing strategies.

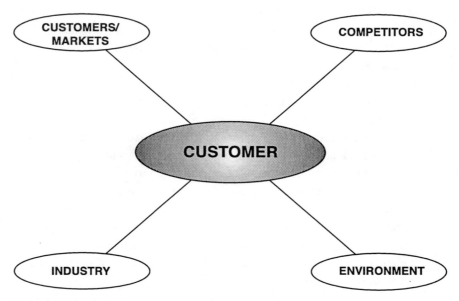

FIGURE 3.1 External forces.

CUSTOMERS

> **Key point:** Understand your customers — if you expect to sustain growth and maintain a comfortable lead over hard-driving competitors.

The customer is the center of marketing's attention. To produce want-satisfying products and services, you must know what your customers want, where they can find what they want, and how to communicate to them that you are able to meet their needs and solve their problems.

Thus, understand your customers — if you expect to sustain growth and maintain a comfortable lead over hard-driving competitors. Beyond wishing for a brilliant idea to flash into your mind, there is a step-by-step process you can follow to trigger marketing innovations:

1. *Define your customers by demographic, geographic, and psychographic (behavioral) characteristics.* Observe changes in the character of your markets. For instance, look for any unmet customer needs that would enable you to respond rapidly in the form of products, services, methods of delivery, credit terms, or technical assistance. Talk with customers to detect their most troublesome problems and frustrations. Meet with salespeople and draw them out on ways to innovate.
2. *Examine customer usage patterns or frequency of purchase.* Watch for alternative and substitute products that could represent an opportunity to re-

place competitive products. Also observe deviations in regional and seasonal purchase patterns. Check for changes from past purchasing and usage practices that could translate into opportunities.

3. *Review selling practices.* Innovations often occur in selling. Stay tuned to current trends in promotional allowances, selling tactics, trade discounts, rebates, point-of-purchase opportunities, or seasonal/holiday requirements — and the evolving strategies associated with the Internet. Here, again, stay close to salespeople for such information. Encourage them to input all behavioral information about perceptions dealing with your product, delivery, company image, complaint handling, and any other factors that influence a sale and contribute to a long-term relationship.

4. *Survey channels of distribution.* Examine your distribution methods and look for opportunities to customize services consistent with the characteristics of the segment. Pay attention to warehousing (if applicable) and which areas could be fertile possibilities to innovate, such as electronic ordering and computerized inventory control systems. Look, too, at the direct marketing channels and the techniques pioneered by such companies as Dell Computer and Gateway. And experiment with other marketing breakthroughs, such as the Internet, as a new sales and distribution channel.

5. *Look at product possibilities.* Watch for innovative new products and product line extensions to maintain an ongoing presence in your existing markets or to gain a foothold in an emerging segment. Seek opportunities to differentiate or add value to products by harnessing new technology in ways that might broaden your customer base and leverage your company's expertise.

6. *Explore opportunities to cut costs for you and your customers.* Investigate ways to strengthen quality assurance and introduce new warranties to improve product performance and reliability. Also look for possibilities to replace products or systems, improve internal and external operating procedures, and discover new product applications.

COMPETITORS

> **Key point:** Determine how competitors develop strategies against you and how effective they are in defending a market.

Looking objectively at your competitors goes a long way toward plotting their market positions. Armed with such insights, then you can move to a preferred market position and concentrate your resources against their weak spots. The overall aim is to create your own special competitive advantage.

Table 3.2 shows a variety of guidelines and actions to understand competitors.

TABLE 3.2
Guidelines for Understanding Competitors

Guideline	Action
Customer selection	Single out those competitors with whom your customers conduct business.
Competitor segments	Determine how competitors divide their markets.
Behavioral purchase patterns	Learn why customers buy from your competitors and not from you.
Competitor strategies	Find out how competitors develop their strategies against you and how effective they are in defendinga market.
Strengths and weaknesses	Determine competitors' strengths and weaknesses in such areas as product mix, new product development, channels of distribution, promotion, sales force coverage, and overall managerial capabilities.

In short, understand your competitors by examining *customer selection*, *competitor segmentation*, *behavioral purchase patterns*, *competitor strategies*, and *strengths and weaknesses*.

INDUSTRY

> **Key point:** Industry analysis provides insights into future trends so you can stake out opportunity areas for growth.

An industry is the sum of many parts, such as sources of supply, existing competitors, emerging competitors, alternative product and service offerings, and various levels of customers — from intermediaries to original equipment manufacturers (OEM), to after-market end users. Within these assorted parts are 11 powerful determinants that can affect an industry — and consequently influence how you develop your marketing strategy:

1. *Current demand for product:* Measures the demand or usage of your product in sales, units, number of users, share of market, or whatever calculations provide a reliable indication of demand, and which would affect current operations and profitability.
2. *Future potential for product:* Uses a time frame of three to five years to forecast the potential for your product. In turn, that information impacts such decisions as whether you stay in the market, how much resources to allocate to the market, and assesses where your product is in its life cycle (introduction, growth, maturity, or decline) before it becomes obsolete and needs replacement.
3. *Industry life cycle:* Identifies the stage the industry has reached in its life cycle. Industries as well as products have cycles, mostly influenced by rapidly changing technologies, emerging markets, and shifts in buyer behavior.
4. *Emerging technology:* Specifies which technology is currently available or may be in use even on an experimental basis within the industry, and specifically among which competitors. And it determines the sources of

the technology and who holds patents or copyrights.

5. *Changing customer profiles:* Uses segmentation criteria to track any significant changes in demographics, geographics, buyer behavior, or psychographics (life style) of existing and future markets.

6. *Frequency of new product introductions:* Monitors the introduction of new products and determines if there is an industry pattern that can serve as a standard for your own level of product development. Such information helps judge the ability of your organization to keep pace with the flow of new products.

7. *Level of government regulation:* Determines if government regulation is increasing or declining. It assesses the impact on your industry and, most importantly, your company's ability to conform to stringent regulations.

8. *Distribution networks:* Indicates if there are significant innovations in the use of distribution channels. For instance, is there emphasis on pushing the product through distributors, or pulling the product through the channel by influencing the end user, or perhaps eliminating distributors entirely by using a business-to-consumer (B2C) approach? You can then check for evidence of forward integration in which producers are acquiring distributors, or vice versa.

9. *Entry and exit barriers:* Assesses the ease or difficulty of entering and exiting an industry. *Entry* barriers include the amount of capital investment needed, extent of economies of scale, access to distribution channels, and opportunities for product differentiation. *Exit* barriers cover length of time needed in the market to honor labor contracts, length of existing leases, services and parts provided to customers, government regulations, social responsibilities to communities and workers, level of emotional attachment to the business or industry, and outside obligations to warehousing or financial institutions.

10. *Marketing innovation:* Establishes if there are ground-breaking innovations in use that can result in a competitive advantage for you or your competitors, such as electronic ordering systems, computer-driven diagnostic systems, interactive product demonstrations, new promotional incentives, marketing over the Internet, or creative uses of the sales force.

11. *Cost structures:* Evaluates the impact of economies of scale on costs and profits as they relate to new product development, manufacturing, purchasing, R&D, marketing, and distribution. Looks at costs related to applying new technology, flexible manufacturing techniques, the Internet, and warehouse automation. Helps calculate the potential of your industry and your company's ability to compete at a profit.

Using the above guidelines and developing a workable profile gives you a reliable picture of the overall industry. Such an analysis provides insights into future trends so you can stake out promising areas for growth.

ENVIRONMENTAL ISSUES

The powerful forces of demographics, economics, natural resources, technology, legislation, and cultural values can make or break marketing efforts for your business. Through environmental analysis, you can judge the impact on strategy in each of the following categories by asking the question, *"What potential does this factor hold for my product or service?"*

- *Demographic.* Explosive population growth will occur within poor countries. This issue points to great potential markets for foods, medicines, basic machines, clothing, agricultural products, and various low-technology products.
- *Economic.* With the recovering economies and the continuing intensity of competition from the euro zones of Western Europe, the Pacific Rim, and from a growing number of developing countries in Eastern Europe and Latin America, there will be tremendous pressure to stay competitive. And with the continuing trends in e-business, supply-chain management, reengineering, downsizing, and outsourcing, it will be necessary to determine the impact of all these issues on your local economy — and specifically on the buying behavior of groups in your geographic segments.
- *Natural resources.* Diminishing supplies of oil and various minerals could pose a serious problem. By the year 2050, several minerals may become exhausted if the current rate of consumption continues. While firms that use these resources face cost increases and potential shortages, for other firms there is the exciting prospect of discovering new sources of materials or alternative products to replace declining natural resources.
- *Technology.* The often-quoted statistic that 90% of all the scientists who ever lived are alive today sums up the accelerating pace of technological change. In the past few years alone technology has generated a tremendous number of new high-tech products, such as the Internet, and the multitude of audio and video links from workplace to home to other distant locations. New technological advances are changing the way workers are handling their jobs and the way consumers purchase products.
- *Legislation.* Businesses are in various stages of regulation and deregulation. Within the political and legal environment, the number of public interest groups is increasing. These groups lobby government officials and put pressure on managers to pay more attention to minority rights, senior citizen rights, women's rights, and consumer rights in general. They also deal with such areas as cleaning up the environment and protecting natural resources.
- *Cultural values.* Cultural values come and go. The three basic components of culture — things, ideas, and behavior patterns — undergo additions, deletions, or modifications. Some components die out, new ones are accepted, and existing ones can be changed in some observable way. Thus, any cultural environment today is not exactly the same as it was last year

or as it will be one year hence. The cultural environment, therefore, needs constant monitoring to take advantage of new opportunities.

The following case example illustrates many of the concepts and guidelines related to the two parts of a multifaceted marketing strategy: marketing mix and external forces.

CASE EXAMPLE: COCA-COLA

Coca-Cola demonstrates how a company with one of the world's most recognized brands stumbled during the latter part of the 1990s and reinvented itself internally to harmonize with the dynamic changes of outside markets.

SITUATION

Over the past decade, sales of Coke faltered in many parts of the world, in particular in Russia, the Baltics, and India, as consumers turned away from the famous brand in favor of local drinks and flavors. Moreover, the company's worldwide bottler system also became flawed as Coke raised prices of its concentrate during stressful periods of declining local economies, which resulted in strained relationships with bottlers.

Then came the humiliating event that tarnished Coke's venerable image. The company had to implement one of its biggest product recalls in June 1999, removing Coke products from the shelves in four European countries due to quality problems.

ACTION STRATEGY

With newly installed CEO Douglas N. Daft at the helm, audacious moves stirred the corporate giant into action:

- First, there was the radical move to decentralize decision-making from its Atlanta headquarters to local levels, where on-site managers could decide about products, advertising, and other functions that previously were controlled from the home office. Implementing the plan, however, forced the layoff of 6000 workers.
- Second, the company arranged to sell more local brands and flavors than in the past. Consequently, as decision-making moved to the grass-roots levels, managers had to sensitize themselves to regional economies, cultures, and environmental factors. Equally important, Atlanta-based executives began to listen, learn, and react appropriately.
- Third, and built into all actions, there was the uncompromising notion that the consumer is the center of Coke's universe. That means developing and maintaining close relationships at every level of the distribution chain became a deep-rooted requirement for success. Further, there was the full realization that the world is a heterogeneous composition of local choices and cultural behaviors, where a single global standard of measurement cannot be used to calculate results.

Coke's actions to recast itself and continue its dominance in the beverage market illustrates the multifaceted strategy discussed thus far: The use of the marketing mix as a technique to develop appropriate strategies; and the examination of external forces of customers, competitors, industry, and environment as a structured format to gain insight and perspective.

STRATEGY: THE KEY TO SUCCESSFUL BUSINESS PRACTICE

> **Key point:** Strategy is further defined at three levels: higher-level strategy, mid-level strategy, and lower-level strategy.

Keeping in mind the strategy practices illustrated in the EMC and Coca-Cola cases, you can now review the definition of strategy in the beginning of this chapter and further see its relevance to successful business practice.

In turn, this primary definition has implications on how you organize your marketing effort and involves virtually every function of your organization. The definition also parallels the way in which you should think of strategic marketing as:

A total system of interacting business activities designed to price, promote, and distribute want-satisfying products and services to business-to-business and consumer markets in a competitive environment at a profit.

To further understand how strategy can permeate every part of your organization and involve all company personnel, strategy is further defined and implemented at three levels:

Higher-level corporate strategy — At this level, your company's total resources should be directed toward fulfilling company policy. Specifically, that means implementing corporate strategy with a view toward the market's long-range growth potential with a minimum expenditure of company resources.

Mid-level strategy — Here, strategy operates at the division, business unit, department, or product-line level. While contributing to your overall company policy, it is more precise than corporate strategy. It covers a period of three to five years and focuses on achieving quantitative and nonquantitative objectives. Specifically, the purpose is to provide for continued growth in four modes:

- Penetrating existing markets with existing products
- Expanding into new markets with existing products
- Developing new products for existing markets
- Launching new products into new markets

Lower-level strategy or tactics — This level requires a shorter time frame than the other two levels and correlates most often with the annual marketing plan. Think of tactics as actions designed to achieve short-term objectives while complementing your longer-term goals. These are precise actions in such areas as pricing and discounts, advertising media and copy themes, Web-site design and function, sales force deployment and selling aids, distributor selection and training, product packaging and service, and selection of market segments for product launch.

SHARPENING STRATEGY SKILLS

The intent here is to delve into the core principles of strategy and emerge with some useable applications that can be used in running your business or contributing to the decision-making process.

STRATEGY APPLICATIONS

There are five ruling principles that are characteristic of all well-executed strategies. They are *speed*, *indirect approach*, *concentration*, *alternative objectives*, and *unbalancing competition*. A thorough understanding of these practical rules is critical for implementing business-building strategies. Below, are descriptions of the strategy guidelines, examples from actual corporations, and step-by-step procedures for applying the guidelines to your firm.

Speed

> **Key point:** Speed is an essential component of strategy for gaining and exploiting a competitive advantage.

Speed is an essential ingredient in the effective application of marketing strategy. There are few cases where overly long, dragged out campaigns have been successful. Exhaustion — the draining of resources — has killed more companies than almost any other factor.

Extended deliberation, procrastination, cumbersome committees, and long chains of command from home office to the field are all detriments to success. Drawn-out efforts often divert interest, diminish enthusiasm, and depress morale. Individuals become bored and their skills lose sharpness. The time gaps created through lack of action give competitors a greater chance to react and blunt your efforts.

In today's aggressive business environment, it is in your best interest to evaluate, maneuver, and concentrate marketing forces quickly to gain the most profit at least cost in the shortest span of time. In one case, IBM acted quickly to invade Japanese markets while bringing legal action against its Japanese competitor for illegally obtaining IBM's operating codes.

In another situation, Heublein, makers of Smirnoff vodka, moved rapidly to reposition its flagship product and introduce two new brands to envelop three distinct market segments before Seagram could respond with an adequate strategy for its brand of Wolfschmidt vodka.

The proverbs "Opportunities are fleeting" and "The window of opportunity is open" have an intensified truth in today's markets. Speed is essential for gaining the advantage and exploiting the advantage gained.

Organizing for speed and quick reaction

> **Key point:** To make your marketing effort effective, reduce the chain of command. The fewer the number of intermediate levels, the more dynamic the operations tend to become.

Two factors make it possible for the manager to react with speed. First, new technologies in product development, Internet communications, and computerization challenge companies to set up organizations to react quickly and decisively in a ratio of a short span of time to a large amount of space. Second, even with new technology, gathering market intelligence entails long periods of research, experiment, and investment for each marketing situation. Therefore, for maximum speed — the essential ingredient — an efficient organization is needed that simplifies the system of control and, in particular, shortens the chain of command. The Coca-Cola example of sending decision making to the local on-site manager adds credibility to the principle. (Also, see discussion on organization options in Chapter 1.)

Your own experience may well support the obvious conclusion that an organization with many levels in its decision-making process cannot operate with speed. This situation exists because each link in a chain of command carries four drawbacks:

1. Loss of time in getting information back.
2. Loss of time in sending orders forward.
3. Reduction of the top executive's full knowledge of the situation.
4. Decrease in the top executive's personal influence on managers.

Therefore, to make the marketing effort effective, reduce the chain of command. The fewer intermediate levels there are, the more dynamic the operations tend to become. The result is improved effectiveness of the total marketing effort and increased flexibility.

A more flexible organization can achieve greater market penetration because it has the capacity to adjust to varying market circumstances, support alternative objectives, and concentrate on the decisive points. Organizational flexibility is further enhanced by setting up cross-functional strategy teams consisting of junior and middle managers, representing different functional areas of the organization. (See Chapter 1 for a listing of duties and responsibilities of a strategy team.)

Action

To increase the speed of your operations and improve flexibility, follow these guidelines:

1. Reduce the chain of command in your company and increase the pace of communications from the field to the home office.
2. Utilize junior managers for ideas, flexibility, and initiatives for identifying and taking advantage of new opportunities.
3. Use a cross-functional strategy team to tap areas of cultural diversity that may exist in your firm, thereby permitting you to benefit from multiple perspectives.

Indirect Approach

> **Key point:** The object of the indirect approach is to circumvent the strong points of resistance and concentrate in the markets of opportunity with a competitive advantage.

The object of the indirect approach is to circumvent the strong points of resistance and concentrate in the markets of opportunity with a competitive advantage built around product, price, promotion, and distribution.

A familiar example is that of Japanese copier makers attacking Xerox by initially avoiding the big-copier market and focusing instead on the vacant small-copier segment. German and Japanese firms dominating the small-automobile market in North America further illustrates an indirect attack centered on market segmentation and product positioning that avoids a direct confrontation. Other examples have become marketing legends:

- Columbia House initially used an indirect approach centered on distribution to start the first record club.
- Book-of-the-Month Club started in the late 1920s and challenged the traditional bookstore as the "only" way to sell books.
- Sony Corp. entered the North American and European markets with a small TV in the early 1970s, thereby using the indirect approach against the inbred giants that focused only on larger sets.
- Amazon.com has become a legend in its own time by using the Internet and a vast selection of discounted book titles as an indirect approach to outflank most booksellers and cause the market leaders to scramble and attempt to catch up.

Concentration

> **Key point:** Concentration means focusing your strengths against the weaknesses of your competitor.

Concentration has two uses in strategy terms. First, it means directing your resources toward a market or group and fulfilling its specific needs and wants. In modern marketing practice, concentration applies to target marketing, segmentation, and niche marketing. Second, as applied to strategy, concentration means focusing your strengths against the weaknesses of your competitor.

How do you determine the weaknesses of the competitor? When developing your marketing strategy, conduct a *competitive analysis* (see Chapter 4) to detect the strength-weakness relationship. From the analysis, isolate the areas of competitive weakness and thereby determine where to apply your strength.

Action

To concentrate in a market, use as many of the following techniques as appropriate to your company's situation:

1. As with the indirect approach, use competitive analysis to identify your competitors' weaknesses and your company's strengths.
2. Concentrate on a market segment that you have determined represents

growth and, in turn, could help launch you into additional market segments. (See discussion on market segments in Chapter 2.)

3. Introduce a differentiated product (or product modification) not already developed by existing competitors.

4. Develop multilevel distribution by private labeling your product for existing suppliers. Concurrent with that action, establish your own brand. Therefore, if one strategy falters the alternative strategy often wins.

5. Follow up by expanding into additional market segments with the appropriate products so you can envelop the entire market category, providing your firm has the resources to sustain the effort.

Alternative Objectives

> **Key point:** Alternative objectives prevent competitors from detecting your real intentions.

There are four central reasons for developing alternative, or multiple objectives:

First, on a corporate scale, most businesses have to fulfill several long- and short-term goals and require various approaches for their attainment. Therefore, they need a wide range of objectives with a variety of time frames.

Second, as already discussed, the strategy principle of concentration is implemented successfully by having alternative objectives open.

Third, alternative objectives permit enough flexibility to exploit opportunities as they arise. By designing a number of objectives, any of which can be used depending on the circumstances, you hold options for achieving one objective when others fail.

Fourth, and most important, alternative objectives keep your competitors on the "horns of a dilemma" — unable to detect your real intentions. By displaying a number of possible threats, you force a competing manager to spread his resources and attention to match your action.

If you dispersed intentionally in order to gain control, you induce your competitor to disperse erratically, inconveniently, and without full knowledge of the situation — thereby, causing the opposing manager to lose control. You can then concentrate rapidly on the objective that offers the best potential for success.

Since the major incalculable factor is the human will, the intent of alternative objectives is to unbalance the opposing manager into making mistakes through inaction, distraction, wrong decisions, false moves, or misinterpretation of your real intent. You thereby expose a weakness that can be exploited through concentration of effort. This unbalancing or dislocation is achieved through movement and surprise.

To use alternative objectives, follow these guidelines:

1. Consider such areas as customer service, improved delivery time, extended warranties, sales terms, after-sales support, packaging, and management training as sources of alternative objectives.
2. Identify alternative niches in the initial stages of attack to cause distraction among your competitors.
3. Exploit your competitors' confusion by concentrating your efforts on the weak spots that represent opportunities.

Examples

The above strategy guidelines are summarized in the following examples:

- *FurnitureFind.com*, *CarParts.com*, and *Guild.com* are just a few of the growing number of e-commerce firms that are developing indirect approaches to serve a growing buying audience. Using new technologies and services, these companies are helping to overcome customer worries about not being able to squeeze the fruit, feel the fabric, or lie on the bed.
- *Abbott Laboratories* is moving aggressively to improve its line of new products. Its strategy is to concentrate on creating new ways to deliver existing drugs to the body; develop follow-on products by focusing executives' attention toward research, marketing, and manufacturing to give input on new drugs at early stages of their development.
- *Apple Computer* is once again beginning to prosper after years of declining market share. Such snappy products as the iBook portable are once more making Apple a hot brand among consumers. To make sure the momentum continues, Apple is primed to keep turning out hit consumer products and rebuild its presence in the small-business markets. As an alternate objective, Apple is positioning itself to command a leadership role with new noncomputer products — the so-called Internet appliances.

While the actions described may appear as simple moves for expansion or diversification, they actually serve as deliberate strategies that follow time-honored principles to maintain a competitive advantage. Such alternative objectives and strategies cut across a wide range of opportunities that send confusing signals to competitors, thereby permitting maximum flexibility in selecting areas for concentration.

Unbalancing Competition

> **Key point:** Strategy's ultimate purpose is the reduction of resistance.

In many competitive situations victory is not necessarily due to the brilliance of the attacker or defender, but rather to the mistakes of the opposing manager. If brilliance plays a roll at all, it is in the manager's deliberate efforts to develop situations that unbalance the competition.

Those efforts produce the psychological and physical unbalancing effects on the opposing manager through speed, indirect approach, concentration, and alternative objectives. Moreover unbalancing fulfills strategy's ultimate purpose: the reduction of resistance.

You might try an unbalancing action, for example, by announcing a new product that could make the competing manager's product line obsolete. Even a press release about a yet-to-be released product line can "make them sweat" and create panic — and mistakes. This unbalancing is practiced continuously in day-to-day activities that range from the threat of legal action to the effects of mergers and acquisitions.

To unbalance competition, use these guidelines:

1. Identify the areas in which the competition is not able (or willing) to respond to your actions. (See Chapter 4).
2. Make a conscious effort to create an unbalancing effect through surprise announcements, for example, of a new computerized ordering procedure, just-in-time delivery, or technical on-site assistance. The unbalancing effect will have the greatest impact only to the extent that you are able to maintain secrecy until the last possible moment.
3. Utilize new technology to unbalance competitors and make them rush to catch up. Investigate the various technologies applied to marketing, such as the various functions associated with e-business linkages to speed delivery from manufacturer to customer, interactive video systems, and the evolving uses of the Internet to enhance communications for ordering and customer service.

The following case example summarizes the concepts and techniques discussed thus far.

CASE EXAMPLE: GILLETTE CO.

Gillette Co., the world leader in shaving products, exemplifies strategic marketing for the 21st-century business. From its very beginnings when King Gillette invented the safety razor in the early 1900s, to its current status as the marketer of the world's most successful razor, the South Boston company has experienced double-digit annual growth.

Behind its auspicious efforts are finely honed practices of concentrating on:

• Satisfying customer needs and expectations
• Developing cutting-edge new products and services
• Enhancing human resource development
• Maintaining operational efficiencies to serve its product development initiatives
• Strengthening supplier capabilities and satisfying their needs

Central to those practices is innovative product development that cuts across Gillette's entire product line — from its Oral-B toothbrushes and Braun appliances to Duracell batteries. Further, forecasts call for 50% of Gillette's sales to come from products introduced within the past 5 years, up from 41% in 1996 and twice the rate of the average consumer-products company.

Behind this product juggernaut are three forces that embrace both internal and external factors:

First, an ongoing rush to market new products, such as a radical new toothbrush from Oral-B, a line of razors for women, and an innovative new battery.

Second, to maintain suitable profitability, ambitious plans to continue slashing manufacturing costs a full 4% annually.

Third, continued penetration of its overseas markets.

Underlying those forces is Gillette's business strategy of spending whatever it takes to gain technology supremacy by producing innovative products that will capture consumers at premium prices.

From the Gillette case and the principles cited in this chapter, four major strategy lessons stand out:

1. While the tools of marketing (the Internet, advertising, sales promotion, field selling, marketing research, distribution, pricing) are physical acts, they are directed by a strategy process. This is particularly true of product development. Thus, the greater the attention paid to your customers, competitors, industry, and environment the more easily you will gain the upper hand and the less it will cost.

2. Establish long-term bonding relationships with customers, suppliers, and intermediaries. Work together to the profitable growth of your markets. As expounded by management guru Peter Drucker, "The object of business is to create a customer."

3. Don't intentionally seek direct competitor confrontations. It will exhaust resources and divert your attention from your customers' needs and problems. Instead, use the indirect approach. The more intent you are on securing a market entirely on your own terms, the stiffer the obstacles raised in your path. And the more cause competitors will have to try to reverse what you have achieved.

4. When you are trying to dislodge your competitor from a strong market position, leave that competitor a quick way to exit the market. Do so by increasing the gap between you and your competitor through product differentiation and value-added services.

You can apply those actions only if adequate competitive analysis is used. For example, identifying emerging markets is useful to the extent that you can preempt your competition and satisfy the needs and wants of those markets.

Employing areas of differentiation is advantageous to the extent that the competitors cannot or are not willing to respond to your action. The confidence level of your strategy is strengthened by your diligent efforts in using competitor analysis to shape an indirect approach.

BEST PRACTICES

For effective strategy development, use these guidelines for success:

- *Know your market.* Pinpoint the critical strategic points for market entry. Initially, look at geographic location, availability of distributors, and buying motives of the targeted buyers. What entry point would give you the best possibility to maneuver?
- *Assess competitors' intentions and strategies.* Evaluate how energetically competitors will challenge your intrusion into their markets. Are they willing to forfeit a piece of the business to you as long as you don't become too aggressive?
- *Determine the level of technology required.* While technology adeptness often wins many of today's markets, there are still numerous low-tech niche opportunities open to a smaller company. Where does your company fit on the technology issue?
- *Evaluate your internal capabilities and competencies.* One of the cornerstones to maneuvering in today's market is the ability to turn out a quality product equal to or better than competitors. What are your company's outstanding competencies?
- *Maintain discipline and vision.* Attempting to maneuver among market leaders takes confidence, courage, and know-how in developing a winning strategy. How would you assess your company's willingness to challenge a market leader?
- *Secure financial resources.* Upper-level management support is necessary to obtain the finances to sustain an ongoing activity. If competitors detect any weakness, they can easily play the waiting game until the financially unsteady organization caves in. What type of support can you count on?
- *Develop a launch plan to market the product.* Shape a marketing mix that incorporates a quality *product*, appropriate *distribution*, adequate *promotion*, and a market-oriented *price* to attract buyers. Which part of the mix would represent your driving force?
- *Maintain a keen awareness of how customers will respond to your product offering.* Use market research to gain insight about what motivates various groups to buy your product. What immediate action can you undertake to target a niche and avoid a head-on confrontation with a market leader?

4 Market Intelligence: The Cornerstone of Marketing Strategy

INTRODUCTION

The power of market intelligence, which has as its primary component competitor intelligence, is the cornerstone of strategy. To take intelligence gathering and strategy development back to its roots, let's absorb the sage advice that has been handed down from an ancient and authoritative source: Sun Tzu.* Although his advice referred to waging war, transposing *enemy* for *competitor* is justified if you are to internalize the wisdom that has endured for over 2500 years and has nurtured both military and business thinking.

> Know the enemy and know yourself; in a hundred battles your will never be in peril. When you are ignorant of the enemy but know yourself, your chances of winning or losing are equal. If ignorant both of your enemy and of yourself, you are certain in every battle to be in peril.

Within that framework, let's give some practical application to market intelligence. As in the previous chapters, imagine a situation where you are attending a strategy meeting and are asked for advice. Think how you would have participated in the session. What questions you would have raised. How you would have reacted to the recommendations made by others.

After you review the case example below, you will find guidelines that would have prepared you to take a leadership role.

CASE EXAMPLE: WEYERHAEUSER

PROBLEM

How do you rebuild a business besieged by bloated costs, flagging sales, and bad morale?

---

*Sun Tzu, *The Art of War* (translated by S. B. Griffith), Oxford University Press, 1963, p. 84.

SITUATION

Weyerhaeuser's door-manufacturing factory operation is just one part of a vast timber company. In 1995, the Marshfield, WI plant was on the verge of closing its own doors due to spiraling costs, dismal sales, and horrendous morale. The plant was operating at half capacity, yet carrying the operating costs equivalent to full capacity.

That was then. Today the plant is the model of efficiency, with a market-driven orientation embracing virtually every part of its physical and human resources. Revenues are growing at an annual rate of 10 to 15%. And profitability is once again on track as the plant cuts, glues, drills, and shapes customized doors according to each customer's specifications. Follow the company's strategy as it relates to market intelligence.

WEYERHAEUSER'S STRATEGY

- Initiated by far-thinking executives sent in to clean up the organizational mess, Weyerhaeuser installed a state of the art in-house communications network that uses the Internet to compare prices, improve on-time delivery, and track orders moving through the plant.
- The network, known as DoorBuilder, has resulted in the plant doubling output to more than 800,000 doors annually. On-time delivery has improved from 40% to 97%. And the plant's U.S. commercial door market share has skyrocketed from 2% to 27%.
- The DoorBuilder network also links up with key distributors, so that timely communications can speed up the ordering process for customers and eliminate costly errors, waste, and delivery problems.
- As a competitive advantage, Weyerhaeuser offers faster turnaround and, in many cases, lower prices than competitors.
- The key is the ability for the Internet system with its DoorBuilder network to plug into vast databases of information, which link customers' needs to their fulfillment in the form of correct products, delivered on time, at the right price. Considering an amazing 2 million possible configurations of doors with size, style, and color and hardware options, prior to DoorBuilder the paperwork was a nightmare. Now all precise information and detailed calculations are competed in seconds. And, as customers plug into the Network, they can bypass Weyerhaeuser's reps and type in their orders on the Marshfield plant's Web site.
- As the orders flow in, customer profiles, product trends, and buying behavior are recorded, as well as their credit worthiness, average order size, and frequency of purchase. Such data are used to note market behavior and identify competitive moves.

NEED TO KNOW

Key point: Today's uncompromising marketplace requires a continuing flow of market intelligence and facts that link all levels in the chain from supplier to end user.

Market intelligence links the finite information about markets and customers to the internal operations of the organization. Expressed differently, it creates an outside-in effect, whereby satisfying customer needs (the essence of the marketing concept) drives the internal workings of the company.

This point was clearly demonstrated in the turnaround strategy used in the Weyerhaeuser case. Consequently, today's unyielding marketplace doesn't allow for a great deal of management by instinct and intuition. Instead, it requires a continuing flow of market intelligence and documented facts that link all levels in the chain from supplier to end user.

Further, the use of technology, in this case the Internet, is the dynamic tool that links the network. Even with that persuasive evidence, however, many managers still feel compelled to utilize the gut-feel approach because they find information technology overwhelming and intimidating. While it is not easy to work through the vast quantity of information generated by an intelligence system, the alternative of "flying blind" is hardly promising. Thus, a compromise between the two extremes seems to be the answer. That is, instinct and factual market intelligence can combine for effective business management.

Notwithstanding, in a competitive world the give and take should tilt in favor of scientifically based information to support and streamline decision making. To adequately satisfy this need, information sources and flows must be managed. Management can be accomplished by clearly defining your information requirements, which, in turn, will govern the gathering and processing of information.

The process of building a complex marketing information system may start with this simple thought: "If I knew exactly what happened in the past and some insight into what may happen in the future, I would have a better feel for what actions are needed."

That statement reveals the manager's desire to develop a mechanism to supply meaningful and up-to-date intelligence that can improve decision making. You should be able to refer questions to a current and consolidated reservoir of information responsive to the "If I knew…" wishes. Such a reservoir is known as data warehousing or data mining, which is part of an overall process of database marketing and customer relationship management (discussed in Chapter 6). In particular, database marketing is an organized collection of data about individual customers or prospects for the purpose of maintaining a high level of personalized service.

DATA WAREHOUSING FOR EFFECTIVE DECISION MAKING

> **Key point:** Data warehousing helps locate and appeal to higher-value customers, reconfigure their product offerings and increase sales.

Databases often contain huge masses of data of strategic importance to effective decision making and strategy development. But how do you access the information? The newest answer is data warehousing and data mining, which are being used both to increase revenues and to reduce costs. Innovative organizations worldwide are using data mining to locate and appeal to higher-value customers, to reconfigure their product offerings, and to increase sales.

Data mining is a computer-based process that uses a variety of analytical tools to discover patterns and relationships in data that may be used to make valid predictions. For example, data mining might determine that males with incomes between $50,000 and $65,000 who subscribe to certain magazines are likely purchasers of a product you want to sell.

Typically, the data to be mined are first extracted from a company's data warehouse into a data mining database. This process generally is not a do-it-yourself project; numerous companies with the appropriate software are available to install the system.

The following examples illustrate the scope of competitor and market intelligence needed to drive business development, product innovation, and a company's overall marketing strategies:

- Amazon.com relies on information to run its customer-centered business. Doing so permits customers to find what they want, discover what they didn't know they wanted, and buy it fast. The sophisticated market intelligence capability permits Amazon to suggest products each individual buyer might like based on previous purchase patterns. This is significant since nearly 70% of its sales are from repeat customers.

- Yahoo! created powerful portals, or gateways, to the Web. The company drives transactions by hosting stores on Yahoo's site that zero in on likely buyers via e-mail. The information gathering activity is so mammoth that Yahoo! collects some 400 billion bytes of information every day about where visitors click on a site — the equivalent of a library crammed with 800,000 books. Armed with the information, Amazon can calculate which ads and products appeal most to visitors so it can garner more e-commerce sales.

- Webvan, the brainchild of bookseller Louis H. Borders and his second-largest bookstore chain in the U.S., has devised an efficient brick-and-mortar system to deliver groceries ordered from its Web site to customers' homes. The unique system permits workers to fill an average 25-item order — out of approximately 50,000 available products — in less than an hour. The goal: provide reliable, personalized service to customers based on their individual needs and purchase patterns.

- John Hagel, III, co-author of *Net Gain and Net Worth*, sells a concept in his books known as "informediary." An infomediary gathers customers' profiles and seeks our special offers and discounts for them from suppliers on the Net. He cites that an average consumer could save more that $1100 a year, even after paying commissions on purchases. The infomediary makes the rest of its money selling profiles to marketers, who happily pay for the advantages of acquiring customer intelligence to execute precise target marketing.

The above examples are diverse enough to show market intelligence as the bedrock that supports a variety of businesses. Further, the examples demonstrate that the information revolution and the World Wide Web are creating enormous challenges and opportunities to advance the ways to gather intelligence and transform it into action.

THE WORLD WIDE WEB AND THE INFORMATION REVOLUTION

> **Key point:** The purpose of intelligence systems is to improve decision making, conserve resources, concentrate efforts for maximum impact, create a competitive advantage and, above all, establish solid customer relationships with the long-term view of growing and sustaining a profitable marketplace.

The World Wide Web is now the trigger for the explosive level of activity designed to acquire finite information about groups as well as individual behavior. As customers make inquiries or purchases, hidden files or tags called "cookies" are deposited on their computers. Software programs then use those files to track and analyze on-line behavior. Such data become the underpinnings to design a product or service offering built around a one-on-one approach.

The above examples of Amazon.com and Webvan illustrate the diverse applications of the new information technology, from selling books to groceries over the Net. In turn, such information provides vendors with valuable data on usage patterns, expenditures, time of purchase, and numerous other pieces of information that when assembled provide an exacting customer profile.

Further, the proliferation of services and databases are generating huge amounts of business information. For example,

- Corporate directories are used to identify and screen customers, prospects, competitors, and to obtain quick profiles of particular firms and their lines of business, management structure, staffing levels, and sales.
- Detailed financial reports help in assessing the financial health of an individual company, as well as overall industry trends.
- Press releases highlight new product announcements, staffing changes, and quarterly financial results.
- Trade journals and general business publications provide a wealth of information, including company profiles, case studies and analyses, interviews with executives, industry surveys and overviews on emerging technologies, as well as background and expert analysis on broad economic and marketplace issues.

The pioneers in providing business information on the Internet include such professional on-line services as Knight-Ridder/Dialogue, Dow Jones News/Retrieval, Lexis-Nexis, and Information Access/Insight. A typical example of subject coverage advertised by one on-line service providing multi-industry coverage includes such information as:

Company activities and events	Professional business activities
Industry trends and overviews	International trade
Economic/demographic information	Company stock performance
Management theory and practice	Editorials
Legislative/regulatory information	Biographies
Product evaluation and reviews	Financial exchange information
Executive changes and profiles	

Then there are the abundant and popular information sources available from CompuServe, Prodigy, and America Online, which give users access to numerous print publications at a modest fee. For example, on-line directories for U.S. companies and their divisions and subsidiaries typically provide the following information: business description, annual revenues, number of employees, SIC codes, officers names and titles, year founded, and stock-related information.

APPLICATIONS

The World Wide Web presents a fresh and unrivaled approach to marketing research. For example, consider the advantages of acquiring the following information:

- A profile of AT&T, IBM, or Dow Chemical including information on their products, strategies, joint ventures, and sales and marketing activities.
- Information on the automotive industry including information on trends and forecasts, key laws and regulations, alliances, and market share leaders.
- Sales figures of the publishing companies in the U.K.
- Case studies of European companies that have implemented Japanese management techniques.
- Recent press coverage of Bill Gates, CEO of Microsoft.
- Current trends and long-term forecasts in the apparel industry.
- The buying trends of cosmetics in East European countries.

The World Wide Web opens up an unparalleled source for detailed information on industries, companies, company individuals, competitors, and consumer behavior that can add greater precision to your plans and strategies.

DEVELOPING A MARKET INTELLIGENCE SYSTEM

> **Key point:** The cost of intelligence gathering is justifiable as long as it continues to improve decision making.

The purpose of intelligence systems is to improve decision making. For example, the intelligence delivered by an information system will guide you in allocating scarce resources in a manner that will optimize profits. For obvious reasons, the cost of intelligence is justifiable only as long as it continues to improve decision making.

Such an intelligence system can accomplish the following:

- Monitor competitors' actions to develop counter strategies.
- Identify neglected or emerging market segments.
- Identify optimum marketing mixes.
- Assist in decisions to add a product, drop a product, or modify a product.
- Develop more accurate strategic marketing plans.

Figure 4.1 summarizes what a system can and cannot do for you.

Can Do

1. Track progress toward long-term strategic goals
2. Aid in day-to-day decision making
3. Establish a common language between marketing and "back office" operations
4. Consider the impact of multiple environments on a strategy
5. Automate many labor-intensive processes, thus effecting huge cost savings
6. Serve as an early warning device for operations or businesses not on target
7. Help determine how to allocate resources to achieve marketing goals
8. Deliver information in a timely and useful manner
9. Help service customers
10. Enable you to improve overall performance through better planning and control

Cannot Do

1. Replace managerial judgment
2. Provide all the information necessary to make an infallible decision
3. Work successfully without management support
4. Work successfully without a total market-driven mind-set
5. Work successfully without being adequately maintained and responsive to internal capabilities

FIGURE 4.1 Capabilities and limitations of a market intelligence system.

MARKET INTELLIGENCE PLAN

The following guidelines show how to organize data coming into the system from diverse sources. Responsibility for initiating and supporting the market intelligence plan sits squarely on the shoulders of the president or any executive in charge of devising competitive strategies.

In order to understand the flow of data, you need to examine each of the following sections.

Collecting Field Data

At the top of the list is the *sales force*, which represents one of the most valuable sources of market and competitor intelligence. When salespeople are trained to observe key events and oriented to believe their input fits into the competitive strategy process, these men and women are first-line reporters of competitor actions.

You can maintain communications with salespeople by periodically traveling with them, by conducting formal debriefing sessions to gain detailed insights behind the competitor actions they observed, and by creating or expanding a section of the sales call reports to record key competitor information. Where no sales force exists and where the Internet is becoming the central source of data collection, then the appropriate software can be employed.

Collecting Published Data

There are numerous sources of published information, from small-town newspapers in which a competitor's presence makes front-page headlines, to large city or national newspapers and magazines that provide financial and product information about markets and competitors. Monitoring want ads in print and over the Internet provide clues to the types of personnel and skills being sought.

Also, speeches by senior management of competing companies provide valuable insights into their future plans, industry trends, and strategies under consideration. It is astonishing how much sensitive information is provided in speeches given at a variety of trade shows and professional meetings that subsequently get into print.

Compiling the Data

Additional marketing intelligence can be compiled by interviewing individuals who come into contact with competitors. You can create special forms that capture key events, such as trade shows. Or you can subscribe to clipping services that submit pertinent articles clipped from newspapers and magazines on competitors' activities related to such areas as pricing, new product introductions, distribution, or special promotions.

Cataloging the Data

The varied sources of data come together at this point in the system. Depending on the facilities available, the data should be organized and maintained under the overall direction of a senior marketing or sales manager, marketing analyst, and manager of marketing intelligence or marketing research.

Digestive Analysis

The four procedures above are mechanical ways of collecting, compiling, and cataloging data. The creative aspects now apply as you begin to synthesize the data to detect opportunities. At this time, nonmarketing managers from finance, manufacturing, and product development are called in to assist in the analysis.

Communication to Strategist

There are various approaches to communicate the synthesized information: oral reports at weekly staff meetings and the increasingly popular market and competitor newsletter. The primary purpose of communication is to feed the next section.

Competitor Analysis for Strategy Formulation

The single most important purpose of the entire competitor intelligence system is to develop competitive strategies, which, in turn, become an integral component of the strategic marketing plan. To emphasize this point further: Without adequate competitive information no reliable marketing strategy is possible. (See the opening quote from Sun Tzu in this chapter.)

STRATEGY APPLICATIONS

> **Key point:** Your most important role in managing competitive intelligence is to know where to apply the information.

While it is in your best interest to become the driving force behind installing and managing a market intelligence system, your next important role is to know where to apply the information to improve performance through enterprising strategies. For instance, maintaining a strong market presence or expanding into new markets can be viewed through (1) market segmentation analysis, (2) product life cycle analysis, and (3) new product development. All of which depend on a solid foundation of reliable market and competitor intelligence.

For *market segmentation analysis*, competitor and marketing intelligence systems can be used to

- Identify segments as demographic, geographic, and psychographic (life style).
- Determine common buying factors and usage rates within segments.
- Monitor segments by measurable characteristics — for example, customer size, growth rate, and location.
- Assess potential new segments by common sales and distribution channels.
- Evaluate segments to protect your position against inroads by competitors.
- Determine the optimum marketing mix (product, price, promotion, and distribution) for protecting or attacking segments.

For *product life cycle analysis*, output can be used at the introductory stage to

- Determine if the product is reaching the intended audience segment and the initial customer reactions to the offering.
- Analyze the marketing mix and its various components for possible mod-

ifications — for example, product performance, backup service, and additional warranties.

- Monitor for initial product positioning to prospects to determine if customer perceptions match intended product performance.
- Identify possible points of entry by competitors in such areas as emerging or poorly served segments; and by using product or packaging innovations, aggressive pricing, innovative promotions, distribution incentives, or add-on services.
- Evaluate distribution channels for market coverage, shipping schedules, customer service, effective communications, and technical support.
- Compare initial financial results to budget.

At the *product life cycle* growth stage, system output can be used to

- Analyze product purchases by market segment.
- Identify emerging market segments and any new product applications.
- Conduct a competitor analysis and determine counter strategies by type of competitor.
- Adjust the marketing mix to emphasize specific groups; for example, changes in product positioning by shifting from a pull-through advertising strategy directed to end users to a push advertising program aimed at distributors.
- Decide on the use of penetration (low) pricing to protect specific market segments.
- Provide new incentives for the sales force.
- Monitor financial results against the plan.
- Provide feedback on product usage and performance information to R&D, manufacturing, and technical service for use in developing product life cycle extension strategies.

At the *product life cycle* maturity stage, system output can be used to

- Evaluate differentiation possibilities to avoid facing a commodity-type situation, where pricing pressure is prevalent.
- Determine how, when, and where to execute product life cycle extension strategies — for example, finding new applications for the product and locating new market segments.
- Expand product usage among existing market segments or find new users for the product's basic materials.
- Monitor threats to market segments on a competitor-by-competitor basis.
- Evaluate financial performance, in particular profitability (if all went according to plan you should be in a cash cow stage and generating cash.)

At the *product life cycle* decline stage, output can be used to

- Evaluate options such as focusing on a specific market niche, extending the market, forming joint ventures with manufacturers or distributors, and locating export opportunities.
- Determine where to prune the product line to obtain the best profitability.
- Monitor financial performance as a means of fine-tuning parts of the marketing mix.
- Identify additional spin-off opportunities through product applications, service, or by using new distribution networks that could create an additional product life cycle.

For *new product development*, marketing intelligence system output can be used as a preliminary screening device to

- Identify potential market segments and as an idea generator for new product development.
- Determine the marketability of a product.
- Assess the extent of competitors' penetration by specific market segments.
- Develop a product introduction strategy from test market to rollout.
- Define financial performance.

MARKET RESEARCH TECHNIQUES

> **Key point:** Market research is the mechanism to improve the effectiveness of marketing decisions by furnishing accurate information about consumer needs or problems on which to base your recommendations.

When you use market intelligence to plan your strategies, market research provides the primary input to reduce the risks inherent in decision making. Such research is invaluable during every phase of the marketing process: from the onset of a new product or service idea through the stages of its evolution and market life and, finally, to the decision to discontinue the product or service.

MARKET RESEARCH GUIDELINES

Reliable market research comes from two major sources: primary data and secondary data. To gain the optimum use from feedback, market research must be

1. *Accurate.* At stake are critical decisions affecting expenditures of money, human resources, and time.
2. *Timely.* Events have cycles that, once past, may not occur again or whose opportunities pass to competitors who have seized the moment.
3. *Usable.* Data that cannot be applied are irrelevant. They must fill the gaps of information in your marketing plan.
4. *Understandable.* Information is virtually useless unless you can internal-

ize and interpret it with relative ease and then use the data to develop strategies and tactics.

5. *Meaningful.* If the information lacks importance, if it is not significant but is merely nice-to-know information, the vital contribution of market research to survival and growth is missed.

Finally, market research is essential for measuring, evaluating, and projecting various competitive scenarios. A clear understanding of the data plays a key role in maintaining competitive strength in existing markets and in expanding into new growth areas.

TYPES OF DATA

The data needed for market research can be obtained either by turning to existing information (secondary data) or by generating your own (primary data). Initially, you should avoid a primary research study for reasons of time and cost. Instead, many marketing questions can be answered satisfactorily by utilizing secondary data. Only if this avenue proves inadequate should you consider primary research.

The distinction between the two types of data is a matter of purpose and control. Secondary data have been collected for another purpose. That is, you have no control over their gathering, processing, and interpretation. Therefore, check carefully to see how applicable they are to your situation. The unit of investigation may have been different (for example, families instead of households); the sample size may have been insufficient; the wrong people may have been queried; the questions may have been leading; the data may now be obsolete.

Even so, a thorough review of available secondary data is a must before you undertake a primary research project, because these data may provide all the answers you need. For instance, if you must find the heavy users of powdered detergents and where they are located, it would be unwise to collect your own data at great expense. Data of this type are readily available from commercial suppliers. Even if you want to know your own ultimate buyers, you don't necessarily need to generate your own information. A professional data collection organization may already have this information in its files.

GENERATING PRIMARY DATA

> **Key point:** Use three major methods to generate your own data for the specific research: experimentation, observation, and interviewing.

Of course, if you come up with "what if" questions; secondary data are no longer useful. They cannot address the issues of new product information, reactions to advertising, the impact of alternative pricing approaches, or the effect of a package change, among others.

It then becomes unavoidable to generate your own data for the specific research purpose at hand. To help you do so, you have three major methods at your disposal: experimentation, observation, and interviewing.

Experimentation

Experimental research looks at the impact of changes for two variables. One is held constant while the other is an experimental variable and is deliberately manipulated to test its effect on the outcome, usually measured in terms of sales. For example, a typical experiment tests different prices charged for the same product in different cities to determine the direct effect of price on sales.

To be meaningful, such tests require controlled situations. If influences from extraneous, uncontrollable variables (for example, dealer display) are found, the data will have to be adjusted accordingly. Therefore, it is advisable to use control groups in which no changes are introduced, to ensure the reliability of the experimental research. Each experiment must be designed and tailored to meet the specific needs of your project.

Observation

Should you want to know the reactions of consumers to your product, packaging, advertising, or some other aspect of your marketing mix, observation can supply you with the input. Researcher and marketing manager could personally watch a test to obtain a firsthand look at the consumer's reaction to an intended change before implementing it on a large scale.

Observation involves recording the behavior of people or the results of this behavior. At times it can be completed without the knowledge or consent of the subjects, thus allowing them to behave uninhibitedly. Accordingly, learn to interpret meaningful gestures; for example, during prospecting and while observing the purchasing process. And there are the sophisticated electronic approaches that use hidden cameras aimed at supermarket aisles to observe nonverbal buying patterns.

However, for everyday use you can conduct a more modest approach by watching body language as part of your overall observation of market and customer behavior. For example, you could personally observe the behavior displayed by consumers in selecting toys.

Specifically, through observation, you can use the following step-by-step approach.

Step 1: Create a map

Purpose: In this first step you define the physical dimension of the market segment that you have singled out to observe. For the most part, the activity requires you to observe closely and avoid being strapped by biases and preconceptions such as, "We've looked at that market before." Therefore, describe a market segment in non-judgmental terms. Use facts built around the physical layout of factories, stores, warehouses, roads, and other transportation hubs, as well as consumers' locations within specific and well-defined geographic areas.

Procedure: The area you select for observation could include a large office complex in a suburban area, or a 20-block business section of a large or mid-size city, or several blocks of an inner-city residential neighborhood. Initially, without interviewing the people you encounter, describe the area in detail. For instance, if looking at an industrial sector, draw a map and annotate it with items that provide a clear picture of the area, such as architecture, condition of buildings, proximity of buildings to main roads, accessibility to railroad sidings, access to suppliers and services, condition of streets, and other physical details that are pertinent to your business.

In the case of a residential neighborhood, also draw a map of the area and comment on the physical condition and location of stores for purchasing daily essentials, availability of banks and similar services, types of residential housing, condition of schools, adequacy of street lighting, and the condition of main and secondary streets. Also observe any other relevant physical details that would contribute to the validity of your research.

Step 2: Use a special language

Purpose: Our "professional" language can, at times, confine us in a straightjacket. So-called objective business and marketing terms used to define the culture of a segment or the characteristics of a group may be laced with false or misleading assumptions. In which case they would delimit and distort a picture of the actual cultural "web of behaviors, patterns, and rules of a group."

One remedy is to create your own personal descriptive language. Another approach is to use terms, descriptions, or vocabulary borrowed from a neutral field or source that doesn't affect you with emotional or prejudged terminology, such as military, architecture, sports, or agricultural terms. It doesn't matter which terms you use, since the intent is to free your mind of biases. Again, you are attempting to capture accurate, unadorned, and objective characteristics of a segment.

Procedure: Write down in narrative form your description of the segment. Include maps and other appropriate references related to demographics, geographics, and behavior. Again, avoid the standard business jargon and technical terms normally used in your industry. This process will help you redefine the makeup of an existing segment and even reveal fresh opportunities you may have missed by using conventional demographic studies. Or, you may discover the segment no longer fits into your long-term plans.

Step 3: Observe body language

Purpose: Observing body language is not new. It is an art form supported by a substantial number of studies cited in the literature from many of the behavioral sciences, including psychology, sociology, and anthropology. The intent, however, is not to make you an expert in this field. Rather, the object is to equip you with a keen awareness of how to apply body language as a step in the process of defining a segment with greater accuracy. Accordingly, learn to interpret meaningful gestures used; for example, during prospecting and while observing the purchasing process.

There are sophisticated electronic approaches that use hidden cameras aimed at supermarket aisles to observe nonverbal buying patterns, and scientific instruments to measure the dilation of the pupil in the eye when viewing a television commercial. However, for everyday use a more modest approach can be conducted by watching body language as part of your overall observation of market and customer behavior. Of course, not all gestures are readily interpreted unless you have an intimate knowledge of the group. Until sufficient experience is accumulated, you will have to gain expertise through continuous observation and by asking knowledgeable individuals who understand the gestures to decode them for you.

Procedure: Through observation — and outside of hearing range — write down a communication exchange between two or more people. (Where one person is shopping for a product or evaluating a purchase, examine the behavior.) Try to interpret the event, including its social, business, and cultural context. For instance, where two or more individuals are involved, how close or distant did the individuals stand during conversation? Did you observe any cultural implications connected to the stance or gestures? (Arabs tend to stand very close to others in conversation, whereas Northern Europeans and North Americans tend to stand further apart.) What other characteristics did you observe that would give you a clue to behavior? Were there any unusual body movements that would require interpretation by hiring outside experts or using insiders?

Step 4: Observe the ritual

Purpose: This step is likened to the shopping and decision-making "ritual" practiced by a consumer, group, purchasing manager, or senior executive. While much has been written in marketing and sales literature about the buying process, we can now add another layer of knowledge from the formidable body of work accumulated by cultural anthropologists over a period of almost 100 years. As rituals vary with individuals, groups, and societies, so too do distinctive practices exist among consumers, companies, and various institutions.

Procedure: Write an insightful description of the ritual. There are no limitations about which rituals you observe. For example, they can include the purchase of sophisticated capital equipment, a computer system for a home, ordinary office supplies, life insurance, or home furniture. For greater accuracy in targeting various purchasing rituals, you can categorize them by demographic, ethnic, geographic, and all those segmentation categories previously discussed. Also, rituals apply to company promotions, orientations, and training of new employees; or to the handling of employee grievances and customer complaints.

In all cases, you want to find out what practices are important to members of the group. This is a critical point if you are to grasp the viewpoint of the customer, which is the essence of relationship marketing. Therefore, stay flexible as you discover the key forms of behavior associated with an event. Describe (or flowchart) in detail and in proper order the physical setting and record the events that make up the ritual, as in purchasing a product.

Finally, the purpose of this four-step process is to add greater precision to your market intelligence efforts. With resources often limited, competition more intense, and viable segments harder to locate, you now have an additional research tool to aid in your decision making.

Interviewing

Key point: Interviewing is by far the most frequently used approach in primary data generation.

Interviewing is asking questions of selected respondents who might possess valuable insights and represent the group under investigation. Such survey research can be conducted formally or informally, structured or unstructured, and disguised. If it is informal, the results cannot be extended to the underlying population.

If it is structured, a formal list of questions (questionnaire) is used. And if it is disguised, the true purpose of the research is concealed from the interviewee. An example of an informal, unstructured, undisguised questioning technique is the focus group interview (discussed later in this chapter), while a mail questionnaire is a formal, structured, disguised technique.

These various characteristics explain why interviewing is by far the most frequently used approach in primary data generation. It is not as cumbersome and expensive as experimentation, and it digs beneath the observed behavioral surface in perception and motivation.

To get at the truth, however, a great deal of skill is required in executing a survey, because it is subject to even more human bias than either experimentation or observation. Bias on the part of both the interviewer and the respondent adds to any inherent defects in the wording or sequence of questions.

Interview research can be extended over a period of time to monitor changes in your competitive environment. Or, it can provide a one-time snapshot of your market, for instance, highlighting, the impact of a particular advertising campaign. Like the other two methods, you can interview either in the field (in supermarkets, shopping malls, or homes) or in the laboratory (inviting selected consumers into a research facility).

A key rule in interviewing is to ask only necessary questions; every additional question takes time, increasing the risk of consumer refusal. You should, therefore, refrain from asking questions that interest you personally, but contribute little to the understanding of the subject at hand.

Interviewing techniques

Depending on the nature of your research task, the amount of money and time available, and the accessibility of the target group to be surveyed, conclusive interview research may take one of three forms:

1. In-person interview: Interviewer questions respondent face to face in the privacy of the interviewee's home or office, or in a central location by intercepting the consumer in a shopping mall or on the street.
2. Telephone interview: interviewer conducts survey over the telephone in a local market, or over nationwide telephone lines.
3. Mail/Internet interview: survey questionnaire is mailed or sent by e-mail to selected respondents.

In choosing one approach over another, look not only at your budget and time frame, but also at the likely rate of response and the response bias. The rate of response is the ratio of those who respond to the total number of people contacted. It is subject to a possible nonresponse bias because people who are not responding may differ substantially from those who do. If this discrepancy is significant, a question may arise as to whether the results are representative. Response bias, on the other hand, is any distortion in the answers given due to misinterpretation of the questions — or by deliberate misrepresentation. You will want to keep the rate of return as high, and the response bias as low, as the constraints of time and budget will allow.

In-person interviewing: flexibility with depth

In-person interviewing produces not only a relatively high rate of response, but also an unusually high proportion of usable responses. It is the most flexible of the techniques in that it can respond spontaneously to the unique conditions of each interview, as well as incorporate a variety of visual cues such as facial expressions, gestures, and body language. Further, it allows for follow-up questions to clarify answers. Once a respondent agrees to an interview in this mode, a considerable amount of time can be spent and extensive information obtained.

On the other hand, in-person interviews are the most expensive questioning technique and can be rather time-consuming to complete because they involve travel. Unless the interviews are conducted in the evening or on weekends, most respondents could be unemployed or retired persons. Geographic coverage is obviously limited by travel time and expense.

Careful training and instructions can moderate the influence that the interviewer might exert over the interviewee (intentionally or inadvertently.) To prevent investigators from cheating or falsifying reports, supervisors should verify a certain percentage of questionnaires by contacting respondents.

All things considered, in-person interviewing is, in most instances, the best research method because it combines flexibility with depth and visual monitoring.

Telephone interviewing

If the nature of your study does not require consumer exposure to exhibits or product samples, you could interview by phone. In contrast to in-person interviewing, in which control and supervision of the data-gathering process are difficult and expensive, calling interviewees from a central location provides a great deal of control.

Phone interviewing is the least time-consuming of the three questioning techniques. It is generally less costly than face to face interviewing, though it remains more expensive than mail (depending on the response rate). Interviewers can conduct the survey while sitting at a computer terminal, reading the questions from the screen, and typing in the responses directly. This direct input eliminates the time-consuming task of coding and keypunching questionnaire data.

Using the telephone, you can survey a relatively large number of people within a short period of time. This makes the telephone query particularly suitable for measuring customer reaction to your product and that of a competitor.

The response rate with telephone interviewing is good and callbacks are easy. Also, travel is eliminated and interviewer bias is reduced. However, you cannot ask intricate or intimate questions over the phone without the risk of people hanging up.

There is obviously a limit to the amount of information you can obtain in this way, since the maximum amount of time a person is willing to spend on the phone with an interviewer has been found to be 30 minutes. It may actually be considerably shorter, depending on the subject matter. Respondents may give incomplete or inaccurate information in an effort to end the interview.

Nevertheless, because of ease of administration, speed of response, flexibility, and wide coverage, phone interviews are rapidly gaining in popularity among marketers.

Mail surveys: large scale, low cost

Although it is the slowest technique in the fieldwork stage, and the most susceptible to internal questionnaire bias, mail survey research offers the most cost-effective method available — potentially generating input from many people at relatively little cost. No interviewing staff is required and no training or travel expenses are incurred to reach people in relatively inaccessible places.

The respondent can answer the questionnaire at his or her convenience and has time to look up any necessary information. There is no interviewer bias, and questions of a personal, embarrassing, or ego-involving nature (for example, on the use of hair dyes, contraceptives, or feminine hygiene products) are answered more readily through anonymous mail questionnaires.

Probably the most serious problem with mail surveys is motivating people to fill out the questionnaires. If the response rate is less than 20%, it will raise questions about how truly representative the results are with respect to the underlying population. To increase the response rate, follow up your original sample by sending them another copy of the questionnaire with a different cover letter. This action tends to increase returns significantly.

Another drawback to mail interviewing is that you never know for sure whether the questionnaire is actually filled out by the intended respondent. This task may be assigned to another family member or a secretary, who might misunderstand or misinterpret some questions.

In spite of these handicaps, mail surveys are widely used because they can reach thousands of participants at a reasonable cost, offer wide geographic coverage, and can address issues that would otherwise be too sensitive. And now the Internet can be used to speed up the process, providing you have access to a suitable quantity of e-mail addresses.

FOCUS GROUP INTERVIEWS

> **Key point:** Focus groups offer a quick and relatively inexpensive research technique.

Focus group interviews offer a flexible, versatile, and powerful tool for the decision maker. These interviews can furnish valuable information on a variety of competitive and marketing problems in a short span of time and at a nominal cost.

However, keep in mind their limitations. Focus groups are a qualitative research tool, not a quantitative technique, and should not be used as a device for headcounting. The results of focus group interviews cannot be projected to your target market at large. They may not even be representative and, certainly, cannot replace the quantitative research that will supply the necessary numbers. But the interviews can improve the quality of your quantitative research significantly.

When there is no time for a well-planned formal project, you can call upon this technique to supply factual and perceptual input for making reasoned decisions, which otherwise would have to rely exclusively on executive suite conjecture.

Focus group interviewing involves the simultaneous interviewing of a group of individuals — physicians, homemakers, executives, purchasing agents, or any other group of potential buyers or specifiers representative of your market. A session is usually conducted as a casual roundtable discussion with 6 to 10 participants.

Fewer than six individuals pose the danger of participants feeling inhibited. More than 10 could result in some members not being heard. The idea, of course, is to get input from everybody. Although the length of a focus group interview varies, an average session lasts about two hours. Traveling around a region or the country for a week can provide a good demographic and geographic cross section of opinions. Thus, focus groups offer a quick and relatively inexpensive research technique.

Use focus group interviews to:

- Diagnose your competitor's strengths and weaknesses.
- Spot the source of marketing problems.
- Spark new product lines.
- Develop questionnaires for quantitative research.
- Find new uses for your products.
- Identify new advertising or packaging themes.
- Test alternative marketing approaches.
- Streamline your product's positioning.

The key figure in a focus group interview is the moderator, who introduces the subject and keeps the discussion on the predetermined topic. The moderator could be yourself or someone employed by an outside marketing research firm. The job of a moderator is not an easy one and much preparation is necessary, but the information obtained can be substantial and well worth the effort.

IMAGE RESEARCH

Key point: An image represents a "personality" with which the prospective buyer either can or cannot identify.

This final section of market intelligence deals with the image projected by your company, or by an individual product, to the consumer and the business-to-business purchaser. An image is the complex of attitudes, beliefs, opinions, and experiences that makes up an individual's total impression of a product, service, or corporation. An image represents a "personality" with which the prospective buyer either can or cannot identify. Our purchases involve projections of our images of the world and ourselves. We want the products and services we use to reflect those images.

In consumer goods, the Gillette Company has long produced quality products for men. When Gillette introduced a deodorant intended for both men and women, women were reluctant to consider it for their personal use. Only when the company stressed a family theme in its advertising for Right Guard did Gillette attain the top position in this market.

THE IMPORTANCE OF A FAVORABLE IMAGE

Trying to change an existing image is a slow and expensive process that requires considerable patience, skill, and commitment. The best insurance against an unfavorable image is prior testing of strategic and tactical marketing moves. As a manager you know that images, intangible and elusive as they are, cannot be left to chance. Rather, they need careful and skillful management.

Images affect business; a poor image means poor business. That fact is why image research is so important. It represents an essential ingredient in image management, indicating strengths to be capitalized on and weaknesses in need of correction. Thus, image research is an invaluable input into market intelligence and managerial decision making. It is governed by three questions that every manager who is concerned with creating and maintaining a favorable image should answer:

1. How does an image develop?
2. How is it researched?
3. How can it be changed?

DEVELOPING AN IMAGE

An image can come from a multitude of factors. It can be the outcome of a company's own efforts as well as those of its competitors. It can result from the choice of a corporate or brand name, the symbolism used, or any other part of the entire marketing effort including product design, pricing, and distribution. The symbolism may include logos, slogans, jingles, colors, shapes, or packaging.

In a packaging test, for example, housewives were presented with identical samples of a new detergent in three different experimental packages. After using the contents, the housewives reported that the product in the blue package did not possess enough cleaning power, the one in the yellow package damaged the fabric, while the one in the blue package with yellow sprinkles was just right, having enough cleaning power but gentle on the clothes. This example shows that a mere change in packaging colors can substantially influence the image of a product.

If you want to strategically shape your product's image, Table 4.1 offers some useful insights and guidelines. It presents a dozen image ingredients that are under your control and briefly highlights their respective roles in determining your product's overall image.

TABLE 4.1
Marketing Mix and Product Image

Controllable Image Ingredients	What They Can Do
Design	Provides esthetic appeal
Color	Sets a mood
Shape	Generates recognizability
Package	Connotes value
Name	Expresses central idea
Slogan, jingle, logo	Create memorability
Advertising, personal selling	Communicate benefits
Sales promotion	Stimulates interest
Price	Suggest quality
Channels of distribution	Determine prestige
Warranty	Establishes believability
Service	Substantiates product support

GUIDELINES TO IMAGE MANAGEMENT

Here are some of the key questions that you may want to ask yourself with respect to image management responsibilities and efforts:

- What do we know about the image of our company/product/service in the eyes of actual or potential buyers?
- Do we have any image at all? Are we well-enough known?
- Is our image positive or negative?
- Is the perceived image accurate or inaccurate? Are we better than our reputation?
- What does our name suggest? Is it appropriate? Have we outgrown it?
- How does our image compare with that of our competition?
- What are our perceived strengths and weaknesses?
- How can we improve our image?

Favorable images serve to attract investment, talent, and buyers. A company's image can make products stand out that are otherwise indistinguishable. Mostly, however, good images lead to a competitive edge. The following case summarizes the scope of market intelligence and its application in a competitive environment.

CASE EXAMPLE: TOYOTA

Toyota Motor Corp. built its reputation in the U.S. by serving baby boomers when they were buying their first cars. Anticipating a changing marketplace, Toyota initiated market research which revealed the disquieting data that those buyers have a median age of 46. Company managers worry what will happen to sales when that group reaches retirement age.

Provoked to take decisive action, the Japanese automaker moved to build a favorable image with the next generation. Specifically, Toyota set a goal of lowering its customers' average age by 10 years and executed the following strategies.

TOYOTA'S STRATEGIES

- Toyota convened a group of ethnically diverse individuals from within its company who were in their 20s and 30s and who could relate comfortably to the target market. The group, known as Genesis, was given the lofty assignment of launching three new cars to cater to the younger buyers: the entry-level ECHO subcompact, a sporty two-door Celica, and a sleek MR2 Spyder convertible.
- The group is attempting to pursue Toyota's success strategy of capturing entry-level buyers and retaining them through their life cycle by moving them up to its more expensive models.
- To assure an entrepreneurial environment in which Genesis could operate unencumbered by the more traditional corporate thinking, the group was spun off to its own workspace in a building across the parking lot from Toyota's Torrance, CA headquarters. The group continues to gather market intelligence and use it to devise strategies that would make the Toyota brand relevant to the post-baby-boom consumer.

BEST PRACTICES

To fully benefit from Market Intelligence (MI), follow these guidelines:

1. MI must be *accurate*: critical decisions affecting expenditures of money, human resources, and time are at stake.
2. MI must be *timely*: events have time cycles. Past a certain point, an opportunity may not occur again — or competitors may seize the opportunity.
3. MI must be *usable*: data without application become irrelevant.
4. MI must be *understandable*: information that cannot be interpreted with relative ease by the average manager and then applied to developing strategies and tactics is nearly useless.
5. MI should be *meaningful*: if it cannot be translated into scenarios of strategies, it's just nice-to-know information.

5 Products: The Lifeline to Survival and Growth

INTRODUCTION

There are two paramount reasons to get involved with existing and new products:

1. Existing products become obsolete with dazzling speed. That is, the product life cycles spanning introduction to decline become progressively shorter as the rate of new product development increases and new technology emerges. Also, there are the far-ranging effects of flexible manufacturing techniques and computer-aided product design that also accelerate the product development process. Then, there is the external situation where product sales dry up as competitors attempt to outperform your offerings with new packaging, product refinements, new features, or value-added services such as extra warranties or after-sale services.
2. New markets continually emerge due to changing demographics, the soaring penetration of e-commerce, and the increasing attention to cultural diversity that exists in various segments. These variations make for capricious buyer behavior that, in turn, triggers a continuing stream of product innovations.

In light of these pragmatic realities, executives and managers of all levels and ranks should fully internalize these dominant influences and embrace the full significance of actively participating in the company's product output. Conversely, if you don't satisfy customers' needs and resolve their problems with appropriate products, services, and solutions, there is always an eager competitor waiting to fill the gap. More precisely, then, viable products are the lifelines to business survival and growth.

To illustrate the above ideas, review the following actual case. As in previous chapters, pretend you are there, sitting in the strategy meeting and asked to provide advice. Think about how you would react. What comments would you make? What advice would you give about the suggestions made by others?

After you go through the exercise, pertinent information follows that will prepare you in the event a similar situation arises in your company.

CASE EXAMPLE: UPS

PROBLEM

How do you handle the combined problems of competitors capturing a significant amount of revenues, and the need to repair relationships with outraged customers?

SITUATION

United Parcel Service faced the dual situation of first, having to close ranks with their drivers after a traumatic strike; and second, appeasing outraged customers who switched to archrivals FedEx and the U.S. Postal Service. Its 1997 strike was eventually settled to the satisfaction of both management and drivers. Then, fence mending began with human-resource remedies implemented quickly and successfully.

From a marketing viewpoint, however, management quickly realized to reestablish a positive image in the minds of disgruntled customers and to devise ways to recapture lost revenues and market share, that business-as-usual would not correct the acute situation nor prepare UPS for the burgeoning growth expected from recovering and emerging world economies.

UPS' STRATEGIES

UPS management implemented the following strategies. As you review them, identify those that link to the concepts already discussed in the previous chapters. Also, think how you would have advised UPS had you been sitting in on the strategy meetings.

1. UPS transformed its thinking, as it related to market and product development, from a trucking company with technology to a technology company with trucks. That new orientation was not some frivolous play on words. UPS actively committed itself to state of the art technology by pouring money into mainframes, PCs, handheld computers, wireless modems, and cellular networks. In terms of customer satisfaction, the communications technology represented the *product* that permits UPS to track the immediate whereabouts of any given package at any point in its entire system. That means the sender can enter the UPS Web site and learn that the package has been received even before the driver is back behind the wheel of his truck.

2. UPS management observed that the industry was transitioning into a global, knowledge-based logistics business. Opening their minds to interpret the exciting product possibilities associated with *logistics*, managers moved into electronic funds transfer with its new COD program. As an extension of that service, UPS provides customers, such as Gateway Inc., with a cash-on-delivery service whereby it collects payment from the customer and deposits the funds directly into Gateway's bank account. Beyond that service is the additional product application of being able to receive, validate, and securely transmit credit card payments at the point of delivery.

3. UPS managers recognized that speed is an essential component of customer satisfaction and central to a strategy of providing just-in-time delivery. To that end, UPS improved delivery to the point that is takes a mere 15 minutes for parcels at its Chicago hub to move through a vast network of conveyer belts, sophisticated electronic scanners, and then be loaded on to trucks headed to distribution centers near the final destinations. So accurate is all the technological wizardry that UPS has used the system (product) to its marketing advantage by guaranteeing delivery times to its business-to-business customers.

4. Interpreting *logistics* into a further product advantage, UPS expanded into Web retailing with a call center run on behalf of Nike.com. UPS stocks Nike shoes and warm-ups in its Louisville warehouse and fulfills orders hourly, loading goods onto trucks headed to the hub. Nike saves on overhead and gets quick turnaround. As another product extension, UPS adds to its product lineup by providing customers with value-added services ranging from parts repair to inventory management. The product strategy takes on explicit meaning when expressed in its sales theme: "We can help you move more than just packages. We can help manage your inventory and information."

5. Aware of product positioning and its resulting perception in the minds of customers, UPS goes to great lengths to project a responsible and trustworthy corporate image. To that end, drivers are taught 340 precise methods on how to correctly deliver a package. Their appearance also follows a strict regimen of a clean uniform every day, well-polished shoes, hair length above the shirt collar, no sideburns below the bottom of the ear, and trimmed mustaches.

Bottom line: UPS is a mainstay of the U.S. economy, delivering 6% of the gross domestic product. It has become a business model to demonstrate how a company refines its customer-driven practices and backs it up with unique products and services that satisfy customers — and, at the same time, neutralizes aggressive competitors.

Need to Know

What do all these strategies have to do with product development?

First, consider a product as a bundle of benefits. As such, a product incorporates any part of the organization that can add value or provide meaningful benefits to the physical dimension of your company's offerings.

Second, regard a product as new only when it is *perceived* as new by the customer, shifting the emphasis to the user as the final judge of *new* — and thereby reducing your claim of what constitutes a new product.

To fully understand the process for developing and evaluating product strategies, the balance of this chapter describes a framework consisting of five major factors: new products, positioning, product life cycle, product mix, and product audit.

NEW PRODUCTS AND SERVICES

> **Key point:** From a marketing viewpoint, a product is new when the customer perceives it as new.

New products and services are the heart of any business that seeks to sustain growth and competitive advantage. In practice, they are the lifelines to any business, whether categorized as a product or service.

The pace of new product introduction and obsolescence is so fast and rigorous that only one out of five innovations survives long enough in the marketplace to become a commercial success. When the stakes are so high, it pays to improve your odds by gaining a better understanding of the new product process in all its ramifications. Sensitivity and adaptability are prerequisites for success in a dynamic marketplace where needs are constantly changing.

DEFINING A NEW PRODUCT

A product is an object, device, or substance. But that definition hardly suffices in today's environment. It reduces the concept of product to a combination of physical and chemical attributes in line with the old product-oriented concept of conducting business.

This emphasis on tangible characteristics neglects the fact that intangibles — such as quality, color, prestige, and backup services — make a significant difference to a prospective buyer. A consumer perceives a product as a source of potential satisfaction, and may buy your offering to satisfy a particular want or desire rather than for its functional value. Charles Revson, the late founder of Revlon, put it succinctly when he said in his now classic statement: "In the factory, we make cosmetics; in the store, we sell hope."

As indicated earlier, a useful definition of a new product is where a customer perceives the offering as new. A product can mean many things to many people. This definition places the emphasis on perception rather than on objective facts, and leaves much room for interpretation. There is a reverse side to this emphasis on perception, though. If you have a product that has never before been offered for sale but is perceived by customers as more of the same, then you really do not have a "new" product from a marketing point of view.

If you can make a customer believe that you are offering a new product, it is new from the customer's point of view. But you cannot claim newness either indiscriminately or indefinitely. You have to be able to prove reformulation to the Federal Trade Commission, and federal law prohibits use of the expression "new" in packaging and promotion for more than six months. Legal limitations aside, it is really a question of convincing your target market that you have something different to sell.

CATEGORIES OF NEW PRODUCTS

New products come in many different forms. This diversity can be reduced to varying degrees of technological and marketing newness. In terms of increasing degrees of technological change, you may want to distinguish among modification, line extension, and diversification. For increasing degrees of marketing newness, you can differentiate between remerchandising and market extension. Table 5.1 presents the differences among these five categories of new products and points out the benefits of each.

TABLE 5.1
Categories of New Products

Category	Definition	Nature	Benefit
Modification	Altering a product feature	Same number of product lines and products	Combining the new with the familiar
Line extension	Adding more variety	Same number of product lines, Higher number of products	Segmenting the market by offering more choice
Diversification	Entering a new business	New product line, Higher number of products Same product,	Spreading risk and capitalizing on opportunities
Remerchandising	Marketing change to create a new impression	Same markets	Generating excitement and stimulating sales
Market extension	Entering a new market	Same products, New market	Broadening the base

Combined Approach for New Product Categories

Rarely will the five categories of new products presented above be used separately. They lend themselves to combined applications for maximum impact. Moreover, you will probably want to avail yourself of a package approach to maintain steady growth in a rapidly changing environment. Line extension, for example, is often used with remerchandising or market extension. Diversification is often combined with market extension. The use of one category does not preclude the application of other approaches at the same time, possibly within the same market. What remains essential, though, is that the prospective customer perceives a difference worthy of consideration.

NEW PRODUCT DEVELOPMENT

> **Key point:** Rather than rely strictly on internal development or licensing as a source of new products, organizations find it more attractive to acquire strategic businesses.

The techniques of product development have gone through dramatic changes during the latter part of the 1990s. For the most part, product development and production work within the traditional system has been handled internally. That approach began to change with the introduction of innovative technology. One such transition began with the use of Electronic Data Interchange (EDI) that linked companies together electronically so their computers could automatically handle many business chores, from dealing with purchase orders to exchanging engineering blueprints.

EDI is especially important when all phases of product development, from design to final assembly, happen simultaneously and in different locations. The upshot is that hundreds of small manufacturers in the U.S. and abroad joined flexible manufacturing networks. These networks pool talents for jobs too big for any one member of the network to handle alone. The full benefits occur as small companies connect to a shared database and instantly coordinate production schedules and blueprint revisions. Instead of farming out work to internal departments, they assign it to member companies and thereby assume the role of a highly responsive "virtual" company.

The trend began to gain strength as EDI's capabilities brought groups into compliance with orders coming from the Pentagon and major manufacturers. By 2005, EDI is expected to be mandatory for all federal purchases. Also known as flexnets, these flexible manufacturing groups span industries from bookbinding and dressmaking to fishing and logging. In its further application, sales and service is either handled by the companies' existing staffs, or centrally by individuals who work full-time for the group.

In still another approach to product development, PricewaterhouseCoopers' survey revealed that a majority of fast-growing companies advanced their new product efforts by acquiring intellectual property (IP) from others. The survey indicated the following:

- 49% license technologies or intellectual assets from others. This includes 57% of service businesses and 38% of product sector companies.
- 27% are involved in joint ventures where the partners share the risks, costs, and profits from development of new intellectual assets. Of these, 74% say this is a growing part of their business.
- 15% invests in smaller, independent businesses as an extension of their own R&D. Of these, 61% expects to increase their involvement in this kind of activity over the next 12 months.

Those organizations find it more attractive to acquire strategic businesses rather than rely strictly on internal development or licensing as a source of new products. Overall, the main attraction of strategic acquisitions is speed, with 62% saying it is faster to buy than make.

However, where internal product development takes place, the following steps should be followed.

STEPS IN THE EVOLUTION OF A NEW PRODUCT

The beginning of an innovation occurs in a process called new product evolution. It takes place in a four-stage format consisting of initiative, decision making, execution, and control, as shown in Table 5.2.

TABLE 5.2
New Product Evolution

Process Steps	Results
Initiative	
1. Initiate project	Gets action under way
2. Identify problem or opportunity	Pinpoints nature of the challenge
Decision Making	
1. Define objectives and criteria	Sets frame of reference
2. Start comprehensive marketing research program	Feeds decision maker relevant information on continuous basis
3. Examine market data	Provides factual input
4. Begin idea generation	Maps out alternative courses of action
5. Initiate screening process	Weeds out unpromising alternatives
6. Conduct business analysis	Subjects surviving proposals to in-depth scrutiny
7. Begin product development	Converts ideas into products
8. Proceed with market testing	Examines market acceptance
9. Finalize marketing program	Prepares for rollout
10. Start plot production	Fills the pipeline
Execution	
1. Move to full-scale launch	Begins market introduction
2. Examine the product life cycle	Analyzes sales and profit changes
Control	
1. Maintain continuous feedback of results	Compares planned and actual figures
2. Take corrective action	Keeps on course

INITIATIVE

Often an innovative new product idea can reside with some astute manager within your organization who perceives a product concept and triggers the process that results in a profitable addition to your product mix. Or an idea can turn up from the input of a customer who faces a severe problem. Thus, numerous external or internal factors can spur a new product initiative. They may reflect market, technological, competitive, or company developments. In any case, they constitute the motivating forces behind the evolutionary process.

Considering the rapid changes occurring in your market, watch for early indications of potential threats and analyze them carefully for emerging new product opportunities. Forecasting, therefore, plays a crucial role in new product evolution by predicting alternative future environmental conditions or events, as well as the likelihood of their occurrence. Some companies retain the services of an elite group of planners who speculate about such future scenarios.

Yet, there are more basic approaches for obtaining significant insights into market trends. One is the careful examination of consumer preferences and life styles, competitive new product activity, distribution patterns, and — most basic of all — sales and profit data.

Technological developments can be just as stimulating. For example, new applications of lasers, glass fibers, and superconductors offer a host of opportunities for the imaginative manager. Lasers are actively employed in industry, surgery, and communications with remarkable results. Glass fibers are in the forefront of telecommunications. And customized computer chips have spawned an array of specialized new products at affordable prices to expose vast new markets.

Increasingly, we now explore the immense potential of technology transfer. That is, applying to one field the technology developed in another. For example, Rockwell International Corp., a major space contractor, used technology developed for the U.S. space program in designing anti-skid devices for truck braking systems. Similarly, microwave ovens are an outgrowth of the space program.

Events within your firm may also be the source of a new product initiative. Such events may include suggestions by employees concerning improvement of existing products or development of entirely different ones. Purchasing problems involving limited availability of key materials or price increases may trigger a rethinking process. Innovations in your research and development department could lead to important discoveries, which, in turn, may stimulate new product evolution processes. Sales trends can and should bring about a reevaluation of your current and future situation, often resulting in new product programs.

While there are numerous environmental clues, your firm will not profit from them unless someone in your organization is sensitive enough to respond selectively to them. Typically, this person will be the product manager of a given product line. More than any other, this person is called upon to scan facts and developments and identify those that represent a true problem or opportunity. This task requires considerable insight and judgment, since it involves "separating the wheat from the chaff." Only someone with imagination, sensitivity to customers' needs, and conscious awareness of the firm's strategic direction can perform this job well.

DECISION MAKING

The sequence of new product evolution begins with goal setting and ends with initial production. In-between is a series of crucial steps that will determine the success of your venture in the marketplace. Close attention to each of the following steps is essential.

Defining Objectives and Criteria

Objectives give direction and orientation to your effort and serve as a measure of actual achievements. Typically, new product objectives involve growth targets identified as market segments or niches, sales volume, profitability, and market share. Objectives also include categories of products, such as modification, line extension, diversification, remerchandising, or market extension, as described in Table 5.1. Overall, it is the role of objectives and their related criteria to guide your efforts and keep your actions focused.

Research and Examination of Market Data

As its most fundamental job, the definable purpose of maintaining ongoing marketing research is to supply the decision maker with relevant facts. The outcome is to hook up with the consumer and establish communication links that keep the evolutionary process going efficiently and on course.

The body of data generated in the first round of this marketing research program is then screened for usable information capable of triggering dynamic thinking. Creativity that is divorced from the realities of the marketplace often ends up being misguided and ill fated. The following process, attributed to consultants Booz Allen & Hamilton, is a reliable product development system you can emulate.

Step 1: Idea generation

Once a database has been established, idea generation can begin. At this early stage, many ideas are considered for an ultimate yield of one successfully commercialized product. Booz•Allen & Hamilton put this ratio at 58:1. Scrutiny becomes more and more rigorous as a product idea advances from its genesis. All the more reason to generate as many ideas as possible at the outset. The search for alternative courses of action should be limited only by any previously cited facts and should not in any way concern itself with such issues as feasibility or profitability.

The best approach is to tap a wide range of sources for product ideas: internal sources such as top management, research and development people, marketing personnel, and other employees. Also use a variety of external sources such as consumers, middlemen, competitors, scientists, inventors, research labs, and suppliers. The techniques employed in activating these sources range from brainstorming to various surveying methods.

Step 2: Idea screening

After you have generated a wealth of new product ideas, they should then be subjected to a screening procedure. This step aims to weed out unpromising ideas before they become costly in time, effort, and money. Thus, the goal at this step is to eliminate from further consideration as many ideas as possible. Two thirds to three quarters of the original ideas vanish at this point.

The focus now is to examine questions of feasibility and profitability. After all, neither one can exist without the other. Feasible products that are not profitable are simply giveaways; profitable products that are not feasible are fiction. The issue of feasibility may be general (whether appropriate technology exists) or specific (whether your production department can handle the job). Profitability, on the other hand, involves projections of anticipated price levels and unit costs to decide whether there is enough money in a deal to warrant attention.

Step 3: Business analysis

The few ideas that pass the screening test enter the business analysis stage. They now receive in-depth scrutiny. The purpose of this step is to advise top management whether it should authorize certain proposals as development projects. Therefore, a careful impact statement has to be developed for each concept, with thorough projections of what would happen if it were adopted and converted into a real product.

Management must know the consequences to your firm in terms of required technological know-how, production and sales force utilization, image, morale, and —

most of all — finances. A concept test is likely to help you in assessing consumer reaction and preference at this point.

Your financial analysis also has to be much more thorough at this step than during screening, relying on tools such as break-even analysis (to determine the sales volume needed to cover costs) and financial analysis (to compute the return on investment).

Step 4: Product development and market testing

Once a particular idea has tested well and has received top management's blessing, it is assigned to personnel for conversion into a tangible product. Here, your technical and production people go to work with clear-cut specifications spelled out by you on the basis of several rounds of marketing research. They will develop rough drafts that will then be laboratory tested and refined, until they have developed a product that is completely debugged and ready for full-scale production.

Of course, before beginning full-scale production, you have to test a sample quantity among users, asking them to try the product at your expense and then suggest changes to improve its performance or enhance its appeal. This procedure, product testing, is intended to help modify and finalize the product design. The most popular approach to product testing involves matching your product against that of a major competitor to find which product your audience prefers and why. The results cannot be taken as conclusive evidence, however, since you select the participants and give them the products.

Therefore, the true indication of your innovation's full market potential is explored only by means of test marketing. This activity involves introducing your product in a number of test cities (or market segments) to see how well it will sell under real market conditions. It is important that these test markets be representative of your overall market and that you run the test long enough to establish repurchase patterns. After all, it is relatively easy to sell somebody something for the first time. The real test is whether the customer buys it again. This determination cannot be made through sales audits alone, but requires customer interviews as well.

Step 5: Final marketing program and pilot production

Completion of market testing enables you to put the finishing touches on your marketing program by adjusting certain elements of the marketing mix for maximum effectiveness. This adjustment permits you to get ready for a full-scale rollout. Of course, you first have to go through pilot production; that is, produce enough merchandise to satisfy initial demand. This step completes the decision-making phase of new product evolution.

EXECUTION AND CONTROL

Once you complete the internal development and external testing of the new product, you are ready to launch its full-scale market introduction. A revised introductory program should now set in motion the start of your product's life cycle, which goes from introduction through growth and maturity, and then to saturation and decline.

As no one is all-knowing, and even the best planning cannot foresee all possible events, continuous feedback to monitor the effectiveness of your product strategy is necessary. This feedback enables periodic comparisons between planned and actual figures. In turn, you can take corrective action to keep your program on course. Ultimately, this action may result in initiating another evolutionary process that could displace the current product.

Within those steps, there is an intrinsic need, first and foremost, to render superior service as part of your new product strategy. It requires that employees impart an attitude of total commitment to satisfying customers' needs with tangible offerings. Companies that have gained notoriety with their obsession for delivering extraordinary service include Nordstrom, McDonalds, Marriott, and Disney.

What have emerged from those companies committed to a service strategy are the following guidelines for executing a service strategy as part of the new product development effort:

- *Customer obsession.* All levels of employees (those with and without direct customer contact) must understand what makes your customers tick. They should sense what tangible and intangible services would satisfy customers and result in long-term loyalty.
- *Commitment to high standards.* To behave as a service-oriented company, you must set high standards and be able to measure results. For instance, a division of 3M cut its complaint handling time from 49 days to 5 days. Managers then monitored ongoing performance not only within their own operation, but used the new standard as a benchmark of performance against competitors.
- *Procedures to monitor service performance.* A former president of the American Management Association once stated, "Don't expect what you don't inspect." Begin with some easy-to-use methods to monitor your service performance, such as formal surveys among customers, informal visits to customers by marketing and technical personnel, and watching the mail for unresolved problems or clues that may lead to new services. The key, however, is to collect feedback from all sources on a regular schedule. Then, assemble the data into a functional report that measures actual performance against customers' expectations. In the same report, compare the level of service you provide with that of your primary competitors. Finally, share the report with those who can take positive action to improve service performance.
- *Responsiveness to customers' needs.* Speed, accuracy, and effective communication form the foundation for first-class service performance. All that monitoring systems can accomplish is to "red flag" what remedial action is needed. Ultimately, the decisive difference in sustaining customer satisfaction and maintaining a competitive advantage is how your firm resolves product problems, handles quality issues, meets delivery dates, and delivers the myriad of other meaningful services.

POSITIONING

> **Key point:** Achieving a lasting and favorable position is an expensive and time-consuming proposition. Once the commitment is made, you should move rapidly to implement the strategy.

Al Reis and Jack Trout popularized positioning during the 1980s as, "Not what you do to a product. Positioning is what you do to the mind of the prospect." And Professor Philip Kotler (Northwestern University) says, " Positioning is the act of designing the company offer and image so that it occupies a distinct and valued place in the target customers' minds."

Thus, a product's position exists in a customer's mind and is the result of three groups of influences:

1. Your company's total effort to establish an appropriate image, including the use of the marketing mix (product, price, promotion, and distribution) to determine an ideal competitive position.
2. External market influences, including the demographic and behavioral characteristics of your target segment, as well as the market position held by your competitors.
3. Your customers' actual perceptions of your products, services, and company.

To define a competitive position for existing products and to locate a position for a new product, follow these steps:

- First, identify your product's actual position by conducting individual consumer interviews. Also, examine the market positions held by your closest competitors (see Chapter 4). That means you want to learn how customers perceive your product by examining the image it projects, the needs it satisfies, and the solutions it provides.
- Second, once you have determined your product's current position, you have these choices. You can maintain your product's current position, particularly if it commands a strong position in the market — and the particular segment represents an area of continuing growth. Then, you can shift positions to a market segment that is emerging, neglected, or poorly served.
- Third, if you select an all new position, you have two product options. Move the product to a new position, with or without a change in the product itself, or introduce an all new product with the necessary characteristics for new positioning. Leave the current product untouched or withdraw it from the original market. The challenge here is to be certain that any new product you introduce is sufficiently different from the original product. Procter & Gamble demonstrates this approach as it expertly positions its numerous brands of detergents, soaps, and toiletries with little or no cannibalizing of sales from one product to another.

- Fourth, after making your positioning decisions, be certain senior management signs off on the strategy and commits adequate resources to the move. Achieving a lasting and favorable position is an expensive and time-consuming proposition. Once the commitment is made, you should move rapidly to implement the strategy. Along the way, carefully monitor competitors' activities. As you become increasingly sensitive to changing competitive conditions, you may find it necessary to modify or revise your original plan about optimizing your position.
- Fifth, maintain active research with two approaches: Track competitive moves and monitor the impact of your positioning on your customer's mind. Then, periodically conduct follow-up research to compare your product's actual position with its desired ideal position. The reason: competition is not sitting still as you make your moves. It, too, is attempting to position its products favorably in the eyes of customers and is striving to win a dominant share of market. Also, count on customer behavior changing with shifting movements in the economy, ups and downs of the stock market, availability of disposable income, and the overall power of market trends and influential media.

The following case example illustrates how a company positions its products against market leaders.

CASE EXAMPLE: A. SCHULMAN INC.

A. Schulman Inc. produces plastics that go into such diverse products as auto dashboards, moldings, and furniture. The company has produced extraordinary results during a five-year period by doubling sales and tripling earnings. Its performance triumphs in a competitive environment against such mighty companies as Dow, Monsanto, Quantum, BASF, and Hoechst. Let's examine the key success strategies:

- Schulman excels in filling rush orders for customers by making special weekend runs in its U.S. and European factories to satisfy customers' urgent requests.
- Schulman talks quality and product differentiation, not price. While the industry giants focus heavily on commodity plastics, Schulman concentrates on higher-priced specialty products. Managers search for areas of differentiation with features that can't be easily duplicated by competitors.
- In its early years of growth, Schulman established strong customer relationships with smaller organizations that were generally neglected by the market leaders. Now, using superior technology to add value to product offerings and by continuing its customer-driven relationships, it is expanding to serve such names as General Motors, Ford, and 3M.
- Commitment to a market-driven attitude is a hard and fast policy at Schulman. Its labs do not develop compounds and then search for markets. Rather, salespeople and engineers work closely with customers on ideas

that solve problems. Those ideas are then converted into customized products to provide solutions.

- About 65% of Schulman's sales are outside the U.S. Beyond its presence
  in Canada, UK, and Europe, the Akron (Ohio) company cultivates thriving
  relationships with Japanese companies, such as Mitsubishi. These alliances provide unique applications for auto moldings and dashboards for
  Toyota and Honda plants in the U.S.

LESSONS

If you want to position your product effectively against market leaders, consider
some of the following action strategies suggested by the Schulman example:

1. Select a competitive advantage that larger competitors cannot perform
   efficiently. Employ market research, such as customer tracking studies, to
   identify possibilities for differentiation.
2. Commit to quality and service as an organizational priority. Initiate programs that encourage individuals at various functions to strive for quality.
   These are not one-time motivational talks, but continuous training.
3. Focus on specialty products that command premium prices; leave the commodity price segment to others. Practice segmenting your market for specific product applications. Get closer to your customers and their problems.
4. Establish long-term alliances with customers and grow with them to build
   technology and product relationships. Encourage trust with customers or
   suppliers so that sensitive information can be shared for mutual interests
   through the proliferating e-business systems.
5. Maintain a market-driven orientation throughout the organization —
   within all functions — to maintain a competitive advantage. Organize
   strategy teams made up of functional managers. Then, use the teams'
   strategic marketing plans as lines of communications to respond rapidly to
   market opportunities.
6. Seek global opportunities that complement long-term objectives. Through
   joint ventures, licensing, or exporting, develop a global presence if consistent with your corporate mission.
7. Partner salespeople with customers to provide product solutions to customers' problems. Go beyond traditional forms of sales training. Instead,
   teach salespeople how to think like strategists so they can help their customers achieve a competitive advantage.
8. Identify market niches that are emerging, neglected, or poorly served.
   Reassess how you segment your markets. Search for additional
   approaches beyond the usual criteria of customer size, frequency of purchase, and geographic location. Look for potential niches related to just-
   in-time delivery, performance, application, quality, or technical assistance.

PRODUCT LIFE CYCLE

> **Key point:** Use the product life cycle as an effective framework for devising marketing strategies at various stages of the curve.

The classic product life cycle — identified by the stages of introduction, growth, maturity, and decline — offers a reliable perspective for observing a "living" product and market moving through dynamic stages. Each stage is influenced by outside economic, social, and environmental forces, as well as by inside company policies, priorities, and resources.

Your primary interest should be to fully understand that the dominant application of the product life cycle is to shape strategies and tactics that extend the sales life of a product. Life-cycle extenders are the safest and most economical strategies to follow. Thus, your active involvement should focus on helping to identify the best extension opportunities. And then gain the energetic cooperation of key personnel in product development, manufacturing, finance, distribution, marketing, and sales.

There are four approaches to extending the life of a product: (1) promote more frequent usage of the product; (2) locate new users for the product; (3) uncover more uses or applications for the product; and (4) discover new uses for the product's basic material (see Figure 5.1).

The product life cycle remains a reliable indicator to identify when a product enters the various stages, signal when to phase in new product applications, and recognize when to introduce next-level technologies to extend the product's sales life with a fresh innovation. Observing a product moving through its life cycle stages offers these advantages: First, it helps prioritize which projects would enhance a company's ability to compete actively, rather than wait passively as competitors and customers push your product into obsolescence. Second, you can focus attention on the evolving needs of customers with a conscious awareness that their needs and wants also have cycles. Third, you call the shots for timing a response before competitors can push you aside.

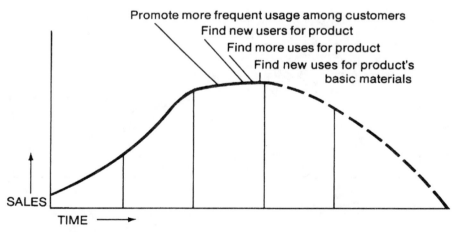

FIGURE 5.1 Strategy application for extending a product's life cycle.

For many companies, monitoring the life cycle curve and knowing when to introduce strategies to extend the life of a product often prevents the severe consequences of allowing a product to reach a commodity status, where price is often the solitary weapon left in the marketing arsenal. Consequently, the product life cycle continues to work as an effective framework for devising marketing strategies at various stages of the curve.

MANAGING THE PRODUCT LIFE CYCLE

If the product life cycle is of any strategic value to you and your firm, you have to determine where in the life cycle — introduction, growth, maturity, saturation, or decline — your product is at any given time. You can identify the product life cycle phase by observing three factors that characterize the product's status, and comparing those results with a typical pattern. You can determine your product's status by examining the three curves shown in Figure 5.2. These curves are

1. Market volume, expressed in units, so as to avoid any distortion resulting from price changes.
2. Rate of change in market volume.
3. Profit/loss, illustrating the differences between total revenue and total cost at each point in time.

Successfully managing your product's life cycle requires careful planning and thorough understanding of its characteristics at the various stages of the curve. Only

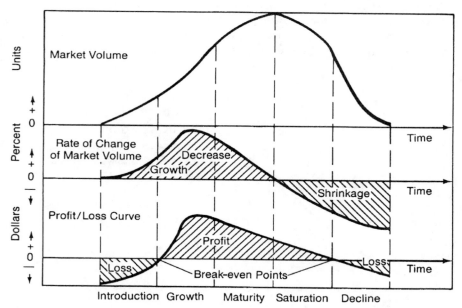

FIGURE 5.2 Curve trends used to measure the life cycle position.

then can you respond quickly and advantageously to new situations, leaving competitors in your wake. Let's examine each of the stages.

Introduction Stage

During the introduction of a new product, market volume usually expands slowly because of initial market resistance. Assuming that your company is the pioneer, and recognizing that the upfront outlay for product and market development is often quite substantial, the introduction stage is generally characterized by costs exceeding revenues, or a loss. Toward the end of this phase, however, your firm should show signs of break-even. Achieving break-even at this early stage will make you more flexible when competitors appear on the scene.

Growth Stage

The growth stage is characterized by sales increasing at a faster pace. While the growth rate will also increase, it peaks about halfway through the stage. Thereafter, further growth occurs at a decreasing rate because of the steadily expanding base. Although profits reach their highest levels in this phase, the trend reverses in the middle of the stage as dwindling prices and rising costs generate downward pressure.

Maturity and Saturation Stages

Market volume moves at a slower pace in the maturity stage, and quickly declines as it reaches the stagnation level at the end of the stage. Profits diminish but are still healthy. As the market enters the saturation stage, all three curves show a negative change rate. Costs and competitive pressure reduce profits further until they cross the break-even line once more at the end of the stage.

Decline Stage

In the decline stage, all signals point to abandonment. The shrinking of market volume is accelerated by booming substitute products. The rate of change becomes increasingly negative. Costs exceed revenue, thereby creating a loss.

STRATEGIES THROUGHOUT THE PRODUCT LIFE CYCLE

> **Key point:** The marketing mix is an effective format to use in developing life cycle strategies.

Now let's look at the strategies throughout the product life cycle. As shown in Table 5.3, different conditions characterize the stages of the product life cycle. This fact suggests continuous monitoring and appropriate changes in your strategic approach to optimize results. These changes include adjustments in your marketing mix — that is, the particular combination of marketing tools that are used at each stage.

TABLE 5.3
Strategies Throughout the Product Life Cycle

	Marketing Mix Elements			
Life Cycle Stage	**Product**	**Pricing**	**Distribution**	**Promotion**
Introduction	Offer technically mature product, keep mix small	"Skim the cream" of price-insensitive innovators through high introductory price	"Fill the pipeline" to the consumer; Use indirect distribution through wholesalers; Enter electronic marketplaces or exchanges on the Web	Create primary demand for product category, Spend generously on extensive and intensive "flight" advertising
Growth	Improve product; Keep mix limited	Adjust price as needed to meet competition	Increase product presence and market penetration	Spend substantially on expansion of sales volume
Maturity	Add value to your product; Expand product offering to satisfy different market segments	Capitalize on price-sensitive demand by further reducing prices	Look for distribution alliances with market leaders; Establish distribution call centers (if appropriate) and have your own sales force call on retailers	Differentiate your product in the minds of prospective buyers; Emphasize brand appeal
Saturation	Customize your mix further to reach viable market segments; Diversify into emerging markets	Keep prices stable	Intensify your distribution to increase availability and exposure	Maintain the status quo; Support your market position through e-commerce
Decline	Prune your mix radically	Carefully increase prices	Consolidate your distribution setup; Establish minimum orders	Reduce promotion activity to a reminder level

Introduction Strategies

In the introduction stage (Table 5.3), your central strategy is to create primary demand for the new product category. Creating primary demand usually consists of an educational process that activates people's needs and focuses them on your product. It also means attempting to alter product usage habits and even reverse supplier loyalties. Also, if the innovation is clearly superior in performance, it is still a monumental task to dissuade consumers from their current relationships. A great deal of "noise" is necessary just to attract the innovators and cross the fine line between success and failure.

During this initial period, keep the product mix small to provide a clear focus and maintain tight cost control. Also, confine the mix to just a few variations that reflect the underlying concept of the entire category. After all, it isn't the breadth of choice but the new approach to the satisfaction of a need or the solution to a problem that attracts the innovators.

Channel decisions are crucial because they lock your firm into long-term commitments to a selected group of middlemen that cannot be changed easily, if at all. The degree to which you know how to secure maximum availability of your product in the right outlets can make or break your participation in the ongoing growth of a new market.

If you do not have an established trade network covering the desired target market, it might prove useful to employ the services of established distributors or link up with the growing number of Web sites that also serve as middlemen to put vendors together with end users through e-mail. This newer approach can achieve fast, widespread connections at a cost far below what would be spent if you had your own sales force calling on individual accounts.

If, however, you do have an established sales force and ongoing business relationships with prospects, you still have to sell them on the merits of your innovation, which is no easy task. To this end, motivate your sales force with a broadly conceived incentive program that will give every individual on the sales force a personal reason to move substantial volumes of merchandise.

Also essential is the support given your product in the form of advertising. Anything less than generous funding and an all-out advertising effort will reduce the product's chances for survival. Giving a new product lukewarm advertising support will reduce its chance of gaining a foothold in its target market.

You are relatively free to decide on your introductory selling price. You can set it fairly low — a strategy called penetration pricing — aimed at creating a mass market and discouraging competitive imitation through low unit profits and large investment requirements. Or you may consider a skimming strategy that starts out with a comparatively high price aimed at recovering your initial outlays for development and market introduction before competitive pressure erodes your temporary advantage.

Growth Strategies

In the growth stage, you will want to modify your basic product to take care of any problems discovered through initial consumer reactions. However, since the product category is selling so well, the product mix can remain small.

With regard to channels of distribution, your goals will include persuading current channel members to buy more and to sign up new channel members. This drive is greatly aided by booming demand, which strains the industry's supply capability and has distributors scurrying for merchandise. Also, following distribution trends, it could aid considerably by connecting with the electronic marketplaces or exchanges on the Web that serve as middlemen between suppliers and their customers.

Your salespeople will continue to sell along the same lines as before, building upon the emerging success story of your innovation. Your advertising emphasis is likely to shift somewhat from creating product awareness to expanding market volume. Where possible, you could try a distribution and promotion partnership with a market leader to assist in greater market penetration. Prices soften as price-cutting competitors enter the market.

Maturity Strategies

Moving into the maturity phase can be traumatic, because the peaceful coexistence of competitors now turns into a fight for market share. At this time, it pays to redesign your product to make it more distinctive and easier to differentiate from competitive offerings. Since product technology is well developed, changes tend to be more cosmetic than functional.

Yet, discriminating customers also demand more variety and a choice of products designed specifically to meet their particular needs and desires. Thus, it is advisable to adopt a strategy of market segmentation: dividing the entire market into smaller submarkets or segments in order to satisfy the unique needs of these fairly homogeneous groups within the market.

As for channel strategy, you may well find yourself reconsidering distribution structure, cost, and control — particularly with the major innovations evolving with e-commerce (discussed in various chapters of this book). If you employed the services of distributors in your introductory thrust, it may now be sensible to eliminate them in order to push your product harder and cut costs. Your product should be well known, and its sales volume high enough to justify your own retail sales force supported by the establishment of brick-and-mortar warehouses and service centers. Your own sales force can be better trained and motivated to do an aggressive job of promoting your product. You also exercise better control over the sales effort and can improve your market feedback system.

Your advertising has to communicate and enhance the drive to differentiate your product. It should put heavy emphasis on brand appeal to presell the product, so that the prospect recognizes and prefers your product even in a competitive environment. The effectiveness of your promotional efforts, however, is likely to decrease sharply as demand becomes less responsive to promotion because of growing brand loyalty and resultant market resistance. (Chapter 8 discusses promotion strategies and e-commerce.)

Since actual differences between substitute products are very slight, price variations between your firm's products and those of your competitors gain in importance. Prices will tend to drop further, but stabilize toward the end of the stage as a result of cost pressures. Insofar as your company has been able to create brand loyalty among its buyers, it will have pricing discretion that permits price adjustments when necessary without losing a substantial amount of sales.

Saturation Strategies

As your product enters the saturation stage of its life cycle, typically a no-holds-barred fight develops for market share. Because market volume has ceased to grow, the growth of a firm's sales volume is achieved at the expense of competitors. As for product strategy, you will find yourself compelled to differentiate further by offering even more choices.

Also, at this stage of limited growth potential it will pay to pursue a strategy of diversification, if consistent with your company's overall strategic direction. Entering another field could reduce risk by decreasing your exposure to the fate of a declining product, as well as add potential revenue and profit to your business.

Your channel strategy remains unaltered in the saturation phase. Attempt to gain even more intensive distribution and, thereby, maximize availability and exposure. Toward this end, your salespeople will have to make a well-planned, concerted effort to obtain more trade cooperation and seek additional alliances. The primary function of advertising at this point is to maintain the status quo. Little new ground can be broken, so highly focused advertising and the use of the Internet should be employed. Elasticity of demand reaches its highest point at this stage. This fact is of little strategic consequence, however, since most possibilities for cost reduction have been exhausted.

Decline Strategies

With consumer interest in the product waning in the decline phase, competitors drop out of the market in droves. If you are still in the market, trim your product offering to the bone, vigorously weeding out weak products and concentrating on a few better-selling items. Similarly, attempt to reduce distribution cost as well as establish minimum orders to discourage small shipments. Your sales effort will tend to be low key, with emphasis on e-commerce. Advertising support will diminish to the low-budget, infrequent-reminder type. To the extent that you are able, your prices stay right about where they are.

The following case example illustrates the impact of positioning and the product life cycle on a company's strategy.

CASE EXAMPLE: FUJI PHOTO

Fuji Photo Film Co. is the second-largest maker of photographic film and paper, behind Eastman Kodak Co. Beyond film, however, Fuji has been moving relentlessly forward to position itself as the leading innovator of digital cameras — introducing a new one, on average, every two months since 1998. Its objective is to become the leader in the still-developing market by staying on the leading edge of the life-cycle curve. In 1999, sales of digital cameras increased 80% over the previous year.

All told, digital products and services will reach about $4 billion in sales by 2004, up from $400 million in 1999. Fuji is committed to securing itself to the introduction and growth stages of the product life cycle — avoiding the maturity and decline stages by investing heavily in a product strategy of continuous improvement and technological innovation.

Underlying the strategy is the recognition by Fuji's astute management that with its control of 70% of Japan's photo-film-paper market, its mainstay business has reached a maturity level of the life cycle curve in that market. Consequently, for growth, it needs a new cycle of sales and a new source of profits.

Fuji's management views the new-wave digital cameras as its dynamic revenue-generating source. Industry experts estimate that the anticipated craze for the new camera is expected to increase usage by as much as six times the pictures currently being snapped.

Beyond picture-taking, however, users are also fascinated with such sophistication as a built-in printer to produce instant photos. The innovation permits users to send their favorite photos over the Net to digital processing centers, which use Fuji photographic paper to prepare prints or postcards, create photo indexes, and load customers' images onto compact disks.

PRODUCT MIX

> **Key point:** In designing a product mix, the object is to prevent cannibalizing sales from one line to another. One relevant strategy to employ is product differentiation.

One of the noteworthy areas of product strategy that should involve your input is the product mix. Reason: To gain a larger share of a total market, you have to consider introducing additional products as competing lines or as private labels. The additional products provide an active defense against intruding competitors. Overall, however, the strategy aims at generating higher revenue than does the use of only a single product.

A central strategy in the product mix is to apply differentiation, so that you don't cannibalize sales from one line to another. Here are useful guidelines:

- *Features and Benefits.* These are characteristics that complement the product's basic function. Start with your basic product. Then visualize adding unique features and services; ideally, these are based on users' expectations.
- *Performance.* This factor relates to the level at which the product operates, including quality.
- *Acceptance.* This characteristic measures how close the product comes to established standards or specifications.
- *Endurance.* This factor relates to the product's expected operating life.
- *Dependability.* This attribute measures the probability of the product breaking or malfunctioning within a specified period. (Dependability is a criterion most often applicable to engineered products.)
- *Appearance.* This factor covers numerous considerations ranging from image, function, look, or feel. Different from performance, appearance integrates the product with all its differentiating components, including packaging.
- *Design.* This factor unites the above differentiating components. While design encompasses the product's appearance, endurance, and dependability, there is particular emphasis placed on ease of use and appropriateness to the function for which it was designed.

Also, within any product mix decision, evaluate the profit advantage of a single product concentrated in a specialized market, or a multiple-product strategy for growth and protection from competitors.

One approach is to consider your company's name or product line, which may have a reputation for quality, performance, after-sales service, or unique applications within an industry. Where a positive image does exist, you can use the following process to exploit your corporate or product name into developing your product mix.

First, keep in mind the definition of a new product. A product is new when it is *perceived* as new by the prospect or customer. Therefore, new products can cover a range of innovations — from minor change to new to the world — if the changes are perceived as new. Perceptions can change by modifying products for specialized applications, developing new forms of packaging, or devising a system for convenience of storage and retrieval.

Further, adding value through field technical assistance, computer-linked inventory systems, and technical/advisory e-mail connections, you also can give the impression of *new*. Use the following checklist to develop your product mix:

1. Review your company's overall product-line objectives. Guard against venturing into line extensions that do not relate to your core business.
2. Define your market by sales and profit volume, customer usage, purchasing patterns, anticipated market share, and investment required.
3. Determine product development requirements, such as using existing company technology, obtaining new technology, licensing finished products, or subcontracting an entire project.
4. Evaluate competitive offerings. Determine how to differentiate your new product to avoid a direct confrontation with look-alike products.
5. Select you product's position. Will it be positioned to *defend* a market niche or be placed on the offensive to secure additional market share? Will it be used as a probe to enter an emerging market or as a preemptive attack on competitors to discourage their entry?

IMPLEMENTING A PRODUCT MIX STRATEGY

First, instill a mind-set in yourself and in those with whom you work that keeps your customers' needs in the forefront of product development and service. Sustaining such an attitude is one part of the success formula. The second is to install a systematic approach that permits you to learn about your customers' business.

Here's one system that works: Explore customers' needs and problems in two broad categories that would appeal to their self-interests: *revenue-expansion* and *cost-reduction* opportunities. This approach will chalk up positive results for your customers. In due course, it should also help you provide applicable products and services. Table 5.4, Implementing Product Mix Strategies, divides the two categories.

TABLE 5.4
Implementing Product Mix Strategies

Revenue Expansion Opportunities

- What approaches would reduce customers' returns and complaints?
- What processes would speed up production and delivery to benefit your customers?
- How can you improve your customers' market positions and images?
- How would adding a name brand impact your customers' revenues?
- What product or service benefits would enhance your customers' operations?
- How can you create differentiation that gives your customers a competitive advantage?
- How would improving reordering procedures impact revenues?

Cost Reduction Opportunities

- What procedures would cut customers' purchase costs?
- What processes would cut customers' production costs?
- What systems would cut customers' production downtime?
- What approaches would cut customers' delivery costs?
- What methods would cut customers' administrative overhead?
- What strategies would maximize customers' working capital?

As you can see, several of those areas in Table 5.4 reach beyond the traditional role of marketing. Therefore, you and other nonmarketing managers should be totally involved in interpreting findings and translating them into product mix decisions.

PRODUCT AUDIT

> **Key point:** Products that no longer earn their keep should be eliminated without delay or sentimentality, provided that such a move has no negative repercussions for the remaining products in the line.

Knowing when to pull a product from the line is as important as knowing when to introduce a new one. The decision has far-reaching implications that impact most functions of the organization, from inventory management to finance to production. Your input as a nonmarketing manager is to consider such internal requirements as profitability, available resources, and new growth opportunities. You should question external factors of sales force coverage, dealer commitment, and customers' needs to determine if a comprehensive line is required.

Efficient use of the product audit is one of the procedures for sustaining product profitability. The following examples illustrate the application.

CASE EXAMPLES

Kraft, Colgate-Palmolive, General Motors, Nabisco, Procter & Gamble, and other marketing-savvy organizations are pursuing a dominant trend. All are focusing on fresh approaches to improve the profitability of their product lines. While many organizations have pursued product profitability over the past decade through downsizing, reengineering, and similar high-profile approaches, what is significant this time are the processes that directly impact their marketing efforts. Increasingly, managers at these high-profile firms (and smaller companies, as well) deal with product profitability by looking to such marketing-related actions as standardizing product packages, reducing trade promotions, pulling back on couponing, trimming product lines, and cutting back the number of new product launches.

For example, Nabisco shaved its product line by 15% and reduced new product launches by 20% during one 12-month period. Kraft initiated moves for the cereal industry to stabilize list prices. Clorox simplified its trade promotions and sliced the number of items it sells. General Motors reduced the number of U.S. car models from 53 to 44.

P&G, in particular, illustrates the significant potential for profitability. It has reduced its product lineup by one third since 1990. In hair products alone, it cut the number of sizes, packages, and formulas in half, while watching with satisfaction as its market share in hair care jumped nearly five points to 36.5%. In the shampoo line, P&G standardized product formulas and packages to just two basic packages in the U.S., saving an extraordinary $25 million a year.

What evidence supports this move toward a simplification of the marketing effort? First, an analysis of consumer goods sales by one consulting firm revealed the enlightening statistic that almost 25% of the products in a typical supermarket sell less than one unit a month. What's more, just 7.6% of all personal care and household products account for 84.5% of sales.

These statistics validate the often-quoted 80/20 rule, whereby 80% of sales (and anything else) come from 20% of customers. But how does all this affect the ruling guide of market segmentation, whereby managers are counseled to target emerging, neglected, and poorly served markets and then cater to each segment with customized products and services?

Does the trend now reverse the use of a segmentation strategy? Not at all. Segmentation, targeting, and concentrating on customers are practical, workable, and successful strategies. Instead, the faults lay, in part, with the lack of attention given to synthesizing and interpreting the vast amount of data generated by today's sophisticated measurement devices. When accurate market information pinpoints those market segments that would respond favorably to your marketing efforts, then implementing product audit strategies should improve your chances for increasing product-line profitability.

Lessons

What can you learn from these case examples? You can initiate one easy-to-install procedure with direct impact on profitability: a product audit. Just as regular physical examinations are essential to maintain the body's good health, likewise, products require regular examination to determine whether they are healthy, need repromotion, or should be allowed to phase out.

Begin your product audit by setting up a Product Audit Committee (see details below). The product audit can assist you in accomplishing the following:

- Determine your product's long-term market potential.
- Assess the advantages and disadvantages of adding value to the product.
- Alter your product's market position compared to that of a competitor's comparable product.
- Estimate the chances of your product being displaced by another product or technology.
- Calculate the product's contribution to your company's financial goals.
- Judge if the product line is filled out sufficiently to prevent your customers from shopping elsewhere.

In addition to the above criteria, consider such related issues as availability of money and human resources, the redeployment of assets to new product and market growth opportunities, and even the effective use of your executives' time. Also, add such factors as your firm's willingness to sustain sales force coverage, obtain dealer commitment, and retain ongoing enthusiasm to respond to changing customers' needs.

Finally, phasing out weak products or exiting a market requires careful consideration of your company's obligations. For instance, there may be significant costs related to labor agreements, maintaining capabilities for spare parts, contractual relationships with dealers and distributors, financial institutions, and so on. In sum, the Product Audit provides a practical approach to the profitability and the decision-making process.

ESTABLISHING A PRODUCT AUDIT PROGRAM

The first step in establishing a regular product evaluation program is to create a Product Audit Committee. This core group, comprised of the top people in the marketing, finance, engineering, and purchasing departments, should control decision-making authority about the design of the company's product mix. Depending upon the dimensions of the product mix and the significance of the products or developments involved, the Product Audit Committee should meet monthly, and every product should have at least an annual review.

How does such a committee operate? To do justice to each product and to have an objective basis for product comparisons, a common rating form should be used. For products that appear dubious, and thus demanding careful evaluation, use a product audit form similar to the one illustrated in Figure 5.3. Using a simple 1 to 5 scoring system, you can assign values for each of 8 criteria. Some of these values will necessarily be subjective in nature, with 1 representing strong grounds for eliminating the product and a score of 5 suggesting retention.

In each case, the score reflects the majority opinion or consensus of the committee. For greater accuracy, each criterion can be given a degree of importance or weight. These weights are then multiplied by the appropriate score and totaled to form the specific product retention index.

	Low		Score		High
Product/Service	**1**	**2**	**3**	**4**	**5**
1. What is the market potential for the product, based on dollar value, unit volume, or other quantitative measures?					
2. What competitive advantage might be gained by adding value, modifying the product, or creating other differentiation features and benefits?					
3. What would be gained by positioning the product differently to customers — and against competing products?					
4. How many resources (materials, equipment, people, and dollars) would be available by eliminating the product?					
5. How good are the opportunities to redeploy re sources to a new product, service, or business?					
6. Based on financial calculations of ROI, profits, and other key financial criteria, how much is the product contributing beyond its direct costs?					
7. What value does the product have in supporting the sale of other company products?					
8. Is the product useful in defending a point of entry against aggressive competitors?					

FIGURE 5.3 Product rating form.

Rating forms are useful for pinpointing weaknesses. Just like thermometers, they indicate the existence of problems but do not supply diagnoses. Quantitative data contained in these forms have to be supplemented and amplified by qualitative information. In order to obtain a complete picture, and make meaningful decisions, the Product Audit Committee must solicit input from all major functional departments of the company.

PRICING YOUR PRODUCT

> **Key point:** Pricing should not be treated as an isolated item. It is but one component of the marketing mix and you should view it within that total framework of marketing strategy options.

Directly related to your product development is selecting a realistic pricing strategy. In recent years, the major influence in pricing a product or service is the arrival of e-commerce. Although negotiated pricing has been around since the dawn of commerce, it is the Internet that has legitimized the technique, making it one of the most powerful economic forces of e-commerce. The concept is being applied to every kind of selling, from airplane tickets to industrial products.

Yet, even with the auction environment that currently exists, you should be mindful of the fundamental principles that are essential in establishing a viable pricing strategy for both existing and new products. The following discussion breaks down pricing strategy into new products and existing products.

PRICING NEW PRODUCTS

There are five categories related to launching new products: skim pricing, penetration pricing, psychological pricing, follow pricing, and cost-plus pricing.

Skim Pricing

The first of the strategies that deal with new products is *skim pricing*. It involves pricing at a high level to hit the "cream" of the buyers who are less sensitive to price. The conditions for using this strategy are

- Senior management requires that you recover R&D, equipment, technology, and other startup costs rapidly.
- The product or service is unique. It is new (or improved) and in the introductory stage of the product life cycle, or it serves a relatively small segment where price is not a major consideration.
- There is little danger of short-term competitive entry because of patent protection, high R&D entry costs, high promotion costs, or limitations on availability of raw materials, or because major distribution channels are filled.
- There is a need to control demand until production is geared up.

The electronics industry usually employs skim pricing at the introductory stage of the product life cycle to the point that consumers and industrial buyers expect the high introductory-pricing pattern. There are exceptions, however. One was Texas Instruments' introduction of its much-touted solid state magnetic storage device for computers that has the capability of not losing stored data when power is cut off. Even with the impressive technology, sales were initially disappointing because potential users were not willing to pay the high introductory price and were willing to wait for price reductions.

Penetration Pricing

Penetration pricing means pricing below the prevailing level in order to gain market entry or to increase market share. The conditions for considering this strategy are

- There is an opportunity to establish a quick foothold in a specific market.
- Existing competitors are not expected to react to your prices.
- The product or service is a "me too" entry and you have achieved a low-cost producer capability.

- You hold to the theory that high market share equals high return on investment, and management is willing to wait for the rewards.

One of the most striking examples of penetration pricing occurred in the early 1980s in the fast-growing market for computer printers, a market pioneered by U.S. manufacturers. But several Japanese makers seized the opportunity and attacked the segment by offering printers at rock-bottom prices and short delivery times. From virtually no U.S. sales in 1979, the Japanese shipped 75% of all units selling for less than $1000 by 1982.

Psychological Pricing

Psychological pricing means pricing at a level that is perceived to be much lower than it actually is: $99, $95, $19.99, and $1.98. Psychological pricing is a viable strategy and you should experiment with it to determine its precise application for your product. The conditions for considering this strategy are

- A product is singled out for special promotion.
- A product is likely to be advertised, displayed, or quoted in writing.
- The desired selling price is close to a multiple of 10, 100, 1000, and so on.

While psychological pricing is most likely to be applied to consumer products, there is an increasing use of the strategy for business-to-business products and services, as in the example of a machine priced at $24,837.00. Note in this example that the traditional "9" is not used. Tests by such organizations as Sears reveal that the "9" doesn't have the psychological impact it once had. In various combinations the "7" has come out on top.

In instances where a prestige product or service is offered, a psychological price may be expressed as "one hundred dollars" to give an elitist impression.

Follow Pricing

Pricing in relation to industry price leaders is termed follow pricing. The conditions for considering this strategy are

- Your organization may be a small or medium-size company in an industry dominated by one or two price leaders.
- Aggressive pricing fluctuations may result in damaging price wars.
- Most products offered don't have distinguishing features.

The most visible example of follow pricing is found in the computer market, in which IBM still holds a strong worldwide position. IBM traditionally set the pricing standards by which its competitors priced their products. However, this situation turned out to be a two-edged sword. The clones of IBM-compatible computers priced at 20 to 40% below IBM reached such high proportions that IBM was forced to reverse its role and use follow pricing against aggressive competitors as a means of protecting its share of the market. However, IBM's use of follow pricing was a holding action in its broader strategy of attempting to regain leadership with the introduction of new products and systems.

Cost-Plus Pricing

Cost-plus pricing entails basing price on product costs and then adding on components such as administration and profit. The conditions for using this strategy are

- The pricing procedure conforms to government, military, or construction regulations.
- There are unpredictable total costs owing to ongoing new product development and testing phases.
- A project (product) moves through a series of start-and-stop sequences.

Cost-plus pricing, unless mandated by government procedures, is product-based pricing. Such an approach contrasts with market-based pricing, which takes into consideration such internal and external factors as:

1. Corporate, divisional, or product-line objectives concerning profits, competitive inroads, market share, and market stability.
2. Target-market objectives dealing with market position, profile of customer segments, current demand for product, and future potential of the market.
3. Marketing mix strategy; for example, how pricing fits together with product, promotion, and distribution components of the mix.

PRICING EXISTING PRODUCTS

You can avoid or postpone price wars by locating untapped market segments and focusing on product improvements. You can also preempt and discourage new competitors by gradually sliding down prices, thereby making the market seem unprofitable. And you can always price according to the flexibility of demand and your production economies. There are six strategies related to pricing existing products.

Slide-Down Pricing

The first in this series of strategies in slide-down pricing that move prices down to tap successive layers of demand. The conditions for considering this strategy are

- The product would appeal to progressively larger groups of users at lower prices in a price-elastic market.
- The organization has adopted a low-cost producer strategy by adhering to learning curve concepts and other economies of scale in distribution, promotion, and sales.
- There is a need to discourage competitive entries.

Slide-down pricing is best utilized in a proactive management mode rather than as a reaction to competitors' pressures. If you anticipate the price movements and do sufficient segmentation analysis to identify price-sensitive groups, you can target those groups with specific promotions to preempt competitors' actions.

Skim pricing, as previously noted with the electronics industry, begins with high pricing and then evolves to slide-down pricing. The downward movement of price usually coincides with such events as new competitors entering to buy market share through low price and then wait as economies of scale begin to take effect.

Segment Pricing

Segment pricing involves pricing essentially the same products differently to various groups. The conditions for considering this strategy are:

- The product is appropriate for several market segments.
- If necessary, the product can be modified or packaged at minimal costs to fit the varying needs of customer groups.
- The consuming segments are noncompetitive and do not violate legal constraints.

Examples of segment pricing abound. The most visible ones are airlines that offer essentially one product, an airplane seat, between two cities. Yet this "same" product may serve different segments, such as business people, clergy, students, military, senior citizens, each at different prices. Then, there is further segmentation according to time of day, day of week, or length of stay at one destination.

To best take advantage of this pricing strategy, search out poorly served, unserved, or emerging market segments.

Flexible Pricing

Pricing to meet competitive or marketplace conditions is known as flexible pricing. The conditions for considering this strategy are

- There is a competitive challenge from imports.
- Pricing variations are needed to create tactical surprise and break predictable patterns.
- There is a need for fast reaction against competitors attacking your market with penetration pricing.

As organizations downsize and reengineer to become more competitive, field managers, who typically are closer to the dynamics of the market, are handed greater pricing authority and accountability for their products. The intent is to allow a flexible pricing strategy when appropriate. In contrast, the opportunity to react is missed where there is a long chain of command from field managers to executive levels, with the detrimental effect of consuming excessive response time.

It is necessary for middle managers to identify competitive situations where flexible pricing may be used. However, remember that flexible pricing, as in all applications of pricing strategy, is not a license to reduce prices to meet competitors' levels. Pricing is still but one component of the marketing mix and you should view it within that total framework of marketing strategy options.

Preemptive Pricing

Preemptive pricing is used to discourage competitive market entry. The conditions for considering this strategy are

- You hold a strong position in a medium or small market.
- You have sufficient coverage of the market and sustained customer loyalty to cause competitors to view the market as unattractive.

The key ingredient to make preemptive pricing a viable strategy is staying close to the market through informal observation and, ideally, a reliable competitive intelligence system. Armed with accurate information that profiles a competitor's typical strategy for entering a market, you have an excellent opportunity to react quickly by meeting a price attack with a preemptive move that blunts the competitor's actions.

Phase-Out Pricing

Phase-out pricing means pricing high to remove a product from the line. The conditions for considering this strategy are

- The product has entered the down side of the product life cycle, but it is still used by a few customers.
- Sudden removal of the product from the line would create severe problems for your customers and create poor relations.

Phase-out pricing does not mean dumping. Rather, it is intended for use with a select group of customers who are willing to pay a higher price for the convenience of a source of supply. For example, Echlin Inc., the producer of auto and truck parts, stocks nearly 150,000 different parts for every auto from the Model T to a Rolls Royce. Customers with old or rare auto models are only too pleased to pay the price for product availability.

Loss-Leader Pricing

Pricing a product low to attract buyers for other products is called loss-leader pricing. The conditions for considering this strategy are

- Complimentary products are available that can be sold in combination with the loss leader at normal price levels.
- The product is used to draw attention to a total product line and increase customers' purchases. The strategy is particularly useful in conjunction with impulse buying.

Loss-leader pricing is one of the most common forms of pricing strategy. It is prevalent in all ranges of businesses, from department stores to auto dealers to industrial product lines. Remember, however, to consider the profitability of the total product line.

THE PRICING PROCESS

Following a defined process increases your chances for success:

1. *Establish your pricing objectives.* These might be to maximize profits, increase sales revenues, increase market share rapidly, or position your product advantageously among competitive look-alike products.
2. *Develop a demand schedule for your product.* Specifically, forecast the probable quantities purchased at various price levels.
3. *Examine competitors' pricing.* This review will determine where you can position your price to achieve your market objectives.
4. *Select your pricing method.* Use the strategies outlined in this section.

BEST PRACTICES

Products and services are the lifeline to survival and growth for an organization. In keeping with that truism, anticipate a competitor's move into your marketplace. Also, recognize early the potential of new technologies, particularly in areas where competitors may choose not to invest. Use life-cycle extensions as the mainstay of your strategy to track product performance and determine when to phase in new activities. Whenever possible, preempt competitors' strategies and blunt their efforts to take market share from you.

To identify strategies and initiate action:

1. Work with all functions to identify your company's best product/service possibilities. Prioritize those product strategies that represent your best opportunities.
2. Indicate what actions are needed from each function and who is assigned the task.
3. Obtain feedback and relate it to your product objectives and the strategies used.
4. List your immediate plans as well as future courses of action to establish a product audit procedure.

6 Customer Relationship Management: Integrating Customer-Driven Marketing with the Internet Age

INTRODUCTION

Technology, specifically the Internet, is sparking a transformation in business that is every bit as profound as the Industrial Revolution. The movement resounds especially among those forward-thinking executives in market-sensitive organizations who commit themselves to total customer satisfaction. That resolve, along with the application of technology, matches perfectly with the traditional definition of marketing as a *total system of interacting forces designed to plan, price, promote, and distribute want-satisfying products and services in a competitive environment at a profit.*

To bring the movement to a real-life setting, act as if you are sitting in on a strategy meeting in the following case example.

> **Key point:** Manufacturing is changing from the "push" model to a "pull" model, where customers decide what they want built.

CASE EXAMPLE: FORD MOTOR CO.

At a Ford Motor Co. strategy meeting the agenda focused on how the company was organized, the problems of costly 80-day inventories sitting on dealer lots, and a 64-day average time from customer order to delivery. Also, there was animated discussion on the growing problem of some disgruntled suppliers complaining about having to manufacture and inventory parts based on last-minute changes in orders resulting from Ford's ever-changing sales forecasts. There was a spirited debate among some individuals at the meeting about the viability of the century-old "push" business model, where the plant builds a predetermined mix of cars and ships them to dealers who rely on aggressive sales tactics or hefty rebates to move cars off the lot.

FORD'S STRATEGIES

Recognizing the depth of those concerns, after a mature discussion Ford management decided to resolutely move forward and create a vision of what a 21st-century marketing-driven company would look like. In fact, Ford had already seized the opportunity, before its competitors could respond, to pull ahead and reinvent manufacturing by changing the "push" model to a "pull" model, where customers decide what kind of vehicle they want built.

The Ford vision encompasses a far-reaching system that integrates the entire supply chain, internal operations, and ancillary services with its customer. In practice:

1. A customer can custom-configure a particular Ford model on-line.
2. Detailed information would be transmitted so that a factory builds the car to order.
3. A dealer delivers the car — and reports any problems instantly so that the plant can make adjustments.
4. Through electronic linkages, suppliers control inventories at Ford factories.
5. The finance unit underwrites the purchase and handles the insurance.
6. Ford designers, watching closely from the sidelines, crank in the customer-driven information into future models.

The entire strategy is a magnificent blend of technology — the integration of every function and activity inside the organization and throughout the entire supply chain. And all activities are linked into a brilliantly conceived web to create customer satisfaction, company growth, and the long-term prosperity of the market.

Executing the plan, however, is not a do-it-yourself activity. Ford began by assembling a high-powered, high-tech group of partners. Oracle provided the software and databases needed to exchange information and conduct transactions seamlessly. Cisco contributed the essential networking expertise. And Microsoft used its CarPoint Web site to offer a build-to-order service.

All told, the integration takes the following form:

- Retailing establishes a Web site where consumers can customize their orders, track their progress, and apply for financing.
- Customer service permits owners to obtain on-line help, follow up their warranty service, and monitor their financing.
- Suppliers set up an on-line purchasing and information exchange network between buyers and dealers.
- Marketing partners with Yahoo!, TeleTech, and others to monitor the behavioral buying patterns of Web-surfing customers.
- Value-added services equip new cars with Web access, satellite phone services, and e-mail capabilities in a digital interior as an extra source of revenue during the lifetime of vehicle ownership.
- Financing repositions much of its Ford Credit services to the Internet for on-line financing and collections.
- Employees are integrated throughout all of its far-flung operations by being offered a computer, printer, and Net access for $5 a month.

What are the tangible advantages? Factories build cars to order, managers tune in to the evolving needs of customers, and suppliers control expensive inventories. The savings alone from streamlining suppliers and distribution by using the Internet are estimated at 25% of the retail price of a car.

Such a system is not unlike the ongoing methods Wal-Mart Stores uses to give suppliers responsibility for stocking its store shelves. Or the practices Dell Computer employs to fine-tune its ordering and manufacturing processes, with the result that it is able to custom assemble more than 25,000 different computer configurations for customers.

Thus, customer relationship management, together with the effective application of technology, becomes the optimum model for marketing in the Internet Age.

CUSTOMER RELATIONSHIP MANAGEMENT (CRM)*

> **Key point:** On-line markets are commerce sites on the public Internet that allow large communities of buyers and suppliers to "meet" and trade with each other.

Central to the entire marketing process is building stronger, more profitable customer relationships. And one of the all-powerful strategies in transforming enterprises — large and small, regional and global — to become customer-focused is Customer Relationship Management (CRM).

CRM pervades the entire organization and involves the alignment of initiatives such as e-commerce, sales force effectiveness, customer service, customer relationship planning, enterprise resource planning, and supply chain management. It is the proliferation of information technologies that makes these intricate alignments possible. For example:

- Tracking software and database programs record how many times Web visitors check out an advertisement or a product — and what they skip over. To do that, Web sites place tags, called cookies, on a visitor's computer disk drive. These cookies, combined with on-line registrations, then add information collected from e-mails and phone inquiries placed by customers. Thus, the value of marketing on the Internet isn't in the click-throughs; it's in the data acquired.
- Software programs compile assorted information about how customers interact with a company through sales calls, meetings, on-line and phone inquiries, or from buying products and services. The outcome: a fine-tuned profile about customers and prospects that includes information on demographics, tastes, or e-mail addresses of millions of people that combine to result in precision targeting.
- Other software programs permit suppliers to automatically reply, route, segment, or forward e-mails to companies, call centers, or specialized sales

---

*Much of the following information on CRM comes from a forum presented by the Gartner Group and is quoted with permission.

reps so they can be more efficient and effective in responding to customers. Additionally, the software pulls together and analyzes information
from systems that companies already have in place, including inventory,
logistics, and sales databases.

- Systems continue to evolve that can understand and interpret customers'
tastes and purchasing patterns. In turn, those data translate into products
and services customized to satisfy buyers' needs and behaviors. In addition
to Ford, such companies as Dell, Cisco, Nestle, and Compaq are on the
cutting edge of reaching the prized goal of mass customization.

B2B

The Ford example highlights specific business-to-consumer and business-to-business applications, with the ultimate goal of creating a unique car or truck (with the
appropriate wraparound financial services) to each customer's specifications. And
the Internet provides the channel through which to accomplish these customer-satis-
faction goals.

While business-to-consumer e-commerce was the first phase and has become
fairly well entrenched, the business-to-business phase is still in its infancy and is
evolving with dazzling possibilities. A Boston Consulting Group report estimates that
Internet-based electronic business relationships will account for $2.8 trillion in sales
by 2003. The Gartner Group places this figure even higher — at $7.2 trillion. Thus,
technology aligns buyers and sellers in product- or industry-focused Internet marketplaces for the exchange of goods and services. These on-line markets, also known as
B2B marketplaces, are commerce sites on the public Internet that allow large communities of buyers and suppliers to "meet" and trade with each other.

According to Ariba Inc., ultimately all businesses will buy on a marketplace, sell
on a marketplace, or be marginalized by a marketplace. B2B marketplaces offer a
compelling entry point into the new economy. They offer buyers and sellers uniquely
powerful forums to reduce transaction costs, enhance sales and distribution
processes, deliver and consume value-added services, and streamline management.
The primary beneficiaries of the B2B wave will be those who use the Web to extend,
deepen, and create business relationships.*

While new information technologies make this alignment possible, it is not technology that drives it. CRM is, above all else, a total business initiative. Figures 6.1a
and 6.1b describe the CRM process.

WHY APPLY CRM

Key point: Personalization means that Web site visitors can specify which information,
products, or other features they want to see regularly. The goal: one-on-one marketing.

---

*Adapted from an Ariba Inc. white paper, "B2B Marketplaces in the New Economy." Ariba Inc., Mountain View, CA,
2000. With permission.

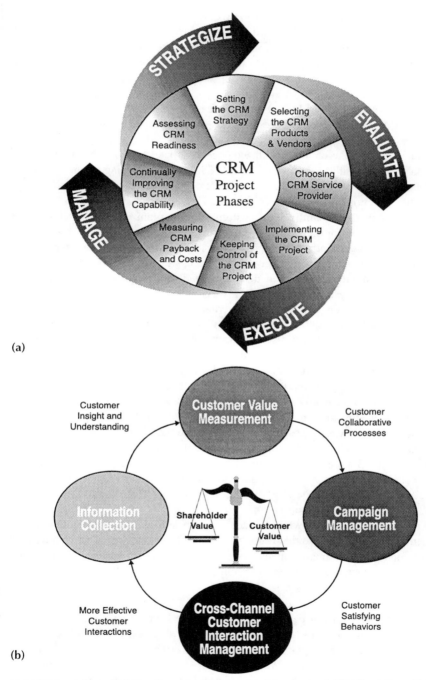

FIGURES 6.1 (a and b) The Customer Relationship Management (CRM) process. Courtesy of the Gartner Group, Inc. Stamford, CT.

As indicated in the Ford case and defined by CRM, the overall aim is to tailor products and services to each and every customer. Thus, every individual is a distinct and unique market. And the resulting personalization has tremendous payoffs. One research report indicates that customization at 25 e-commerce sites boosted new customers by 47% in the first year — and revenues by 52%. For example:

- Music retailer CDnow Inc. lets customers have a Web page designed just for them containing music suggestions based on their particular inclinations, past purchases, and ratings on artists and CDs. Based on a list of CD preferences that appear on the customized pages, shoppers tag CDs they may buy later. Result: sales skyrocketed by 200% in 1999. According to one executive, "It really is a music store for each of our 600,000-plus customers."
- Office Depot Inc. offers small-business buyers personalized on-line catalogs, with the capability that customers can organize a distinct Office Depot catalog for their particular needs.
- Dell Computer Corp. has created some 1500 customized home pages for its best customers so they have direct access to corporate-specified personal computers, negotiated discounts, and records of orders and payments. This system results in Dell's PC unit sales growing over 70% a year, compared with the industry average of 11%.
- Sapient Health Network offers personalized information for some 115,000 sufferers of 20 different diseases, from breast cancer to hepatitis C. After filling out an extensive questionnaire on their own unique conditions, each patient gets a personal "bookshelf" full of symptoms, treatments, and the like, specifically related to their unique ailments.
- California State Auto Association uses market-analysis software to extract customer information from separate databases controlled by its travel agency, emergency roadside service, insurance business, and Web site. Such data give managers a capacity to assign each customer a lifetime value.
- Williams-Sonoma Inc. uses e-mail software to cross-promote its Web site, mail-order business, and Williams-Sonoma and Pottery Barn retail stores. Managers then use the e-mail addresses collected at stores and Web sites to send targeted promotions.
- Consolidated Freightways utilizes its Web site to offer rate quotes on trucking jobs and provide routing guides. When the query is made a help window automatically opens. As customers obtain assistance, Consolidated collects insightful information from them which they use to target them for increased business.

The above examples of personalization illustrate how diverse organizations use technology and databases to tailor a Web site, trace users' past behavior and tastes, and track meaningful demographic and geographic criteria. Thus, personalization is based on the active choices that Web site visitors use to specify which information, products, or other features they want to see regularly. Again, the goal is one-on-one marketing — similar to the small-town, buyer-seller relationships of yesteryear.

CUSTOMER RETENTION

> **Key point:** Retaining the loyalty of a customer is far more cost-effective, since the acquisition costs are sharply reduced or eliminated altogether.

Favorable statistics associated with CRM have already been cited. There is, however, within the framework of CRM still another compelling statistic: it can cost up to 10 times more to attract a new customer than to retain a current one. Consequently, sales models that focus on attracting as many new customers as possible — at the expense of properly servicing existing ones — have become outmoded. Customers can move quickly to more competent suppliers when they are not completely satisfied.

Let's look at the average cost for acquiring a new customer in a business-to-business market:

Cost of an average sales call	$290
(including salary, commission, benefits, and expenses)	
Average number of calls to convert a prospect into a customer	× 5
Cost of acquiring a new customer	$1450
(advertising/promotion expenditures are not included)	

Now, let's look at the projected lifetime value of a customer:

Annual customer revenue	$5000
Average years as a customer	× 2
Average profit margin	× .10
Customer lifetime value	$1000

Conclusion: it costs more to acquire a new customer than you will gain in lifetime value; that is, unless you can find a way to decrease selling expenditures, reduce the number of sales calls, or increase lifetime value. Therefore, retaining the loyalty of a customer is far more cost-effective, since the acquisition costs are sharply reduced or eliminated altogether.

Let's examine how to install a customer retention program:

- Measure retention rate over a sustained period. If you have a few large customers, the calculation is simple. With a large customer base, the use of percentages or actual customer counts will give you a clear measurement.
- Isolate the causes of customer defections. Customers that discontinue business or move to an area not serviced by your firm are one thing. Those leaving because of poor product quality, excessive pricing, shabby customer service, or faulty order processing are quite another matter and cause for concern. Then, focus on specific corrective actions and incorporate them into your marketing plan.
- Calculate how much profit you would forfeit from lost customers. This is expressed as a customer's lifetime value, as illustrated above.

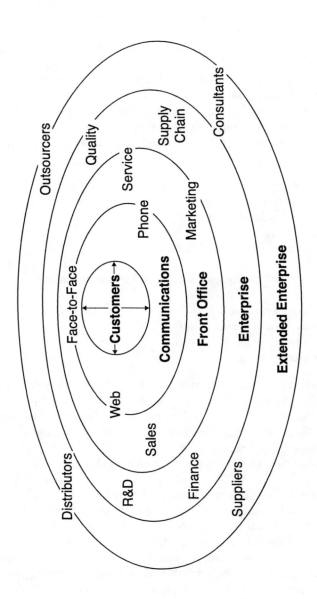

FIGURE 6.2 CRM: "ripple effect" through the enterprise and beyond. Courtesy of the Gartner Group, Inc., Stamford, CT.

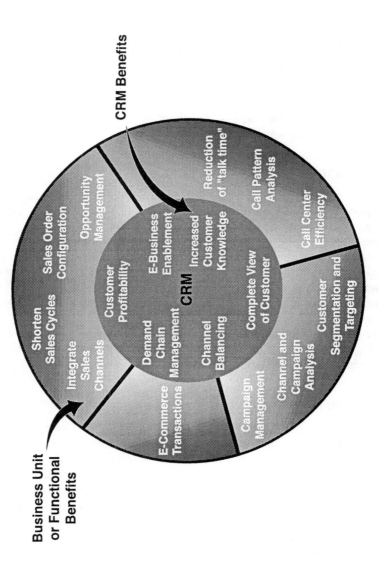

FIGURE 6.3 Benefits of CRM. Courtesy of the Gartner Group, Inc., Stamford, CT.

- Determine what it would cost your company to reduce the defection rate. As long as the cost is less than the lost profit, the expenditure is justified.

Thus, to retain customers, your organization must serve them better than competitors do. An effective way to do this is by investing in the technology and procedures to integrate all relevant information on each customer across the enterprise. Doing so gives you the ability to facilitate more effective planning, marketing, selling, and servicing decisions throughout the customer life cycle.

As customers' value requirements and expectations are met, loyal customers are created and CRM is initiated. Enterprises lacking a compelling CRM strategy risk losing both new and existing customers to more nimble, customer-centric bricks and mortar as well as bricks and clicks competitors. Figure 6.2 and Figure 6.3 illustrate the overall process and advantages of CRM.

PATTERNS OF CUSTOMER BEHAVIOR

> **Key point:** A framework for understanding the behavioral cycle consists of stimulus, sensation, need and predisposition, perception, motives, and behavior.

A core component that is embedded in CRM (and highlighted in the above case examples) incorporates patterns of customer behavior. Highlighting behavior raises these questions: How is a customer likely to think, behave, and make decisions regarding your products and services? How can you use that information to reach and attract potential customers — and retain them? What impact does behavior analysis have on selecting customer-centered marketing strategies?

The following case example involving medical services illustrates the relevance of these questions to CRM and to the larger issue of marketing strategy.

CASE EXAMPLE: TECNOL

Tecnol needed a point of entry to penetrate the crowded health-care market. Larger competitors not only dominated it with sizable market shares, but also commanded superior resources in R&D, production, and marketing to maintain a continuing presence.

To overcome those formidable barriers, Tecnol managers initially concentrated on two major factors: customer behavior and competitor characteristics. To find a point of entry, managers canvassed the medical products industry to catalog the various product lines and the segments each served.

Their search revealed significant changes in surgical procedures driven by new technology. Along with the changes, they observed a sharp rise in health-related fears that were unnerving operating room personnel. For example, they noted the soaring anxiety about AIDS, the concern about the increasing use of lasers in surgical procedures, which produces airborne particles of bacteria from diseased tissue, and the worry about the swelling number of TB cases in hospitals. From the investigation, Tecnol managers reasoned that if they entered the market with a single product line of medical supplies, there could be a reasonable chance for success. Their conclusion: enter the surgical mask market.

Next, Tecnol managers evaluated two dominant competitors serving that niche: 3M and Johnson & Johnson. They judged that those leaders were satisfied with their market performance and, in Tecnol's opinion, were taking the surgical mask market for granted. Further, they calculated that those companies weren't keeping up with rapidly changing surgical technology nor addressing the physical/emotional needs of the users — namely, surgeons and nurses — by lagging behind in developing innovative surgical masks. Using those customer behaviors and competitive characteristics as a framework for implementing its market entry strategy, the Texas-based company launched into "high tech" surgical masks.

Most of the Tecnol specialty masks had patented screens to filter out submicron-size particles of bacteria, smoke, and other airborne tissue fragments. Tecnol also developed a shield made of plastic that attaches to a mask and protects the surgeons' and nurses' eyes from blood and other fluids splattered during surgery. Imaginative products continued to roll out from Tecnol's continuing responsiveness to customers' behavior, changing technology, emerging hospital hazards, and awareness that the market leaders would eventually rise to meet the competitive challenger. Result: Tecnol now commands over 50% of the surgical mask market.

LESSONS

What can you learn from the Tecnol case? First, it takes diligent research to understand customer behavior and translate the findings into market entry, product development, and CRM strategies. Tecnol's track record in those areas is exceptional and offers some of the best lessons for entering a new market that has high-profile competitors. For example:

- Locate the optimum product/market entry point through a methodical probe of customer behavior and competitors' dispositions. (Also, review segmentation guidelines in Chapter 2.)
- Sustain growth with a continuous flow of new products, applications, and services.
- Monitor existing products that are currently being sold to your existing markets. Where possible, quantify those products by sales, profits, market share, position in the market, and any other pertinent criteria that permit you to appraise market performance.
- List new markets (or applications) in which your existing products can be sold. (As Tecnol did, rank those segments by competitive performance, rate of segment growth, and level of technology changes.)
- Identify new services or value-added products that can be sold to existing customers. These new products could include any new systems you have licensed, private-labeled items, or modified products with wraparound services that customers perceive as new.
- Launch new products into new markets. While this is the riskiest of the

steps, it allows you to test emerging segments that have opened up through expanding applications of technology, government regulations, or unique requirements tied to customers' behavior. (This step was successfully executed by Tecnol's perceptive actions.)

An additional useful framework for grasping the behavioral aspects of customer relationship management consists of the following elements: stimulus, sensation, need and predisposition, perception, motives, and consumer behavior.

Stimulus

A stimulus is any external or internal force or event that arouses one or more senses. An example of an internal stimulus is a grumbling stomach, while external stimuli can come from any element of the environment outside the body. Whatever its nature, a stimulus is relevant only if it reaches at least one sense and brings about a sensation.

Sensation

A sensation is the arousal of a sense and is a prerequisite for perception. Sensations are involuntary and thus not under the control of the consumer, but rather are controlled by the stimulus and its source. Once a shopper is exposed to a given stimulus situation, such as walking down a supermarket aisle or being lured by an enticing Web site, a variety of stimuli activate the senses. Short of closing your eyes, you cannot prevent packages or blinking signals from making a visual impression. Sensory discrimination is based on the ability of the stimulus to stand out and attract attention.

The ability to attract attention is dependent on (1) the level of stimulation present (for example, some viewers charge that TV commercials are louder than the programs they interrupt), and (2) the consumer's ability — or inability — to distinguish among similar stimuli (studies show that most consumers cannot identify their favorite brand of beer, cigarettes, or cola drink in unlabeled tests.)

Need and Predisposition

Once a sensation has been created, it has to evoke a response from a need or predisposition before it can produce perceptions and, ultimately, conscious consumer behavior. A need is an inactive condition within an individual that will be expressed by active behavior when properly stimulated. One example is an increased appetite in response to a need for food. Because needs are often both dormant and vague, it is a challenge to every marketer to awaken and focus them. The process leading to a desire for a particular product or service is called motivation.

A predisposition is an attitude, a tendency to react in a particular way to a stimulus. It can be favorable or unfavorable and it reflects a consumer's receptiveness to a certain type of stimulation. For example, some consumers are reluctant to buy pre-sweetened cereals because they are thought to hasten tooth decay. Taken together, needs and predispositions are filters for selecting favorable stimuli to be acted upon or for discriminating against unfavorable stimuli, which, under normal circumstances, would not even reach the level of consciousness.

Perception

If a stimulus passes through the filters of need and predisposition, perception will occur. Perception is the interpretation of sensations. It involves conscious mental processing relating sensory impressions to an individual's frame of reference and, therefore, varies from one person to another. Thus, perception is subject to personality influences and cultural factors. As such, it can result in a considerable distortion of reality. In fact, continual change is the norm and the perception at a particular point in time is a type of snapshot, since no cultural behavior remains completely static year after year.

Apart from any defects a product may have, the way in which a consumer views a product or service will determine whether it will be bought. Further, the crucial factor in determining who makes the sales is not so much the inherent features of the product but rather the skill of the marketer in understanding the dynamics of the transaction "ritual" between the company and the customer. More than any other element in the model, consumer perception warrants careful study and constant attention.

Motives

A stimulus that is perceived may result in a motive. A motive is a state of tension (want, desire, urge, and drive) that causes an individual to act to reduce or eliminate the tension. In the Tecnol case, there was a clear-cut motive on the part of doctors and nurses to eliminate the tension that existed in their feelings about exposure to disease in a hospital work environment. As such, a motive represents an activated and focused need that is now oriented toward the achievement of a goal.

The problem for the marketer is that consumers act rarely, if ever, from a single motive. Rather, multiple and, at times, even conflicting motives govern most behavioral acts. The purchase of a car, for instance, may be influenced by the motives of prestige, comfort, safety, and economy. It is unlikely that all these motives will point to the same choice. Consumers, therefore, have to assign priorities to their motives to decide which ones are more important. The central idea is to determine your customers' motives, as well as their priorities, and be able to address and trigger them properly with stimuli in the form of advertising, packaging, incentives, and other elements of the marketing mix.

Consumer Behavior

How a consumer behaves toward a product is an attempt to decrease or eliminate tension. As such, a response may take three major directions: the consumer: (1) decides to purchase and use your product, (2) determines that he or she needs more information and so begins a search effort, or (3) decides to drop the whole matter and take no action.

Once a purchase has been made, the consumer compares expectations and fulfillment in a process called *feedback*. The outcome of this comparison affects future behavior. A single positive experience produces satisfaction that leads to reinforcement. Continued reinforcement results in the formation of a habit, which is an ideal situation because it means repeat purchase of your product and results in brand loyalty. A negative experience, on the other hand, may wind up with the consumer changing brands, avoiding an entire product category, or, as in the Tecnol case, create a negative morale situation.

USING THE BEHAVIOR MODEL

One of the major benefits of understanding basic behavior is that it is highly adaptable to specific situations. You can substitute or add individual components to fit special conditions. For instance, it applies equally well to selective behavior (where a choice is made when a product is first considered) and to repetitive behavior (where successful actions are habitually repeated). In the case of selective behavior, motive turns into a more or less decision-making stage.

Although the model is based on the behavior of the individual consumer, it can, nevertheless, be used to explain the behavior of entire market segments. If your customers are business-to-business buyers, the model is equally applicable to their behavior as individuals or as group decision makers.

Table 6.1 reviews the different factors in behavior analysis and tells how to influence consumers in each of these areas. For example, regarding motives, the chart counsels you to investigate how consumers choose the brand they will use, and then to use this information in designing your product and advertising.

TABLE 6.1
Applying the Behavioral Model

Factor	What You Should Do to Influence Consumers
Stimuli	Test, in a competitive environment, how much attention your stimuli create (e.g., product design, advertising, packaging)
Sensations	Unless you can create sensory impressions, no action is likely to follow. Stimuli must stand out from their environment to be distinguishable.
Needs/predispositions	Look at your product design, advertising, or Web site as you consider the most pressing current need(s) or most positive predispositions.
Perception	Ask consumers what your advertising and packaging tell them about your product.
Personality	Consumers try to match the personality profiles of the products they buy with their own. Make sure that yours has a clear-cut profile. It cannot be all things to all people. Where possible, use the new CRM software and technology to accomplish such a match.
Social factors	Be aware of social and environmental factors and seek acceptance by others to your advertising.
Image	Unless you can create a positive image for your product, consumers are unlikely to buy. Ask them how they view your product and adjust its image if necessary.
Information search	Provide informative and persuasive booklets, free for the asking.
Motive	Investigate what ultimately makes consumers choose one product over another. Build this argument into your product and advertising.
Decision making	Make the decision atmosphere easy and pleasant. For instance, offer financing or other special incentives for making a decision before the specified date.
Behavior	At this point, your product's package is probably the most powerful influence on consumer behavior, the "silent salesperson" on the store shelf. Make sure that it encourages purchase and consumption.

Goal orientation   Explain how your product gives desired results.
Feedback   Using tracking software, find out who is repurchasing or abandoning your prod-
                          uct and why.

UNFILLED WANTS AND NEEDS

Another component of customer behavior is determining the unfilled wants and needs
of various customer segments. The analysis, however, goes beyond simply identifying
these wants. It specifies ways to fulfill them by examining how consumers adopt a
new product and how you can communicate your offerings to them. The following
case example illustrates how one progressive company shaped its strategy.

CASE EXAMPLE: BALDOR ELECTRIC

Baldor Electric Co. considers customer relationship management and total orientation toward satisfying unfilled wants and needs as more than just a management
buzzword. In the mid-1990s, the Fort Smith, AR company was dwarfed by two stalwart rivals, Reliance Electric and General Electric, competitors in electric motors for
power pumps, fans, conveyor belts, and the variety of automated components used in
modern factories.

"If you have good relationships, you can weather the bad times," declared Baldor
CEO Roland Boreham, Jr. Relationships, according to Boreham, extend beyond customers and include workers at Baldor, where there has not been a single layoff since
1962. Even during the recession of 1991, workers were busy increasing inventory
and expanding the product line in readiness for the eventual upswing in business.
Since 1991, sales have skyrocketed by 46%.

LESSONS

> **Key point:** Your optimum goal for CRM is to achieve a preferred supplier status with
> 100% conformance to expectations.

Focusing on fulfilling customers' wants and needs at Baldor means providing customers with the motors they need — on time, and according to specifications. The
company accomplishes this by building up ready-to-go inventory early in the production cycle, permitting it to fill an order overnight for the numerous motors it
stocks — ranging in size from 1/50 to 700 hp. It assembles other sizes on short order
from a database that includes over 20,000 different specifications.

The core ingredients behind Baldor's ability to sustain sound customer relationships are

1. A bulk of its inventory is stored in 31 warehouses strategically located
   around the country in close proximity to customers' locations.
2. Each warehousing facility is owned and operated by an independent
   Baldor sales representative who is in continuing contact with other reps
   around the country.

3. Each facility is linked by computer to respond to a customer's urgent request for a motor to prevent, for instance, a potential manufacturing interruption.

Result: unsurpassed customer relationships for reliability, responsiveness, and flexibility where almost any size of motor ships on virtually an overnight schedule, exceeding the capabilities of most of its formidable competitors.

With the customer as the centerpiece behind Baldor's success, the following eight steps of a customer satisfaction program are recommended for your own organization:

1. *Define customer requirements and expectations.* Begin by establishing continuous dialogue with customers to define their current and future expectations. Gather information by both personal customer contact and using the Internet. Then match customer expectations against promises made in the sales presentation and advertising. The feedback often falls into such basic areas as orders being shipped complete and on time, and complaints being handled rapidly and to the customer's satisfaction.

2. *Maintain an organized system of customer relationship management.* Ongoing customer contact is a key component of the program. It means assigning permanent customer contact people such as customer service, sales, and technical service to selected customers. Each contact person is then empowered to initiate actions to resolve customers' problems. Other features of customer relations include toll-free telephone lines and on-line "expert systems" that connect customers to information on inventory, production, and technical problem-solving assistance. Overall goal: achieve a preferred supplier status with 100% conformance to expectations.

3. *Adhere to customer service standards.* All quality plans, product performance, and customer relationships are driven by customers' standards. Most often, those standards are measured by the time it takes to handle complaints, the number of on-time shipments compared to previous time periods, and the amount of invoicing errors, freight claims, and product returns. Once indexed, the information is forwarded to a steering committee made up of various functional managers for evaluation and action.

4. *Make the commitment to customers a company ritual.* A commitment means guarantees that include, for example, stock orders shipped the same day received, technical service teams sent to customers' locations when needed, specialized training provided to customers' employees, products that conform to data supplied by customers, and a 24-hour "hot line" for support services.

5. *Resolve complaints to achieve quality-improvement results.* Empower customer-contact personnel to resolve customer problems on the spot. In particular, sales reps should follow up complaints and make a formal report to a Customer Satisfaction Committee.

6. *Determine what constitutes customer satisfaction.* Develop an index to

measure customer satisfaction. With customer feedback as the input, as-semble information from various sources, such as direct customer contact, customer audits, independent surveys, quality assurance cards about ship-ments, suggestions, inquiries, and complaints.

7. *Customer satisfaction results.* Circulate the results so functional managers can design customer satisfaction objectives for the following year.

8. *Compare customer satisfaction levels.* Contrast your results with those of competitors and with industry standards through formal and informal benchmarking. Then share the results with intermediaries to help them improve their customer satisfaction ratings.

HOW CUSTOMERS ADOPT A NEW PRODUCT

Key point: Diffusion is the spread of a new idea from your company to its ultimate users or adopters. Adoption is the decision-making process that prospective users go through after they learn about an innovation.

The Baldor case shows how one company met the overall needs of the electric mo-tors industry by fulfilling the individual needs of customers through a well-defined program. The underpinning of such a program is a process of diffusion and adoption.

When a new product is introduced to the marketplace, two interrelated processes are brought into play: *diffusion* and *adoption*. Diffusion is the spread of a new idea from your company to its ultimate users. Adoption, on the other hand, is the decision-making process that prospective users go through after they learn about an innova-tion. In the final stage of the adoption process the consumer decides whether to purchase your new product on a regular basis.

Because innovations are vital to the growth of your firm, it is essential that you understand the methods by which information and opinions about your product are communicated, and then either accepted or rejected. In order to achieve the maxi-mum flow of communication about your innovation, you need to be knowledgeable about the processes involved in the diffusion of innovations. You also should know what decision-making stages individual customers go through in making up their minds about your new product, and what the possibilities are to influence their deci-sions in your favor.

DIFFUSION

Diffusion means spreading the word about your new product and is initiated by you. But it is only partially under your control. A great deal of discussion occurs in face-to-face encounters and exchanges between customers, over which you have no direct influence. Thus, it is important to give them every reason to think and speak favor-ably about your innovation. In this context, it is particularly crucial to understand the nature of innovation and communication.

An *innovation* is an idea perceived as new by customers. This fact has far-reaching implications. First of all, *ideas*, not products, are spread in the diffusion process. Only if you can convince customers to accept the new idea underlying your product will they consider the product itself. If customers view your new product as being the same as all the others, they will not consider it worth a try. Again, it makes very little difference whether or not your product represents a substantial departure from other products on the market. The only thing that counts is what customers *think* your product is.

ADOPTION

Effective diffusion of your new idea is a prerequisite for adoption. Only after a customer has learned about the existence, availability, and desirability of your innovation can he or she decide about its adoption.

Information and persuasion are passed on from your firm via mass media, the Internet, and through various opinion leaders to individual consumers who, in turn, go through several phases of decision making. Besides that mainstream of information and influence through which consumers first become aware of and interested in your innovation, other sources of communication come into play at different stages of the adoption process. Therefore, although the diffusion process reaches into every stage of the adoption process by means of a communication flow, adoption is essentially an individual matter. In the end, it is the consumer alone who must make the decision after considering outside factors.

In adopting your company's innovation, a consumer passes through five distinct phases: awareness, interest, evaluation, trial, and adoption.

1. *Awareness.* At the awareness stage, product information flows to the customer with no initiative on her part. She receives it passively but experiences little emotional response. Her information at this point is incomplete in that she may not be sufficiently informed about your innovation's availability, price, and features. The efforts of the mass media and the Internet are particularly well-suited to creating such widespread awareness because of the relatively low cost considering the size of the audiences.
2. *Interest.* As the information received in the awareness stage is absorbed, a customer may say to himself, "That sounds interesting. Let me find out more about it." Thus, the interest stage is initiated. It represents a turnaround from the indifference of the awareness phase. The customer is now turned on, at least sufficiently so to investigate the matter further. He conducts an active search for more information. The purpose of this effort is to obtain a comprehensive picture of your innovation. While folders and brochures from your company will be helpful, and other sources may be consulted, particular emphasis and confidence are likely to be given to independent impersonal sources such as consumer reports, professional journals, and government studies.
3. *Evaluation.* Having collected as much additional information as possible, the customer examines the evidence and ponders whether to try the prod-

uct. In the evaluation stage, after weighing the pros and cons of a purchase the prospect solicits the advice of relevant individuals who are trusted personal sources. Two groups of people are involved here: "experts," that is, friends who possess some degree of knowledge in the subject and can be consulted from a functional and financial point of view, and members of the social system (for example, family) who will be affected by a purchase decision and whose acceptance becomes crucial, even though they may not have any expertise. Since the customer perceives both a financial risk (that your product may not perform to his satisfaction, thus resulting in a loss of money) and a social risk (that the innovation will not be accepted by her reference group, bringing about a "loss of face"), she will be strongly influenced by these two factors, which override any influence on your part at this point.

4. *Trial.* During the trial stage, a prospect will test your new product, often by purchasing it on a small scale. While many items can be sampled in small quantities, difficulties arise in the case of durable goods that require trial under conditions of normal use, which is all but impossible unless the product is rented or purchased.

5. *Adoption.* When he completes his personal trial of your innovation, your buyer will determine whether or not it has proved to be useful and desirable in his particular situation. If the decision is positive, the customer will adopt — that is, continue using or consuming your product. Besides his own trial experience, your company and product image as well as his social environment will influence the final decision.

Of course, your target market can reject your innovation at any stage. A prospect can eliminate your product idea even at the awareness stage as being of no interest. This dismissal may result from a misunderstanding, if your advertising message was not persuasive enough. During the course of information gathering, she also can decide your product is inappropriate or unaffordable. Evaluation of the benefits and drawbacks may cause her to reject it. She may even discard it as unsatisfactory after the trial period.

A rejection after adoption, however, represents a *discontinuance* because it follows an earlier commitment. An understanding of the interplay between adoption and discontinuance is of great importance for the design of a successful market strategy. Many firms restrict their analysis to a study of the adoption rate, which is simply the ratio between the number of actual and potential adoptions.

An increasing adoption rate, however, can be misleading because it suggests growing popularity of your product, which may not be the case. If you investigate the interplay of adoption, discontinuance, and readoption, you may well find that even though more and more of the original nonadopters convert to adoption, a certain percentage of former adopters discontinued using your product.

Adopter Groups

A useful component of the adoption process incorporates adopter groups. They are characterized as:

- Innovators: venturesome individuals and leading-edge companies that are first to try new ideas and generally are insensitive to price.
- Early adopters: opinion leaders with high visibility who adopt new products early but only after careful scrutiny, since their reputations are on the line.
- Early majority: individuals or companies that buy before the masses. However, they are rarely industry leaders.
- Late majority: individuals who are skeptics and adopt after a significant number of people or companies have tried the product.
- Laggards: tradition-bound groups that are cautious, price sensitive, and last to buy.

By pinpointing the characteristics of these adopter groups, you can launch an intensive promotional effort targeted at innovators and early adopters, with emphasis on the latter group. If possible, try offering free trials of your product or service. You can use the test results to develop sales strategies for other adopter categories that are waiting and watching the purchasing patterns of the early adopters.

HOW SOCIAL SYSTEMS INFLUENCE DIFFUSION AND ADOPTION

> **Key point:** The perceptions, motives, values, habits, attitudes, and beliefs that are prevalent in any social system may make or break your new product.

While volumes have been written about social systems, suffice to say for our purposes that a social system makes up an integral part of the target market you are trying to address. Social systems play a major role not only in diffusion, but also in the adoption of your innovation. For example:

- In many instances, a consumer will purchase a new product because other members of his or her social set acquired them. The keep-up-with-the-Joneses syndrome explains this tendency for conspicuous items such as swimming pools.
- A certain type of innovation may require prior acceptance by the majority of a social system's members before individual adoption decisions can be made. A charter flight is a good example; the individual still has a choice, but can adopt only if the group supports the idea.
- Another type of innovation is adopted by the majority of a social system and is subsequently forced on those who opposed it — local zoning laws, for example.

- In some situations, customers, regardless of the decisions of other individuals in the social system, will adopt some innovations. In such cases, the items involved are typically inconspicuous or universal, such as toothpaste, soap, canned vegetables, and refrigerators.

These few illustrations make it clear that the diffusion and adoption of innovations are shaped, and often initiated, by the interaction of the people belonging to the social system that you are trying to penetrate. The perceptions, motives, values, habits, attitudes, and beliefs that are prevalent in this social system may make or break your new product.

The adoption of innovations is often governed by behavioral patterns of the consumer, with the features of the product taken for granted and playing only a minor role. Of necessity then, psychology, sociology, cultural anthropology, and other behavioral sciences serve as important tools for senior executives, marketing executives, and product developers.

In particular, cultural anthropology is beginning to emerge as a major contributor in understanding the culture of various groups and the behavioral patterns exhibited by groups of buyers. For instance, Gary Ferraro* writes:

> Most innovations introduced into a culture are the result of borrowing from other cultures. This process is known as cultural diffusion, the spreading of cultural items from one culture to another. The importance of cultural borrowing can be better understood if viewed in terms of economy of effort. That is, it is much easier to borrow someone else's invention or discovery than it is to discover or invent it. In fact, anthropologists generally agree that as much as 90% of all things, ideas, and behavioral patterns found in any culture had their origins elsewhere. Individuals in every culture, limited by background and time, can get new ideas with far less effort if they borrow them.

According to Everett Rogers** the rapidity with which an innovation is adopted, or whether it will be adopted at all, is affected by the following five variables:

1. *Relative advantage:* the extent to which an innovation is thought to be superior to whatever it replaces.
2. *Compatibility:* the extent to which an innovation is perceived to be congruous with the existing cultural values, attitudes, behavior patterns, and material objects.
3. *Complexity:* the ease with which an innovation can be understood and utilized.
4. *Trialability:* the degree to which an innovation can be tested on a limited basis.
5. *Observability:* the extent to which people in the society can see the positive benefits of the innovation.

---

*Ferraro, G., *The Cultural Dimension of International Business*, Prentice-Hall, Englewood Cliffs, NJ, 1998, p. 25.
**Rogers, E., *Communication of Innovations: A Cross-Cultural Approach*, Free Press, New York, 1971.

Thus, we can see from these two references from cultural anthropology that the patterns of diffusion and adoption have a solid correlation with standard marketing practices.

To summarize, the following case examples illustrate the sweeping and powerful effects of customer relationship management and clarify the far-reaching effects of integrating customer-driven marketing with the Internet Age:

- General Electric has performed superbly in virtually every market it serves — from aircraft engines and medical systems, to nonbank finance services. As a priority issue in its strategic plans, GE has forged an all-out push to capitalize on the Internet. Its e-commerce initiative is transforming the way GE interacts with customers and how it sells everything from home mortgages to highly sophisticated medical-imaging machines via the net.

- Yahoo! expanded from a simple search engine into a strongly branded consumer brand service. As a result, the number of people visiting Yahoo tripled in 1 year to 105 million monthly. And it has become a powerful magnet for advertisers, merchants, and consumers since it is the largest Internet portal, with sites in 21 countries. To maintain the momentum, Yahoo is forming relationships to become a major player in non-PC devices that access the Web.

- Cisco Systems Inc. has grown 10 times in revenues and profits since 1994. Its managers have an obsession with customer satisfaction. Even CEO Chambers will take a call from a customer at 2:00 a.m. The company sells routers and switches that direct data across the Net and around corporate networks. Latching on firmly to the Internet explosion, Cisco has broadened into strategic businesses in such growth areas as software, consulting, and fiber-optic communications.

- Martha Stewart Living Omnimedia established alliances "to be the only place you need to go to get things for your home." Its sales vehicles include a monthly magazine, radio, TV, a newspaper column, and a flourishing Web site with more than 1 million registered users. Also, there is a Kmart alliance that forecasts sales of more than $1 billion for Martha Stewart brand merchandise.

- America Online Inc. has firmly established its presence in the fast-moving world of e-commerce. With its base of 22 million subscribers and advertisers generating record-breaking profits, the company is looking to such new vistas as mobile phones, TV screens, and handheld computers. It is creating a host of partnerships with such companies as 3Com, Motorola, and Eastman Kodak.

- Qualcomm's founder and CEO, Irwin M. Jacobs, is credited with some of the outstanding signal-processing breakthroughs. Qualcomm's technology is used in about 50% of new digital handsets sold in the U.S. And such giants as Ericsson are slated to use Qualcomm's technology for a new generation of digital wireless phones.

- Siebel Systems Inc. produces sales-management and customer-service software, which includes a total backup support system. Engineering SWAT teams typically work around the clock when a problem comes up. The corporate culture is one of making employees focus with intense eagerness on achieving total customer satisfaction. Recognizing the movement of markets and the way in which business transaction will be conducted, the company moves relentlessly forward to generate products that power e-commerce sites.

BEST PRACTICES

1. Manufacturing is changing from the "push" model to a "pull" model, where customers decide what they want built. The change encompasses a far-reaching system that integrates the entire supply chain, internal operations, and ancillary services with the customer.
2. Customer Relationship Management (CRM), together with the effective application of technology, is the optimum marketing model for the Internet Age. It is one of the all-powerful strategies in transforming enterprises — large and small, regional and global — to become customer focused.
3. Electronic marketplaces offer buyers and sellers uniquely powerful forums to reduce transaction costs, enhance sales and distribution processes, deliver and consume value-added services, and streamline management. The aim is to tailor products and service to each and every customer. Thus, every individual is a unique market.
4. Retaining the loyalty of a customer is far more cost-effective, since the acquisition costs are sharply reduced or eliminated altogether. And as customers' value requirements and expectations are met, loyal customers are created and retained.
5. A framework for understanding the human aspects of how consumers buy is evident in a behavioral cycle consisting of stimulus, sensation, need and predisposition, perception, motives, and behavior.

7 Supply Chain Management: A New Era in Logistics and Distribution

INTRODUCTION

Supply chain management encompasses an array of logistic and distribution activities employed by the most competitive and marketing-savvy organizations. The supply chain begins when an organization conceptualizes a product. The product concept is then forwarded to a contract manufacturer. Characterized as a new breed of supercontractors that are currently revolutionizing manufacturing, these firms manage the customers' entire product line and offer a multitude of services from design to inventory management to delivery and even after-sales services.

The contract manufacturer is emerging as an integral component of the supply chain: it participates in the purchase of raw materials, components, and equipment; converts them into finished products; and either distributes them directly to a final destination or forwards them through a distributor to the end user. Figure 7.1 illustrates the supply chain.

To examine the workings of but one link in the chain, let's look at Owens & Minor, an intermediary that has redefined the traditional role of the distributor and expanded its functions. As in other chapters, act as if you are participating in the company's strategy session and are asked for input to solve the following problem.

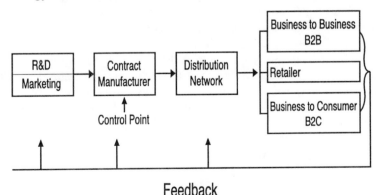

FIGURE 7.1 Supply chain management.

> **Key point:** The purpose of tying together the manufacturer and distributor over the Net is to link them as partners, allowing them to share business data and even combine forces for product design and development.

CASE EXAMPLE: OWENS & MINOR

PROBLEM

As a distributor, how can we command a competitive advantage in the channel system, while maintaining our rate of growth and profitability?

SITUATION

Owens & Minor, a distributor of hospital supplies, has been examining the emerging role of the intermediary in the distribution channel. The Richmond, VA company has also come to the conclusion that to survive as a viable organization it would have to embrace a strategy that combines technology and customer service as the centerpiece of its long-term thinking. Traditionally, manufacturers have retained an unchallenged position by taking commanding control of the distribution channel.

Owens & Minor managers also observed that in numerous other industries customers often considered distributors obsolete, believing that buying direct would result in big savings. Manufacturers reinforced this opinion with, "We can price it lower because we've eliminated the middleman."

That approach is changing. Increasing numbers of distributors in a variety of industries are responding to their customers' calls for help, after being pounded by intense competition and high operating costs that put them in a cash bind.

How are distributors shaping their strategies? Let's break down some of the activities already implemented by Owens & Minor:

1. *Inventory.* Owens & Minor's employees take a daily inventory at its customer hospitals using hand-held electronic devices linked to the hospitals' computers. The computers then transmit orders directly to Owens & Minor's regional distribution centers where daily deliveries are scheduled. In one hospital where this managed inventory system was installed, inventory that includes everything from catheters to garbage bags and was once valued at $250,000, dropped to $50,000. With cash-strapped hospitals seeking relief, the managed inventory system satisfies the customer, strengthens the distributor-buyer relationship, and gives Owens & Minor's marketing and sales strategy a commanding edge.
2. *Management efficiency.* With inventory control and just-in-time delivery in place, hospitals benefit further by less paperwork, fewer employees, less stockroom maintenance, and reduced spoilage from such products as baby formula. One customer, UCLA Medical Center, figures it saved $9 million in 3 years by using the system.

3. *Consultation.* Owens & Minor advises its customers on ways to reduce waste. In one instance, its personnel observed that a hospital was spending $600 on products for each open-heart operation, compared with $420 spent by other customers for the same procedure. Altering the contents of one sterilized package saved that hospital the difference.
4. *Growth.* Pyramiding on its efficient distribution system already in place, Owens & Minor managers capitalize on their dominance by adding products to their line. Result: more profitable sales volume with only incremental costs, while satisfying customers with one-stop shopping.

STRATEGIES

> **Key point:** When a company opens its Intranet (internal network) to suppliers, distributors, business partners, and other authorized users, it becomes an Extranet.

What are the marketing implications of the Owens & Minor case for distributors and manufacturers?

If you are a distributor take control of the distribution channel by becoming more than just a conduit for supplying products from the manufacturer to the customer. Utilize technology to manage customers' inventories, improve delivery times, solve customers' problems related to waste, and reduce costs in order processing and shipping.

If you are a manufacturer recognize that if you decide to bypass the middleman you will have to deliver the above services. With distributors taking the initiative, it may be a prudent alternative to select a distributor and provide maximum support, even to the extent of supplying capital to purchase or update the distributor's technology. Such an alliance accepts the middleman not as a weak link in the supply chain, but as a powerful coupling to activate a marketing strategy. For example, chip maker National Semiconductor Corp. saved its distributors $20 million in one year by encouraging them to order products on-line, while at the same time asking them for precise sales projections through the Web site.

Tying together the manufacturer and distributor through an Extranet extends a company's internal network or its Intranet to key business partners over the Net. The purpose is to put together more formal business links among partners, allowing them to share business data, and to even combine forces on product design and development.

A prime example is Trading Process Network developed by General Electric Co. TPN consists of an expansive electronic marketplace that includes a dozen large buyers, including Con Edison, and 2000 suppliers. The network also includes creating on-line catalogs that corporate buyers can peruse to make purchases. GE alone bought more that $1 billion in goods and services through the network in 1999.

Even in vertical industries, such as electrical parts, the power, speed, and efficiencies of the Extranet dazzle manufacturers and distributors with the colossal opportunities. For decades, companies within that industry have struggled with archaic manual approaches in handling tens of thousands of different parts — from light-bulb sockets to pipe connectors. And they endured the profit-draining financial burden of absorbing huge expenditures for processing orders and correcting numerous errors.

Finally, they took the quantum leap. Some 225 companies in the electrical parts industry banded together to enter the Internet with Idxchange, a state of the art private network linked to a huge database that catalogs electrical parts and carries orders between manufacturers and distributors in a flash. The point-and-click system synchronizes the manufacturers' data with those of the distributors' so that errors in price and product identifications are eliminated. Idxchange is estimated to cut labor and telecommunications costs by some 50% a year.

DISTRIBUTION FUNCTIONS

> **Key point:** With the backward and forward flow of activities and information throughout the supply chain, different participants in the channel assume distinct functions.

Regardless of your position in the supply chain, there are key functions you have to deal with in shaping a distribution strategy:

- Information: collect, analyze, and disseminate market intelligence about potential and current customers, competitors, and other forces affecting the market.
- Communication: combine various forms of communication including literature, videos, and workshops to attract and retain customers.
- Negotiation: seek agreement on price, terms of delivery, and other value-added services as they relate to preferred customer status and long-term relationships.
- Ordering: set up procedures for the efficient (electronic) transmission of ordering information.
- Financing: develop the means to fund a managed inventory system (similar to Owens & Minor).
- Risk taking: assume the responsibility for risks associated with the expanded role of middleman activities.
- Physical possession: develop the capability to store additional varieties of products for customers and manage increases in inventory turnover.
- Payment: design an effective system for payment including the selective financing of inventories for the buyer.
- Title: develop a system to pinpoint the transfer of ownership from seller to buyer. In some situations, inventory is held at the buyer's location and title changes only when usage occurs.

With the backward and forward flow of activities and information throughout the supply chain, different participants in the channel assume distinct functions. Therefore, whether you are a manufacturer or distributor, form a relationship that clearly defines the role of each channel member.

THE NEW ROLE OF THE INTERMEDIARY

> **Key point:** With the use of inventory management systems and the Internet, the intermediary plays a key role in the chain by sorting through the numerous choices of suppliers — and most important, staying close to the customer.

The full benefits of managing and participating in the supply chain is achieved through the explosive use of the Internet. To demonstrate the workings of technology from a logistics and distribution viewpoint, let's examine additional techniques.

First, to show the broad impact of the Internet and e-commerce on conventional brick-and-mortar businesses using traditional distribution networks, consider the much-publicized Amazon.com and eToys Inc. sites. Each of these relative newcomers to their respective industries now command multibillion-dollar market caps and have seriously challenged the stalwarts of their respective fields, Barnes & Noble Inc. and Toys 'R' Us Inc.

For instance, Amazon.com has experienced remarkable cost efficiencies by selling over the Web without the fixed expenses of stores. As of 2000, it has spent only $56 million on fixed assets such as computers and warehouses, while Barnes & Noble has spent $472 million on its 1000 stores. Also, estimates indicate that Amazon's investment in new warehouses can support $15 billion in sales. To further illustrate the striking effect of the Web, Cisco Systems Inc. obtains 78% of all its orders over the Net. It then develops the product specifications and electronically turns them over to contract manufacturers for order fulfillment.

Conclusion: recommending a major review of your existing logistical and distribution channel systems would go far in determining if building expensive time-consuming in-house capabilities would add or detract from developing a competitive market advantage. If undertaken, such a review begins with examining your company's core competencies by asking, "What are our inherent strengths?" If, for instance, shipping and logistics come up as a weakness, you would need to ask, "Should we locate the best shipper who can provide exceptional delivery service and apply the saved resources to build on our strengths to sustain growth and profitability?"

What, then, is the new role of the intermediary? While the exact boundaries between direct and indirect distribution may become indistinct in the supply chain, there are considerable advantages to outsourcing distribution, warehousing, and logistics to a partner. As demonstrated by Owens & Minor, using inventory management systems and the Internet the intermediary plays a key role in the chain by sorting through the numerous choices of suppliers and, most important, staying close to the customer. In turn, suppliers need to be where the vast number of buyers gather, which is not at a single company's site but more often at the increasing number of e-markets.

CHOOSING CHANNELS OF DISTRIBUTION

> **Key point:** Depending on the degree of market exposure desired, choose from exclusive, intensive, and selective distribution strategies.

As described above, supply chain management is the 21st-century model, with its interconnections of suppliers, producers, intermediaries, and end users on the Internets, Intranets, Extranets — all tied to the accelerating proliferation of e-markets or exchanges in virtually every industry. Yet, there are underlying concepts about the workings of channels of distribution that still endure as brick-and-mortar establishments continue to retain a solid place in the movement of goods in the meandering pathway from product concept to end user. To that end, let's examine the bedrock characteristics of a distribution system.

MARKET EXPOSURE

One fundamental consideration for your company is determining how much and what type of market coverage is appropriate for your product or service. Depending on the degree of market exposure desired, you can choose from exclusive, intensive, and selective distribution strategies (see Table 7.1).

TABLE 7.1.
Choosing the Degree of Market Exposure

Factor	Exclusive Distribution	Selective Distribution	Intensive Distribution
Degree of coverage	Limited	Medium	Saturation
Degree of control	Stringent	Substantial	Virtually nil
Cost of distribution	Low	Medium	High
Dealer support	Substantial	Limited	Very limited
Dealer training	Extensive	Restricted	None
Type of goods	Specialty	Shopping	Convenience
Product durability	Durable	Semidurable	Nondurable
Product advertising	Yes	Yes	No
Couponing	No	No	Yes
Product example:	*Automobile*	*Suit*	*Chewing gum*

Exclusive Distribution

If you sell a prestige product, you are likely to grant exclusive rights covering a geographic area to a specific distributor or retailer, protecting that firm against territorial encroachments by other companies carrying your products. This policy severely limits the number of middlemen handling your products and should be adopted only if you want to exercise substantial control over your intermediaries' price, promotion, presentation, and service. It results in a stronger commitment on the part of your dealers and generally produces a more aggressive selling effort.

Frequently practiced in the automobile business, exclusive distribution can lead to potential legal problems. For instance, an exclusive dealer contract signed between your firm and a specific retailer prevents the middleman from selling competitors' products. However, changes are taking place in the industry as the so-called superdealers are beginning to sell products of several auto makers.

In a parallel consideration, closed sales territories, a term referring to a vertical territorial restriction between a supplier and an intermediary, frequently come under scrutiny. Ever concerned with maintaining competition, the courts have generally agreed to such arrangements when the manufacturer in question is not a market leader. Tying contracts, which permit exclusive dealers to carry other suppliers' products, violate the Sherman Antitrust Act and Clayton Act if they preclude competitors from entering major markets.

Intensive Distribution

Intensive distribution is the direct opposite of exclusivity. Popular among producers of convenience items, this strategy aims to make these goods available in as many outlets as possible. As the category name suggests. buyers of such products expect them to be conveniently accessible and will not expend much shopping effort. Products in this category are frequently purchased, low-ticket nondurables, such as cigarettes and chewing gum.

Selective Distribution

Between the extremes of exclusive and intensive distribution falls selective distribution. This policy involves setting up selection criteria and deliberately restricting the number of retailers that will be permitted to handle your brand. More than one, but less than all applicants in an area will be selected. This approach implies quality without the restrictions of exclusivity.

Selective distribution is far less costly than intensive distribution and affords greater control. In particular, it is suitable for such retail goods as name-brand clothes, which fall into the semidurable category (in contrast to the expensive durable specialty goods that are best handled through exclusive distribution.) Selective distribution lends itself to cooperative advertising, in which manufacturer and retailer share the cost.

While the use of e-commerce tends to overshadow the sharp distinctions of market coverage made here, the three categories are valid in determining how and where to target your primary prospects and customers. Also, it serves as a promotion consideration for developing a suitable image by nature of the product's availability by type and location of outlets. The marketing consideration here is to be customer-focused and sensitive to the buying behavior of individuals and customer segments.

SELECTING DIRECT VS. INDIRECT DISTRIBUTION

> **Key point:** Using a multichannel design is often essential to increase market coverage and create greater impact in the marketplace.

Another basic distribution consideration parallel to market coverage that should be decided relatively early in your planning is whether to handle the distribution of your product alone or enlist expert help. The former method is called direct distribution and the latter, indirect distribution. While there are numerous e-markets, along with their auction formats proliferating by industry or product category, these trends do not alter the need to make a conscious choice between direct and indirect distribution.

Direct Distribution

As the name suggests, direct distribution involves a direct transfer of ownership from the producer to the consumer. As Figure 7.2 shows, this method does not ban various types of facilitators from entering into the picture. As long as they do not assume title separate and distinct from the manufacturer, the channel still remains direct. Thus, producers can sell through the mail, over the phone, door to door, the Internet, through a factory outlet, through their own retail stores, or even through an independent agent, and still be involved in a direct transaction. Direct distribution obviously involves a greater degree of control than indirect distribution, but it cuts off a producer from the widespread coverage that the latter approach can offer.

Indirect Distribution

On the other hand, indirect distribution always incorporates middlemen or resellers, who are basically of two types: wholesalers and retailers. Figure 7.2 presents a graphic comparison of the direct and indirect approaches.

What you see in Figure 7.2 is typical of the most frequently encountered channel designs. It is evident that in the direct distribution channel there is never a third party who takes title to the goods in question. For indirect distribution, the opposite situation is clearly the case, even though the manufacturer is likely to have a sales force to call on intermediaries.

The illustration does not propose to exhaust the variety of channel structures. Instead, it delineates the most frequently used multichannel designs. As can be readily seen, multiple channels (also known as multiplex marketing) are entirely possible and are often essential to increase market coverage and thereby create greater impact in the marketplace. However, selecting more than one route to the consumer can lead either to complementary or competing and, thus, conflicting channels. Where it results in conflict, this growth policy can defeat its own purpose.

Function vs. Institution

In distinguishing between direct and indirect distribution, a basic distinction ought to be made between the functions and institutions of wholesaling and retailing. The function of wholesaling is to sell those items necessary for use in the conduct of a business (for example, word processors) or for resale. The function of retailing, in contrast, is to sell for personal, nonbusiness use. In a retailing transaction the buyer of an item is a consumer who intends it for private use or consumption.

The respective institutions are business firms specializing in each particular type of transaction. An institution of wholesaling — a wholesaler — is a firm whose primary business is buying merchandise in large quantities at substantial discounts and reselling it in unaltered form at a relatively modest markup to industrial or institutional users, or in somewhat smaller but still sizable quantities to other wholesalers or retailers.

As an institution of retailing, a retailer's primary activity is buying merchandise in medium-size quantities (cases vs. the wholesaler's truckloads) and reselling it in small quantities (frequently in individual units) to consumers, often at substantial markups.

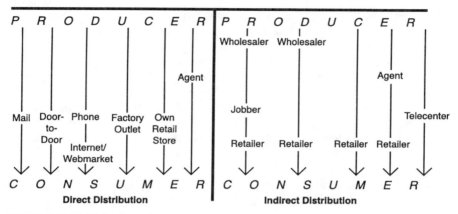

FIGURE 7.2 Multiple channel designs.

The reason for drawing these rudimentary distinctions between function and institution is that *institutions can be eliminated, their respective functions cannot.*

When you first enter a new market, it is generally advisable to go the indirect route, involving intermediaries who can deliver quick and widespread coverage at a reasonable cost.

Later, though, as your product moves into the maturity stage of the life cycle, you may want to eliminate your wholesalers in order to gain more immediate access to your retailers and better control over the selling effort. It is at this point that you often discover that one can eliminate the institution but not the function of wholesaling (or retailing, for that matter). The question, therefore, is not whether to perform these functions, but who is to perform them.

MAKING THE DECISION

When the time comes to make the channel decision for your product, you should consider several factors. Initially, an important consideration is where does the customer expect to find your product or service? Therefore, the industry's prevailing distribution pattern is a powerful guide in making such a channel decision. If your current sales force has related experience and appropriate business contacts, you may want to follow established routes.

Other elements to take into account can be grouped as company, competitive, and customer factors:

- *Companies* that are strong financially have the option of direct distribution, while weaker firms have to use middlemen. If your product line is broad, you are in a better position than a specialized supplier to consider going direct. And, in keeping with marketing's prevailing credo of staying close to the customer, i.e., practicing Customer Relationship Management (CRM), the fewer intermediaries you will want to have.
- Competitive practices will often encourage you to meet competitors head-on in the very same outlets they use. Therefore, you have to assess your

firm's strengths and weaknesses and determine how to create a competitive advantage with your distribution strategy. Your choices vary from just-in-time delivery, inventory management, consultation, and those other strategies described in the Owens & Minor case.

• Customer characteristics include the number of buyers, their geographic location, and their buying patterns. You are better off going direct when you have a limited number of prospects. Again, if they are concentrated in only a few areas you can send your own sales force out to do the job. Should they buy often and in small quantities, you had better let others handle the selling.

Channel members are a vital link in your effort to satisfy distant customers. By making them your partners and serving their best interests, you will find that they will help you achieve your goals.

As discussed in this and other chapters, there is still another factor that is making a significant impact on channel-related decisions: the Internet. By 2002, businesses are expected to exchange at an estimated annual rate of $327 billion in goods and services through that explosive new channel.

Buying electronically isn't new to many companies that have been using an older technology called Electronic Data Interchange, or EDI. But that technology is rather pricey and difficult to set up. The Internet, on the other hand, lets businesses not only consummate a sale, but permits quick and inexpensive transfer of all kinds of data: sales contacts, product brochures, and even engineering drawings.

As a channel of distribution, doing business via the Internet shows cost savings in the range of 5 to 10% of sales (an average based on the experience of a wide variety of companies in 1998.) In more dramatic numbers, some companies reported huge advantages from on-line business relationships. Chip maker National Semiconductor Corp. reported saving its distributors $20 million in 1998. Boeing Co. booked $100 million in spare-parts orders from airlines in 1 year through its Web site. And networking giant Cisco Systems Inc. booked $11 million in orders each day on its Web site from resellers, or about $4 billion a year.

The following international case illustrates the blend of market coverage, channels of distribution, supply chain management, and technology.

CASE EXAMPLE: YAMATO TRANSPORT

Yamato Transport Co., Japan's largest home-delivery firm, established a special unit to handle distribution services for those Net retailers that ship merchandise directly to consumers. Not only does the firm handle deliveries, but also customers' warehousing, stock management, and packing functions.

Another part of Yamato's business consists of two on-line specialty sites — one for books, the other for toys. Consumers have the choice of picking up their purchases at a convenience store or having Yamato deliver them to their location. As a parallel activity, the driver also can collect payment from the buyers, passing it on to the merchants. The service also permits customers with Net-ready cell phones to access Yamato's on-line tracking system. (The strategy is similar to those of Federal Express and United Parcel Service. Both have set up warehouses near key air hubs and invested huge amounts of money in computerized and net-ready package-tracking systems.)

Yamato's management accurately envisioned the bright future of e-commerce in Japan and planned for the company's active role in supplying logistics and distribution know-how. E-commerce is about to explode in Japan, from 1999 sales of $82.7 billion to a projected $683 billion by 2003. Behind that skyrocketing growth is the rapid movement of the Japanese to connect with the Internet. From an estimated 17 million users in 1999, the increase is expected to jump to 35 million in just 2 years.

YAMATO'S DRIVING FORCE

Yamato's corporate culture links its current success to the company's past. It has a history of always being an innovator and leader of its competitors. In the mid-1970s, it was the first Japanese transport company to offer home delivery. That service expanded to include Saturday and Sunday delivery, which was followed by offering two-hour delivery service to time-sensitive customers.

The company then executed a niche strategy of transporting sporting equipment, such as bulky golf club, to and from resorts. By the mid-1980s, it expanded services once again by collecting payments on behalf of companies that shipped goods to customers. Once again, Yamato niched the market by shipping frozen foods.

CHANNEL CONTROL

Channel control is another marketing imperative that relates to the search for an optimum distribution system. The factors include:

1. The introduction of a new product into new markets.
2. Desire to intensify market coverage.
3. Need to replace existing distributors.
4. Industry movements that trigger changes in methods of distribution.

SELECTING DISTRIBUTORS

Given the high degree of specialization found among distributors, your firm's management must decide how selective or comprehensive it wants to be in its market coverage. Only with the appropriate distribution mix can you satisfactorily achieve your company's marketing goals.

Your distributors will perform as expected only if you carefully manage and constantly update your relationship with them. Therefore, develop and consistently apply well thought out criteria for selecting the right distribution partner in a given area.

To help determine how many and what kinds of distributors you need for a particular territory, and to facilitate the selection process, you will want to conduct a market review to estimate its sales potential. Fortunately, however, you rarely have to choose a completely new set of distributors, unless your existing distributors are not tuned in to the workings of e-commerce, e-markets, Extranets, and the accompanying technologies. (The Owens & Minor case exemplifies the new role of the distributor.) Otherwise, your own firm's present distributors should be able to handle most new product innovations.

However, as you introduce new products and systems, you may find that your current distributors are ill equipped to sell and service them, or that it already handles competitive products from other manufacturers. Also, you may be addressing a new kind of clientele not serviced by your current network. Or if you enter into new geographic markets, the need for knowledgeable representation may become apparent.

Further, as you review your share of business in a given segment, you may conclude that your firm is underrepresented. Or you may determine that your present outlets are not going after the business aggressively enough to satisfy you. As a result, you need to add more distributors in the territory, based on population, sales, buying potential, buying behavior, or other relevant considerations.

In some instances, an area may be growing so quickly that your current distributor is simply no longer in a position to service the market adequately. In any event, the addition of new distributors in existing territories needs considerable thought and diplomacy. Be aware, however, your motive for maximizing territory coverage can prove counterproductive if it demoralizes your current distributors.

By far, the most frequent reason for appointing new distributors is the turnover of existing outlets. These changes may be due to natural attrition, the death or retirement of principals, the sale or collapse of a distributor, or the inability of a distributor to stay current on the dynamics associated with e-commerce. The recent trend toward more specialization or limited-line selling has also led many distributors to drop a certain manufacturer's line.

Changes in the distributor mix come about more often by inadequate distributor performance that leaves the manufacturer, or even both sides, dissatisfied rather than through attrition. Yet, such a move can prove painful and disruptive and should be undertaken only in extreme cases. In some instances you may try to rekindle an existing relationship, as long as there is a willingness to recognize the dynamic changes of the marketplace and consequently the changes required in blending distribution strategy with a Web strategy.

EXAMINING YOUR DISTRIBUTION STRUCTURE

Where you have to revamp your entire distribution structure, the restructuring may require adding or eliminating an intermediary step in distributing your company's products. If you decide to make a change from direct to indirect distribution, you will have to build a national distributor network from scratch — a formidable challenge requiring analysis, search, and organization.

Once you establish a need for a new or additional distributor representation, the next task is to develop a list of candidates. You usually have a number of sources for this list, including your own field sales force, your manager of distributor sales, trade associations, and present distributors and dealers.

The intelligent selection of distributive outlets requires more than the good judgment of a few key people. Since so much is at stake, the selection process should be directed by a set of carefully chosen guidelines consistently applied. These selection criteria have to be customized to suit the particular conditions and goals of your firm.

Table 7.2 highlights the selection criteria most often mentioned by some 200 leading U.S. manufacturers in a study on this subject. Look at how the numerous considerations are classified and summarized into a limited number of categories that can apply to any distributor selection task.

It is a monumental task to both formulate and apply a set of selection criteria suited to your particular circumstances. But it is well worth the effort, since it should lead to a satisfying and long-lasting relationship.

Selecting a distributor is by no means a one-way street. Rather, it is a matter of both sides choosing to work with each other. Thus, once you have made a selection, you have to persuade the prospect to join your team. It may well be that your prospec-

---

TABLE 7.2
Criteria for Selecting Distributors

Criterion (Category)	Reasoning
Financial aspects	Only a distributor of solid financial strength and practices can assure adequate, continuous representation
Sales organization and performance	The sales strength and record of a prospect is essential to your potential relationship
Number of salespeople (in the field and on the inside)	The general rule: the more salespeople, the more sales and the more effective the market coverage
Sales and technical competence, particularly in the total workings of e-commerce	Salespeople with adequate technical and sales skills
Sales performance	A track record speaks for itself
Product lines carried	Pick your bedfellows carefully
Competitive products	Generally discouraged, sometimes okay
Compatible products	Tend to be beneficial
Quality level	The higher, the better
Number of lines	Will your line get enough attention
Reputation	You are judged by the company you keep
Market coverage	Exposure means sales
Geographic coverage	Avoid overlap and conflicts
Industry coverage	Major user groups must be covered
Intensity of coverage	Infrequent calls mean lost business
Multichannel management	Ability to build, manage, and participate in existing and new channels
Inventory and warehousing	Ability to perform just-in-time delivery is often crucial
Kind and size of inventory	You want the right mix and a willingness to maintain adequate stock
Warehousing facilities	Automated storage and handling facilities, ideally integrated with supply chain management and e-commerce technologies
Management	Proper leadership spells success
Ability	You want competent leadership
Continuity	Succession should be assured
Attitudes	Look for enthusiasm and aggressiveness

tive distribution partner is scrutinizing your firm just as carefully. Welcome that, and be willing to supply information as freely as you expect to receive it. A well-analyzed commitment is bound to last longer than a hasty decision.

EVALUATING DISTRIBUTORS

Once you have secured the services of a sought-after distributor candidate, you must then ensure that your association brings maximum benefit to both parties. You need to perform periodic evaluations designed to be continually informed about the relative performance of your various distributors. These evaluations may be in the nature of current operating appraisals or may take on the form of overall performance reviews. If they are simple and limited in scope, you could conduct them monthly. Thorough analyses, however, should be undertaken only at infrequent intervals: annually, biennially, or even triennially.

If you engage in selective rather than exclusive distribution, the amount of evaluative input you can readily obtain from your distributors is quite limited, forcing you to rely mostly on your own records, observations, and intelligence. If your product is a high-volume, low-cost item with little need for after-sale servicing, you can restrict yourself to a more limited evaluation than in the case of complex systems installations.

If your team is composed of many hundreds of multiline distributors, you will tend to take a closer look at a particular reseller only if his sales trends are way out of line. This procedure is called "evaluation by exception." If, in contrast, your firm employs only a moderate number of outlets, the analysis can be more thorough. There may not even be a need for formal evaluation if you have a close, continuous working relationship.

If you have examined the new role of the distributor in supply chain management, you may not need to eliminate a particular distributor's services. Elimination is truly the last step, after all attempts to reestablish a satisfactory relationship have failed. The expense, time, and trouble involved in dropping a distributor and appointing an established outlet, or even appointing an additional distributor, are considerably less appealing alternatives.

BEST PRACTICES

The following practices summarize the diverse actions that surround supply chain management, logistics, and distribution:

- Look for viable outsourcing opportunities or possible joint relationships with firms that offer state of the art logistical services and that provide linkages along the supply chain.
- Devote time and energy to develop value-added services. For instance, initiate emergency "red flag" delivery, offer private-label packaging, install computerized inventory control systems and ordering procedures, reduce time to resolve complaints, or connect a 24-hour hot line for technical assistance.

- Work jointly with suppliers to find new applications for products that would open up new market niches to sustain growth.
- Examine opportunities for multiplex marketing channels. Adding new segments to your core markets can achieve larger economies of scale and competitive strength. A dependable distribution system can be cost-effective.
- Make use of new technologies. Look to the immense opportunities to create a competitive edge and relieve yourself from the commodity problem. For instance, reach for high performance with computerized order-entry systems and warehouse automation.
- Connect with supply chain management and link up to Internets, Extranets, and e-markets.

8 Marketing Communications: Your Link to the Outside World

INTRODUCTION

Marketing communications is the total process of maintaining ongoing contact with present and potential customers, distributors, suppliers, investors, and the general public. In particular, it is the communications effort along the entire supply chain. One central objective of a communications strategy is brand building, which is the broad development of a product's image. Its construction usually requires some or all of the following forms of communication: TV/Cable, Internet, print advertising, direct marketing, licensing, sponsorships, public relations, sales promotion, and personal selling.

To sample the workings of the communications process and, in particular, brand building, put yourself in a position of helping the following company solve its problem.

CASE EXAMPLE: EDDIE BAUER

PROBLEM

How do we retain the integrity of our brand name as we expand into new market segments?

SITUATION

Eddie Bauer Inc., a Seattle-based maker of casual apparel and furniture, had been following the dominant marketing trend by establishing a brand identity over the Internet and relished the notion of participating in the big bonanza of e-commerce. Yet, this 80-year-old company still detected the long-term advantages of maintaining its infrastructure of brick-and-mortar stores to serve those existing customers whose buying behavior were geared to the touch-and-feel of a traditional retail experience.

At first, managers tried Internet banner ads to drive surfers to its Web site. But results indicated that such advertising was expensive and conversions to sales were low. Then, after learning that half the consumers who visited the Web site had never before shopped at Eddie Bauer, management had to be certain that the experience would go well beyond just duplicating a catalog page on the screen.

How, then, could they exploit the uniqueness of the Internet, tap into a new market segment, and integrate all aspects into a viable marketing strategy to build the Eddie Bauer brand?

EDDIE BAUER'S STRATEGIES

The solution came through the following creative applications:

- Develop an on-line virtual dressing room where shoppers can click on a sports jacket and drag a colorful sweater or striped pants to view the style effects.
- Offer on-line customers a reminder service that signals them by e-mail about forthcoming birthdays, anniversaries, and holidays. The service also permits users to create an electronic shopping list of items they want relatives to buy for them.
- Identify groups and individuals by buying patterns. Then use tailored e-mail to communicate special savings on selected merchandise to match the buyers' fashion profile. Also, direct follow-up promotion to specific groups or special events, such as working women or back-to-school. The objective is 24/7 round-the-clock shopping, all anchored to brand name recognition.
- Apply a similar interactive experience for its furniture line. For instance, on-line shoppers can plug in the floor plans for their homes and see how Eddie Bauer furniture designs look room by room.

Taking the multifaceted approach to building its brand and expanding into new market segments, Eddie Bauer managers integrated all forms of communications such as its Web site, catalogs, advertising, sales promotion — as well as its stores — to build a total brand strategy. For example, the Eddie Bauer catalog promotes its Web site with all the interactive on-line services. In turn, the on-line services inform visitors about taking products they wish to return to its brick-and-mortar stores, where ample cross reference is also made to the Eddie Bauer Web address.

BRANDING

Key point: A brand is the emotional shortcut between a company and its customer that cannot be easily replicated.

The Eddie Bauer case focused on the construction of a brand. Why should there be such emphasis about a brand? With new products being thrust on the market brandishing similar features and benefits that are at times indistinguishable, it is becoming increasingly difficult to differentiate one's product from that of the competitor. Certainly price can make a meaningful difference to some groups, as can such value-added services as just-in-time delivery, technical support, or inventory control systems.

But what emerges as the rock-solid issue, and one that cannot be easily replicated, is the intrinsic value of a brand. As evidence, look at what has occurred in a relatively short space of time with the first batch of recognizable on-line brand names: America Online, Amazon.com, Yahoo!, eBay, and Netscape Communications. All have come from virtual obscurity to achieve an impressive score in the 50% range on unaided brand-recognition surveys. "A brand is the emotional shortcut between a company and its customer," states an executive of a brand-marketing firm.

With the enormous potential of e-commerce capturing the attention of many executives, the question of building a brand using the Internet has become a primary objective of a communications strategy. As illustrated in the Eddie Bauer case, one of the vital building components for constructing a viable long-lasting brand on the Internet is interaction. It creates the emotional bond between seller and buyer.

The following examples illustrate a variety of interactive techniques:

- General Motors Corp.'s Saturn includes a lease-price calculator, an interactive design shop for choosing options, along with an on-line order form. In contrast, its TV commercial is used to deliver a traditional emotional brand appeal.
- Dell Computer lets customers configure and price a computer system online.
- Yahoo! and America Online provide numerous options for customizing their respective services.
- Amazon.com focuses on building its site with interactive features such as one-click ordering and software-generated book recommendations.
- Macy's online services offer a gift registry and personal shopping assistance via e-mail. (As with Eddie Bauer, the Internet presence reaches shoppers who were not shopping at Macy's stores.)

Variously defined as rational branding or experiential marketing, the interactive experiences induce perceptions that, in turn, shape attitudes toward brands. Projections from experts estimate that spending on experiential marketing will skyrocket from $1.1 billion to $11.2 billion by 2003. Where does conventional advertising fit into the total business strategy? The American Advertising Federation asked senior executives to rank marketing tactics in order of importance. Only 10% put advertising at the top. The survey revealed the following:

Product development. 29.4%
Strategic planning 26.8%
Public relations 15.5%
Research and development 14.0%
Financial strategies 13.6%
Advertising 10.3%
Legal 3.4%

IMAGE

> **Key point:** An image represents a "personality" with which the prospective buyer either can or cannot identify.

Still another identifiable phase of a brand-building strategy is the image a product or service projects. In the context of a brand, a purchaser buys an image as well as a product or service. The image comprises a complex of attitudes, beliefs, opinion, and experiences. These make up an individual's total impression of a product, service, or organization.

Consequently, an image represents a "personality" with which prospective buyers either can or cannot identify. Moreover, their purchases project images of the world and themselves. In effect, buyers want products and services to reflect those identifiable images. Taken together, these complex images are entwined inextricably with the assorted behaviors, attitudes, and practices of diverse cultures represented by various and market segments.

DIVERSE CULTURES

Increasingly, cultural diversity is gaining attention in managers' thinking and planning. There is greater awareness that a one-size-fits-all image doesn't work in a culturally diverse marketplace. Some of the findings from the Hudson Institute's *Workforce 2000* study of the work force of the future, commissioned by the U.S. Department of Labor, reveal that between 1985 and 2000, of the more than 25 million who joined the workplace 85% were minorities and women, while white males counted for only 15%. The 85% were made up of white females, and immigrants and minorities of various black, Hispanic, and Asian origins. This work force diversity also means that they comprise a significant segment of a buying public.

Coming to grips with cultural diversity correlates precisely with the movement of getting closer to the customer — or practicing customer relationship management (CRM). As a result, managing diversity means paying greater attention to segmentation, targeting, and positioning. (See Chapter 2 for a comprehensive review.)

Cultural Values

Consider the following concepts to determine what potential they hold for your product or service:

1. Cultural values come and go. The three basic components of culture (things, ideas, and behavior patterns) undergo additions, deletions, or modifications. Some components die out, new ones are accepted, and existing ones can be changed in some observable way. Although the pace of cultural change varies from society to society and market to market, the absolute constant is change. This pragmatic insight should remind the business person that any cultural environment today is not exactly the

same as it was last year nor will it be the same one year hence. Consequently, the cultural environment that envelops a marketplace needs continual formal monitoring and personal observation.

2. Society holds a variety of values. Some are classified as primary beliefs and values and tend to be long lasting. These values relate to work, marriage, charity, and honesty. They are usually passed on from parents to children and are reinforced within the institutions of schools, churches, businesses, and government. A range of secondary beliefs also exists and is within the marketer's ability to influence. Such beliefs can range from when individuals get married and how much debt should be carried, to the frequency, quality, and brand of products and services they purchase.

3. Subcultures rise and fall, from the flower children of the 1960s, to the yuppies of the 1980s, to the variety of religious cults that flourish in various geographical locations, all expressing different beliefs, preferences, and behaviors. Each has a major impact on hairstyles, clothing, sexual norms, and the types of products and services purchased.

DEVELOPING AN IMAGE

Developing or attempting to change an existing image is a slow process that requires considerable patience, skill, and commitment. The best insurance against an unfavorable image is prior testing. Before you attempt to establish or change an image, it is a valuable investment to use image research to provide input. To that end, you should be conversant with three questions that impacts creating and maintaining a favorable image:

1. How does an image develop?
2. How is it researched?
3. How can it be changed?

An image can come from a multitude of factors. It can be outcomes of a company's own communications efforts as well as the actions of competitors attempting to shape a distorted image of your product or company. It can result from the choice of a corporate or brand name, the symbolism used, or any other part of the entire marketing effort including product design, pricing, and distribution. Further, the symbolism may include logos, slogans, jingles, colors, shapes, or packaging.

For example, when computer maker Gateway Inc. decided to move its administrative offices from the prairies of North Sioux City, SD to the shores of San Diego, the company was attempting to create a new corporate image. Gone was its folksy trademark Holstein cows featured in many of its award-winning ads, which alluded to its homespun, grass-roots character. The modifications in advertising, logos, and company location were part of the total image makeover. Behind the strategic decision was the relentless need to grow into new markets or suffer the consequences and retreat into a commodity niche. Also behind the decision was the unyielding aggressiveness of its chief rival, Dell Computer, attempting to take away hard-earned market share. An additional driver was the compelling need to attract much-needed key employees who could not otherwise be tempted to relocate to South Dakota.

Then there is the now-famous packaging test where housewives were presented with identical samples of a new detergent in three different experimental packages. After using the contents, the housewives reported that the product in the blue package did not posseses enough cleaning power; the one in the yellow package damaged the fabric; while the one in the blue package with yellow sprinkles was just right, having enough cleaning power but still gentle on the clothes. This example shows that a mere change in packaging colors can substantially influence the image of a product.

If you want to strategically shape your product's image, Table 8.1 offers some useful insights and guidelines. It presents a dozen image ingredients that are under your control and briefly highlights their respective roles in determining your product's overall image.

TABLE 8.1
Image Ingredients and Their Impact on a Product

Image Ingredients	Impact
Design	Provides esthetic appeal
Color	Sets a mood
Shape	Generates recognizability
Package	Connotes value
Name	Expresses central idea
Slogan, jingle, logo	Creates memorability
Advertising, personal selling	Communicates benefits
Sales promotion	Stimulates interest
Price	Suggests quality
Channels of distribution	Determines prestige
Warranty	Establishes believability
Service	Substantiates product support

RESEARCHING AN IMAGE

> **Key point:** The three projective techniques most frequently used in marketing research include sentence completion, word association, and picture association.

In view of their largely emotional nature, images are best researched by using projective techniques that present the respondents with a stimulus (such as a cartoon character) and ask them to interpret it. While ostensibly talking about this stimulus, the interviewees will unknowingly project their own feelings into the interpretation, thus revealing a true image that could not be obtained by straightforward questioning. The three projective techniques most frequently used in marketing research are *sentence completion, word association, and picture association.*

Sentence completion — This test is made up of 10 to 20 sentence fragments that give only a partial direction of thought and encourage the respondents to complete the sentences in any way they think appropriate. The statements should be balanced with respect to personal ("I think CitiBank is …") and neutral ("Colgate toothpaste is …") direction. An equal balance should be achieved between negative ("The worst thing about the Ford is …") and positive ("The thing I like best about the Ford is …"). The major benefit of this technique rests in the awareness that respondents express their own feelings in their own words. Sentence completion tests can be administered either by personal interview, computer, or by the pencil and paper method.

Word association — This test is a high-pressure technique that presents an interviewee with key words, terms, or names, one at a time, and insists on the respondent's immediate reporting of whatever comes to mind upon hearing a given word. In order to avoid second-guessing, the subject is not presented for casual reflection or deliberation. A brief series of about five responses per trigger word is generally registered. The main advantage of this method is that it produces spontaneous association. This technique is best administered through personal interview.

Picture Association — This test presents respondents with drawings or photographs of different people representing potential product users. The interviewees are asked to identify the prospective users of products A, B, and C. The interviewer then probes for characteristics of the pictured people, thus developing a personality profile of the perceived typical user of a particular product, which is in turn reflective of its image. The prime payoff of this approach is that it elicits a wealth of uninhibited information that would otherwise be impossible to obtain. Like the word association test, picture associations is best administered by personal interview.

While these three projective techniques benefit greatly from professional interpretation, budget-conscious managers can attempt their own analyses using plain old common sense.

A method more suited to the do-it-yourself approach is the *semantic differential*. As illustrated in Figure 8.1, it uses pairs of adjectives with opposite meanings. Respondents are required to express the strength of their attitudes by checking off the

	1	2	3	4	5	
Well-known	O	—	—	X	—	Unknown
Modern	—	X	—	—	O	Old-fashioned
Reliable	—	—	O	—	—	Unreliable
Expensive	O	—	X	—	—	Inexpensive
Prestigious	O	—	—	X	—	Low-class
Attractive	—	X	—	O	—	Unattractive
Economical	X	—	—	O	—	Wasteful

Legend: X ——————— Product A
         O – – – – – – – – Product B

Competitive strengths and weaknesses emerge as average scores and are graphically connected.

FIGURE 8.1 Semantic differential profiles of two competing products.

appropriate position on the scale connecting a given pair of adjectives as it applies to the product in question.

The various positions on the scale are usually assigned numerical values (1 through 5 in the figure) and the individual results for each pair of adjectives are averaged for all respondents. When these averages are connected, a product profile emerges.

If this procedure is applied to other products in the same category, a graphic comparison of competitive profiles can be undertaken that highlights the strengths and weaknesses of the different products involved. This technique enables you to capitalize on your product's advantages and to correct, or at least play down, its disadvantages in your marketing approach.

CHANGING AN IMAGE

If you determine that your product's problem is an unfavorable image, you can correct this situation by first being concerned with quality and prepared to offer generous and uncomplicated guarantees. Chrysler Corporation achieved a tremendous improvement in its image by offering a 5-year/50,000 mile warranty. A&P, in an unprecedented move, admitted in its ads, "We have let pride (quality) slip a little," and promised market improvement to a wary public. Quality extends into every controllable image ingredient listed in Table 8.1. The product's design, color, shape, package, name, slogan, jingle, and logo all must connote this characteristic and commitment.

Examine the quality of your sales force and service organization to improve the presentation and quality of product performance. There have been occasional instances when an entire sales force has been replaced in an attempt to strengthen company image and sales. And the availability of reliable, competent, and friendly service is a factor that frequently makes or breaks a sale.

In addition, advertising messages and news releases can obviously go a long way toward improving an image and restoring public confidence by communicating improvements that have been made and correcting any false impressions. Some companies are taking advantage of the environmental controversy over ozone depletion by communicating the fact that they have changed from marketing the possibly harmful aerosol sprays to nonpressurized pump sprays.

GUIDELINES TO IMAGE MANAGEMENT

Here are some of the key questions that you may want to ask yourself and others with respect to image management responsibilities and efforts:

- What do we know about the image of our company/product/service in the eyes of actual or potential buyers?
- Do we have any image at all? Are we well-enough known?
- Is our image positive or negative?
- Is the perceived image accurate or inaccurate? Are we better than our reputation?

- What does our name suggest? Is it appropriate? Have we outgrown it?
- How does our image compare with that of our competition?
- What are our perceived strengths and weaknesses?
- How can we improve our image?

Favorable images serve as a magnet to attract investment, talent, and buyers. In particular, a favorable company image can make even commodity products stand out that otherwise would be indistinguishable. In the main, however, good images lead to a competitive edge that cannot be easily replicated.

Having set the stage for communications with brand-building and image, let us now focus on the place of the traditional and dominant forms of promotion; namely, advertising and sales promotion.

ADVERTISING

> **Key point:** Advertising interacts closely and continuously with the other elements of your marketing mix such as product, pricing, and distribution. In turn, its impact is enhanced by sales promotion activities.

As the tantalizing outcomes associated with conducting e-commerce capture the attention of an increasing number of executives, and a concerted effort exists to make Internet initiatives harmonize with their current marketing strategies, more traditional forms of communication approaches are playing a significant role in those efforts. In particular, the time-honored advertising principles should not be ignored if you are to advise others on the expenditures of corporate funds to achieve a total marketing effort. In fact, they should be mastered so that you can make informed judgments on the types, formats, and messages that are conveyed through the various media.

Initially, be precise about the job you want advertising to accomplish. For example, it can:

- Support personal selling.
- Inform a target audience about the availability of your product.
- Persuade prospects to buy.

Once a dominant job is identified, choose media and copy themes to match those objectives. As a result, your advertising becomes realistic, measurable, and results-oriented.

The following case shows the realistic application of promotion where a company introduced a new product into a new market dominated by strong competitors.

CASE EXAMPLE: MICROSOFT

Microsoft gained notoriety with its Windows operating system for desktop computers. At one point in its campaign to expand market coverage, it targeted large corporations handling multilevel tasks in accounting, inventory management, and transaction processing (mainframes or minicomputers usually perform such tasks).

Microsoft launched into the corporate market with Windows NT, software designed for client-server networks that can handle a multitude of tasks through networks of desktop computers (clients) that obtain data and programs from hub machines (servers.) Anticipating the Window's NT launch, aggressive competitors such as IBM, Hewlett-Packard, and Sun Microsystems were unwilling to give up a single market-share point or a customer to Microsoft without a fight.

Overcoming such anxious competitors was only one part of Microsoft's launch strategy. The second part was convincing dubious corporate customers that it could handle their huge multitasking needs. Let us summarize the obstacles Microsoft faced when it decided to wander outside its secure niche. Understanding the nature of the barriers will sensitize you to the issues connected with developing a successful product promotion.

First, while Microsoft was firmly entrenched in one segment of the software market, customers in the corporate segment perceived the company as inexperienced and without a track record. Second, some corporate customers were cautious about making a wholesale conversion to Microsoft's new product, mostly due to the costs associated with switching from one system to another. Instead they opted for a minimal order, far from their full sales potential. Third, another group of prospects, unwilling to be first to try a brand-new system, indicated concern about a product that might not be fully debugged.

Finally, competitors were swift to learn of Microsoft's product launch and had time to develop a counter strategy. This condition resulted from the wide publicity and the prolonged waiting period for Microsoft to receive test results from customers.

LAUNCH STRATEGY

To overcome those obstacles, Microsoft decided to promote Windows NT using the following approach:

1. The company introduced two versions of NT: a desktop edition and an advanced edition for more complex applications. Each was sharply discounted during the introductory period. The plan was to probe two user niches and find the best opportunities and the fewest obstacles. Also, by launching two editions Microsoft hoped to recover losses if one edition failed and the other scored.
2. Microsoft announced the product with great fanfare to maximize the effects of publicity and gain extra mileage from its advertising campaign.
3. It selected a group of customers with high visibility in their respective industries to test Windows NT. The intent was to obtain operating results and testimonials that the sales force could use to target additional prospects on an industry-by-industry rollout.
4. Microsoft moved rapidly to sign up 65,000 application software developers, over 200 distributors, plus more than 20 computer makers. This strat-

egy accelerated the launch into numerous geographic and industry-specific segments.

5. Microsoft monitored the marketplace with precision. For example, surveys of 200 big corporations revealed that 59% said they would likely buy NT. That compared with such competitors as Unix scoring 39% and IBM with 36%.

What can be learned from the Microsoft case? A useful component in promoting a product launch is the adoption process. Adoption is the decision-making process individuals go through from first hearing of a new product or service until becoming buyers. (Microsoft saw its relevance with the initial resistance to NT among specific groups of potential customers.) Adopter groups are characterized as:

- *Innovators:* venturesome individuals and leading-edge companies that are first to try new ideas and generally are insensitive to price.
- *Early adopters:* opinion leaders with high visibility who adopt new products early but only after careful scrutiny, since their reputations are on the line.
- *Early majority:* individuals or companies that buy before the masses, however, they are rarely industry leaders.
- *Late majority:* individuals who are skeptics and adopt a product or technology only after a significant number of people or companies have tried the product.
- *Laggards:* tradition-bound groups that are cautious, price sensitive, and last to buy.

KNOW YOUR PROFITABLE CUSTOMERS

By pinpointing the characteristics of these adopter groups, you can launch an intensive advertising effort targeted at innovators and early adopters, with emphasis on the latter group. For instance, you can offer free trials of your product or service. Then, you can use the test results to develop sales strategies for other adopter categories that are waiting and watching the purchasing patterns of the early adopters.

There is yet another dimension of adopter groups that is becoming more attractive to executives: knowing the cost of doing business with your customers and then calculating their profitability. While tracking the value of customers is an exercise practiced by many sales managers, there is now a more sophisticated approach.

Companies such as U.S. West, Bank of America, and The Limited collect extensive quantities of precise customer data that allow them to compare the varied types of marketing and servicing costs that go into retaining each individual consumer vs. the revenues he or she is likely to bring in. In effect, it equates to building a profit and loss statement for each customer.

The pure benefit of such an approach lies in a company's ability to determine how much to spend on marketing campaigns, and where, for example, to focus advertising dollars. For example, U.S. West periodically goes through its customer list looking for money losers who have the potential to be more profitable in the future, or those that should receive minimal advertising attention. The company starts with 200 observations about each customer's calling patterns. By reviewing demographic profiles, plus the mix of local vs. long-distance calls, or whether a customer has voice mail, U.S. West managers can estimate a customer's potential telecom spending.

ADVERTISING TECHNIQUES

Now, imagine that you have administrative responsibility for developing an overall advertising strategy and implementing it through an advertising department or an outside advertising agency. To make prudent assessments, here are key points you should know.

First, direct advertising at informing your target audience about the availability and features of your product or service. Second, once that audience has been informed, use advertising to persuade your prospects to buy your offering. In this two-step process, advertising interacts closely and continuously with the other elements of your marketing mix, such as product, pricing, and distribution. More specifically, it reinforces personal selling efforts. In turn, its impact is enhanced by sales promotion activities.

Obviously, then, advertising cannot be developed in a vacuum. Your advertising plan is but one component of the communication plan and to the broader strategic marketing plan. Accordingly, planning an advertising campaign is quite similar to other business planning activities. It requires, as does all planning, anticipating market and competitive conditions, developing objectives, designing strategies and tactics, and establishing controls to monitor performance.

Table 8.2 details the steps involved in developing an advertising campaign. It highlights how continuous marketing research is the foundation of a sound campaign.

PRE-CAMPAIGN PHASE

To effectively monitor the advertising effort, understand the following planning techniques and carefully assess overall market conditions before approving an advertising campaign:

1. Conduct a market analysis that surveys the competitive field as a first step in the pre-campaign phase. For instance, this analysis should examine the range of competitive offerings, their positioning and media choices, their distribution and usage patterns, as well as related market trends. You will want to find out who competitors' customers are and when, where, and for what purpose they make purchases. This background information will provide the necessary perspective for choosing appropriate promotion strategies.

2. Focus subsequent product research more intensively on your own product. The principal purpose is to find out from actual or potential users of the product which features they consider desirable and the benefits they asso-

TABLE 8.2
Developing an Advertising Campaign

Campaign Step	Advertising Activities Pre-Campaign Phase	Research Activities
1. Market analysis		Study competitive products, positioning, media, distribution, and usage patterns
2. Product research		Identify perceived product characteristics and benefits
3. Customer research		Conduct demographic and psychographic studies of prospective customers; Investigate media, purchasing, and consumption patterns
	Strategic Decisions	
4. Set advertising objectives	Determine target markets and user profiles, as well as exposure goals	
5. Decide on level of appropriation	Determine total advertising spending necessary to support objectives	Investigate competitive spending levels and media cost necessary to reach objectives
6. Formulate advertising strategy	Develop a creative approach and prepare a "shopping list" of appropriate media	Examine audience profiles, reach, frequency, and costs of alternative media
7. Integrate advertising strategy with overall marketing strategy	Make sure that advertising supports and is supported by other elements of marketing mix	
	Tactical Execution	
8. Develop detailed advertising budget	Break down overall allocation to spending on media categories and individual media	
9. Choose message content and mode of presentation	Develop alternative creative concepts, copy, and layout	Conduct concept and copy tests
10. Analyze legal ramifications	Have chosen copy reviewed by legal staff or counsel	
11. Establish media plan	Determine media mix and schedule	Conduct media research, primarily from secondary sources
12. Review agency presentation	See entire planned campaign in perspective for approval	
	Campaign Implementation	
13. Production and traffic	Finalize and reproduce advertisement(s), buy media time and space, and deliver ads	
14. Insertion of advertisements	Actually run ads in selected media	Check whether ads appeared as agreed and directed
	Campaign Follow-Through	
15. Impact control		Get feedback on consumer and competitive reaction
16. Review and revision	Adjust advertising execution or spending levels to conditions	Check whether changes made yielded desired results

ciate with its use. Such information will help you make the right positioning decision and formulate effective appeals. In this context, study the
usage patterns in depth.

3. Concentrate your follow-on research on the customer. Here, you attempt
to develop demographic, life style, and behavioral profiles of actual or
prospective buyers. For instance, recognize the frequent and infrequent
users of your product, how old they are, where they live, how much money
they have at their disposal, their educational backgrounds, their occupa-
tions, their marital status and family size, and the cultural group they
belong to.

You will also want to know how they think and act; that is, to the extent that you
can access experts who can provide you with insightful profiles. Ongoing research
provides answers regarding their attitudes, interests, and opinions, which should help
determine what motivates them.

You must then analyze their media habits. Knowing who your customers are and
how they behave is of little value unless you know what they watch, listen to, and
read. You need to know how to reach them. It is also helpful to find out where they
purchase, how much, and how often, and who does the purchasing.

Additional insights can be gained from a look at consumption patterns. At that
point, you can determine who ultimately consumes your product, when, how much,
how often, and under what circumstances. Only after all of this preliminary information has been gathered, interpreted, and internalized should advertising planning be
initiated.

While this pre-campaign work may seem like overkill, think about the time, effort, and funds being expended. Also, the uncomfortable fact remains that much advertising fails because of inadequate pre-work.

ADVERTISING DECISIONS

Once the relevant data have been assembled and examined, you are ready to make a
number of strategic decisions that will guide the detail work that follows. As in all
planning activities, the first major decision is to set advertising objectives.

Developing Objectives

Objectives are guidelines for action that spell out what you want to achieve. You
could say that the basic objective of all advertising is to sell something — a product,
service, idea, or company. To that end, advertising is effective communication, resulting in positive attitudes and behavior on the part of the receivers of the message
that results in increased sales.

However, the objective of increasing sales is too broad to be implemented effectively in an advertising program. Rather, you should formulate more specific and limited aims that you can nail down with greater precision and which you can measure
with accuracy. For example:

• Support a personal selling program.

- Achieve a specific number of exposures to your target audience.
- Address prospects who are inaccessible to your salespeople.
- Create a specified level of awareness, measurable through recall or recognition tests.
- Improve dealer relations.
- Improve consumer attitudes toward your product or company.
- Present a new product and generate demand for it.
- Build familiarity and easy recognition of your company, brand, package, or trademark.

The list is truly endless and as varied as companies and situations. It illustrates some of the possibilities and pinpoints the need for precision to derive maximum guidance from objectives. Because objectives imply accountability for results, they often lead to an evaluation of individual or agency performance.

Advertising Spending

Having determined where you want to go, you must now decide how best to get there. Marketing executives can choose from a number of alternative approaches for setting the level of total advertising spending.

- *Affordable Method* ignores your objectives and is simply an expression of how much you think you can afford to spend. This viewpoint makes your level of appropriation subject to whim and may grossly over- or underestimate the amount in relation to your needs.
- *Percentage of Sales Approach* is probably the most widely used because of its simplicity. That is, it ties your advertising allowance to a specified percentage of current or expected future sales. This procedure, with its built-in fluctuations, not only discourages long-term advertising planning but also neglects current business needs and opportunity.
- *Competitive Parity Method* proposes that your company match competitive spending levels. This simplistic outlook is no more sophisticated or justifiable than the two preceding approaches.
- *Objective and Task Method* produces the most meaningful results. You proceed in three steps: (1) define your advertising objectives as specifically as possible; (2) identify the tasks that must be performed to achieve your objectives; and (3) estimate the costs of performing these tasks. The sum total of these costs represents your level of appropriation. While this approach does not examine or justify the objectives themselves, it nevertheless reflects a reliable assessment of your perceived needs and opportunities, which you can translate into a workable budget.

MAKING ADVERTISING PAY OFF

Advertising remains a key element in a total communications package. Remember, however, no matter how good your agency or advertising department is, you bear the

ultimate responsibility for results. Therefore, it pays to be skeptical, to be more independent, and not to be intimidated by the creators of your advertising.

Also remember that advertising can run into a significant sum of money in terms
of total outlay, so you will want to make sure that your ads are working hard for you.
Work more intelligently and effectively with your advertising people, and offer more
precise guidance as to what they should stress. The following fundamental guidelines
apply primarily to print advertising:

1. *Examine your product's position in the marketplace.* Consider positioning
   your product or service as an alternative way (less expensive, faster, or more
   convenient) of doing things compared with the competing product in the
   field. Also, emphasize a major customer benefit that is unique, meaningful,
   and one that can truly and convincingly be delivered by your product.

2. *Maintain a personality for your brand.* If you want your ads to command
   attention and produce results, try for a uniqueness that makes them stand
   out from the flood of competing messages. Identify a symbol, logo, or
   other repetitious element that will be remembered by customers. The idea
   is to use your advertising to make a positive contribution to the brand
   image.

3. *Excite your audience.* While it is difficult, and at times rather risky, to start
   a trend, do attempt to innovate rather than imitate the style of competing
   products. Your message has only fleeting moments to capture interest and
   communicate a memorable idea.

4. *Be factual and convey benefits.* One powerful way to present factual material is to use a problem-solving approach. Choose a problem that your
   customer can relate to and show how your product can solve it. While this
   guideline is most often associated with business-to-business advertising,
   digging below the surface into emotional themes at times can be combined
   with factual material for greater impact on your audience.

5. *Formulate effective headlines.* Use simple, understandable language. As
   for length of headlines, department store advertising research has shown
   that headlines of ten or more words sell more merchandise than do shorter
   ones. Further, recall is best for headlines of 8 to 10 words.

6. *Reinforce your advertising with illustrations, particularly of demonstrations.* Most often, pictures with story appeal and a human factor awaken
   the interest of the readers and tempt them to read the text. Some research
   indicates that photographs invariably pull better than drawings. They attract more readers, generate more appetite appeal, are more believable, result in higher recall and coupon redemption, and produce more sales.

7. *Use captions, the capsule explanations beneath pictures, to sell.* Expect a
   greater impact from your pictures if you include your product's brand
   name and the major benefit you promise.

8. *Generate an informative atmosphere.* Experiment with a variety of formats
   to provide useful information. For instance, some advertisers give their ads
   an editorial appearance rather than using elaborate, "creative" layouts.

9. *Determine the optimum size of your ads by number of words.* According to some advertising research, readership falls off rapidly in ad copy of up to 50 words but shrinks only insignificantly in copy of 50 to 500 words. Although relatively few people read long copy, those people generally represent genuine prospects. Especially, business-to-business ads with more than 350 words are read more thoroughly than shorter ones.

10. *Don't replace your advertisements before they have had a chance to develop their full potential.* The most basic learning theories stress the importance of *repetition* in affecting behavior. Repeat your winners until the desired effects start to wear off.

SALES PROMOTION

> **Key point:** While advertisements are a long-term investment in the image of a brand, sales promotion campaigns are temporary measures that should be used with discretion. Consider sales promotion as an incentive to buy, whereas advertising offers a reason to buy.

Sales promotion consists of all those promotional efforts of a firm that cannot be grouped under the heading of advertising, personal selling, publicity, or packaging. More precisely:

Sales promotion includes those activities or objects that attempt to encourage salespeople, resellers, and ultimate buyers to cooperate with a manufacturer's plans by temporarily offering more value for the money — or providing some special incentive related to a specific product or service.

While somewhat lengthy, this definition points up a number of essential features:

- Sales promotion includes both *activities* — such as demonstrations and contests, and *objects* — such as coupons, premiums, and samples.
- It may be directed at one or any combination of three distinct audiences: a company's own sales force; middlemen of all types and levels, such as wholesalers and retailers; and consumers or business-to-business buyers.
- In contrast with the continuous, long-term nature of the other elements of the promotion mix, sales promotion campaigns are *temporary measures* that should be used with discretion. (Legendary advertising guru, David Ogilvy said, "an advertisement is a long-term investment in the image of a brand.")

However, unless used wisely, sales promotion can easily become self-defeating and counterproductive. While there are no hard and fast rules, a brand, that is "on deal" one third of the time or more is likely to suffer image problems. In fact, if yours is a leading brand in a mature market, use sales promotion most sparingly because it is improbable that you will gain any lasting advantage from a more generous application.

It is important to remember that sales promotion is costly and should thus be judged from a cost/benefit point of view. So, don't overuse it — even if the temptation is great to yield to internal pressures or external competitive challenges.

In all situations, you should look to integrate sales promotion with your advertising and sales force objectives and strategies. Use sales promotion to encourage more product usage, induce dealer involvement, and stimulate greater sales force efforts.

Although a great deal of money is spent on it, sales promotion often receives less funding than advertising. Consequently, it exists as a poor relative — grudgingly acknowledged but unenthusiastically integrated into the total communications effort. Given such neglect, this potentially powerful tool is often poorly understood, planned, and applied, leading to considerable waste and inefficiency. It can, however, work as an effective component of most any communications mix, ranging from consumer goods to industrial goods and even services, dynamically supplementing and complementing the more sophisticated advertising and personal selling efforts.

Nevertheless, sales promotion has experienced a phenomenal growth that can be expected to increase rapidly. Both internal and external factors have contributed to this impressive record. Among the internal propellants: (1) senior management in many cases has come to view sales promotion as an acceptable and effective stimulant to sales, abandoning the long-held premise that hawking one's wares cheapens the brand; (2) a more professional approach to sales promotion seeks to employ better-qualified individuals and upgrade their status within the organization; and (3) product managers tend to be more receptive to the "quick fix" aspects of sales promotion that help them achieve fast and impressive results, which in turn may lead to personal advancement.

Some important external reasons for the increased use of sales promotion include:

- The number of products in the business-to-business and consumer marketplace have proliferated, leading to intensified competition and the need to create more "noise" at the point of purchase.
- There is a need to respond to competitive increases in promotion spending, although clearly accompanied by the danger of escalation into a "war" in which all sides lose.
- In a down market, manufacturers are more willing to use rebates to shrink inventories and improve cash flow, just as consumers are more responsive to sales stimulation measures.
- The growing power of and pressure from the trade produce more promotional allowances and support from suppliers.
- Some managers feel a certain disenchantment with advertising, where they don't have the funds to carry on a sustained campaign. Or they feel there is a decline in efficiency and effectiveness owing to a disproportionate rise in cost and in competing messages.

ATTRIBUTES OF SALES PROMOTION

Consider sales promotion as an incentive to buy, whereas advertising offers a reason to buy. Also, while sales promotion is part of an overall marketing program, it involves a variety of company functions to make it work effectively. Sales promotion permits tremendous flexibility, creativity, and application. Consider the following applications:

- Consumer promotions: which consist of samples, coupons, cash refunds, premiums, free trials, warranties, and demonstrations.
- Trade promotions: which include buying allowances, free goods, cooperative advertising, display allowances, push money, video conferencing, and dealer sales contests.
- Sales force promotions: which employ bonuses, contests, and sales rallies.

As indicated with advertising (and all other components of the marketing mix), sales promotion is not a stand-alone activity. Instead, make it an integral component of the tactical portion of your strategic marketing plan. Further, establish sales promotion objectives to support the broader strategic vision.

Such objectives include entering new market segments, gaining entry into new channels of distribution, encouraging purchase of larger-size units, building trial usage among nonusers, attracting prospects away from competitors, building brand loyalty, stimulating off-season sales, and winning back former customers.

BEGINNING A SALES PROMOTION CAMPAIGN

In developing a planned approach to sales promotion, it is profitable to follow a series of logical steps for maximum impact and efficiency. The latter can be achieved only if a sales promotion campaign is undertaken not in isolation, but rather as a part of a long-term communication plan, carefully coordinated and integrated with the other elements of your firm's promotion mix and, ultimately, with its marketing mix.

As already stated, sales promotion complements, supplements, and often amplifies other communications tools, and it should always be used in concert with them. For example, displays that tie in with TV commercials produce more sales than unrelated ones.

The following steps are involved in the evolution of a sales promotion campaign:

1. Establish your objectives.
2. Select appropriate techniques.
3. Develop your sales promotion program.
4. Pretest your sales promotion program.
5. Implement and evaluate your campaign.

This sequence contains all four major elements of the marketing management cycle: analysis, planning, execution, and control. Following this pattern slows down the process in comparison with "shooting from the hip," but it makes success considerably more likely.

Establish Sales Promotion Objectives

While the main purpose of sales promotion is to increase the sales volume of a product or to stimulate traffic in a retail outlet, more specific objectives can be identified depending upon the type of audience and the nature of the task involved. Sales promotion efforts directed at your company's own sales force aim to generate enthusiasm and zeal. It is important, then, that you offer your salespeople special incentives to excel and provide the desired support.

A second targeted group is your company's dealers or distributors, without whose active cooperation your entire marketing effort and, more specifically, a sales promotion campaign, would falter. Lastly, while the support and loyalty of your sales force and dealer/distributor network are certainly crucial, a sales promotion campaign would hardly be complete if it failed to stimulate buyer action.

Consider these objectives:

- Identify and attract new buyers.
- Encourage more frequent and varied usage of current products.
- Motivate trial and purchase of new products.
- Educate users and nonusers about improved product features.
- Suggest purchases of multiple and/or larger units of your product.
- Win over buyers of competitive products.
- Reinforce brand loyalty and purchase continuity.
- Create customer enthusiasm and excitement leading to word-of-mouth recommendations and referrals.
- Diminish fluctuations by encouraging off-season usage.
- Counter competitive raiding.
- Generate more traffic at your dealers' outlets.

Although sales promotion campaigns represent short-term stimulation, they are most effective when used in a long-term framework. Further, as shown by the scope of the above list of objectives, sales promotion ties in with opportunities associated with longer-term marketing strategies.

Your sales promotion objectives should be audience-specific and should be spelled out in quantitative form to facilitate later evaluation. For example, software systems can now help packaged-goods companies and supermarket chains target their coupons to individual shoppers. Using loyalty cards to track purchases, supermarkets send the information over the Net to a printer, and a unique package of coupons is mailed out to each customer. The amount of the discount on each product can be varied according to how much customers usually buy.

Select Appropriate Techniques

Once you have decided which market segments you want to address, you can select specific techniques for motivating the dealer, introducing new products, and promoting existing products.

Motivating the dealer — With dealers (or any intermediary in the business-to-business, consumer, and service sector), the most powerful spoken language is still money, that is, profit. Among many available techniques, sales promotion for motivating dealers can include buying allowances, cooperative advertising, dealer listings, sales contests, specialty advertising, and exhibits at trade shows.

Introducing new products — Another meaningful way to break down the variety of approaches is to group them according to their major application area. Sales promotion techniques particularly well-suited to the introduction of new products include free samples or trial offers, coupons, and money refunds.

Promoting existing products — You may want to use one or more different tools when attempting to promote established brands, such as premiums, price packs, contests and sweepstakes, trading stamps, and demonstrations. These tools aim to attract competitors' customers and build market share, introduce new versions of established brands, and reward buyer loyalty.

Table 8.3 will aid your selection process by presenting the pros and cons of these sales promotion techniques.

TABLE 8.3
Advantages and Disadvantages of Various Sales Promotion Techniques

Technique	Advantages	Disadvantages
Free samples	Induce trial	Expensive
	Attract new customers	Lacks precision
	Speed up adoption	Cumbersome
Free trial	Overcomes market resistance	Costly to administer
Door-to-door couponing	Very selective	Time-consuming
	High redemption rate	Needs careful supervision
		Lead time needed
Direct-mail couponing	High targetability	Needed
	At-home coverage	Costly
	High redemption rate	Dependent upon list quality
Newspaper couponing	Quick and convenient	Low redemption rate
	Geographically targetable	Retailers may balk
	Low cost	Requires careful planning
Magazine/supplement couponing	Targets audience	Can become expensive
	Effective coverage	Consumers neglect to clip
	Increases readership	Slow redemption rate
Money refund	Generates new business	Results can be slow
	Reinforces brand loyalty	Modest impact
In-or-near-pack premiums	Increases product sales	Bonus to loyal buyers
	Modest distribution cost	Pilferage problem
Self-liquidating premiums	Low cost	Modest sales impact
	Boosts brand image	May be too popular
Price pack	Moves merchandise	Not selective
	Keeps up visibility	May cheapen brand image
Contests/sweepstakes	No purchase required	Expensive
	Increases brand awareness	Modest participation
Trading stamps/ promotional games	No extra expense for consumer	Consumer boredom
	Creates Store Preference	Expensive
Point-of-purchase displays	Effective stimulation	Requires dealer cooperation

DEVELOPING YOUR SALES PROMOTION PROGRAM

> **Key point:** Sales promotion should not be used as a substitute for advertising, but rather as a complementary effort.

Having selected (or advised others about) the techniques most suitable for accomplishing your objectives for one or more of your prospective audiences — sales force, dealers, and consumers — you must now work out the operational details of your campaign. This activity includes determining the budget for your program, which has to take into account three types of costs:

1. *The administrative cost:* covering creative aspects, production of the promotional material, mailing, and advertising.
2. *The incentive cost:* which includes the cost of the premium, coupon, price pack, and sales force or dealer incentive and also reflects the likely rate of redemption (which can vary greatly, depending upon the method of delivery).
3. *The marginal product cost:* such as the cost of a different package or imprint, or of overtime or supplementary purchases required by the temporary increase in output.

Of necessity, the budget for a specific campaign will be set according to the promotional needs of the product during the remainder of the year, as well as with the needs of other elements of the communications mix. Also, the specific budget is bound by the size of the overall annual appropriation for sales promotion, which is usually spelled out as a percentage of a company's communications budget and may run anywhere from 20% for business-to-business firms to 60% for consumer goods.

When deciding on the length of your campaign, you will find yourself at a critical point. If the promotion is too short, neither you nor your target audience will derive sufficient benefit from it. On the other hand, if it is too long, your brand's image is likely to be cheapened and your campaign's "act now" urgency will be diluted. A related issue is frequency — that is, how often you should promote a given product. Generally, the rules are not too often, not too short, and not too long.

The final steps in developing your sales promotion program include the following:

PRETEST YOUR SALES PROMOTION PROGRAM

Having determined the budget for running your campaign, make sure the plan ties in smoothly with the other elements of your marketing plan as well as with the plans of your purchasing and production departments. You should now proceed to *pretest your campaign* on a limited scale. This activity will help to reassure you that you have chosen the most appropriate techniques (outlined in Table 8.3) and are delivering it in the most effective manner.

IMPLEMENT AND EVALUATE YOUR CAMPAIGN

Once your campaign has been fine-tuned, put it into motion. If you are introducing a new product, you may want to demonstrate it at a national sales meeting to motivate your sales force to go out and excel.

For an established product, send your salespeople kits that spell out the objectives of your campaign and its operational details as well as the nature and size of the incentives offered to them, your dealers, and your consumers.

It will be helpful to equip your salespeople with audiovisual aids and samples of the promotional materials. They also need persuasive arguments to support their efforts, and a schedule specifying dates for sell-in, shipping, advertising, mail drop, and expiration of the deal. A well-informed, enthusiastic sales force is vital to the success of your program.

As an astute manager, closely and continually monitor the progress of your campaign. Poor execution can cause it to backfire by creating frustration and ill-will. Therefore make every effort to achieve the objectives of your campaign.

You can measure the extent of goal attainment and campaign effectiveness in various ways; the essential ones are in the form of product movement or market-share figures. But it is here that you must keep in mind the limitations of your sales promotion campaign. Namely: sales promotion is a short-term tool that can support long-term goals only in a supplementary capacity. It cannot build a consumer franchise. To the contrary, if it is used too often it can destroy the image of a brand. Thus, it should be used not as a substitute for advertising, but rather as a complementary effort.

MARKETING OVER THE INTERNET

Key point: With the projected revenue growth into the 21st century projected to skyrocket into the billions of dollars, establishing a solid presence on the Internet will pay off in sales growth and market expansion.

While e-commerce has been discussed in several chapters, here is a more precise usage of the Internet within the framework of the communications mix. Let's track the workings of a particular transaction where a computer maker is searching for the best price and delivery of a memory chip in an open-market networking system:

- A computer maker needs 10,000 memory chips to assemble its new models.
- The purchasing department logs on to the Internet network and enters information about the chip. The system shows a list of available chips with price, quantity, and other specifications.
- The computer maker puts in a price; e-mail notifies the suppliers and other buyers interested in the same part of the bid.
- The seller indicates the selling price. The buyer is alerted by e-mail and accepts or negotiates the price in an auction format.

The above example illustrates the workings of Internet bidding exchanges for a wide array of products, connecting buyers and sellers in both consumer and business-to-business transactions. For example, transactions can be as diverse as the following: *Aucnet* attracts wholesalers to a used-car auction and helps buyers judge the quality of the cars; *Narrowline* provides an electronic exchange that brings together media buyers with Web sites looking to sell available advertising space; and *Eworldauction* holds monthly online auctions of old books, maps, and medieval manuscripts.

The big area of growth in e-commerce is business-to-business, or B2B. Total sales using B2B e-commerce have exploded from almost zero a few years ago to a staggering estimate that 91% of U.S. businesses will do their purchasing on the Net by 2001, up from 31% in 1999. The bottom-line payoff is the B2B bonanza could lead to lower prices, higher productivity, and reduced labor costs.

The ability to utilize the Internet is not confined to the large organizations; small companies with limited sales resources can establish a home page as a way to communicate a product message, offer special deals, announce a new service, or launch into foreign markets.

Regardless of company size, follow these guidelines to make the Internet work for you:

1. Register a "domain name." A domain name uses the familiar format of *www.yourcompany.com*. The name is an address that establishes an Internet presence. Numerous Web site marketing services exist to help you register a domain name.
2. As illustrated in the Eddie Bauer case, utilize e-mail to develop a dialogue between buyer and seller. E-mail can distribute information, survey customers, update prices, develop a quote bidding system, and close the sale.
3. Set up "links" or electronic connections to tie your own and noncompeting Web sites. This helps build an inexpensive on-line referral network that attracts customers with common interests in both companies.
4. Offer genuine information that is useful and applicable to customers and prospects. The object is to follow the marketing-driven approach of solving customers' problems and forming long-term relationships. Such information might indicate new applications for your product, a diagnostic menu for solving the most common operating problems, or providing training materials to hone customers' skills.

Having established your Internet presence, the next step is to market your on-line service and have customers and prospects visit your site. The following guidelines will assist you in gaining visibility:

- Promote your Web site in all advertising media, including sales promotion brochures, technical manuals, letterheads, and business cards.
- Display your Web address on packages, in-store displays, and counter tops.
- Use your Web address on press releases and any articles written for or about your firm.
- Develop dedicated promotions that "sell" the recipient on the advantages of visiting your Web site. This goes together with the guidelines of offering genuine information to the visitor.
- Register with Web search engines — the means by which individuals lo-

cate sites that interest them. You can also buy a banner ad in a popular search engine in the particular section in which your company is classified. Interested users can then link or connect to your site, thereby increasing your traffic at a modest cost. The major search engines include Yahoo, Excite, Infoseek, WebCrawler, Alta Vista, Magellan, Lycos, and OpenText.

This exciting promotion medium is still in its infancy. And with the projected revenue growth into the 21st century projected to skyrocket into the billions of dollars, establishing a solid presence on the Internet will pay off in sales growth and market expansion. The bottom line: make the Internet an integral component of your communications plan.

BEST PRACTICES

Observe the following points to maximize the impact of your communications. Speed is the essence of promotional success. There are few cases, if any, of a profitable campaign that was prolonged. A campaign may lack ingenuity, but it has a chance for success if delivered with extraordinary speed. Effective use of promotion can force competitors to react to your moves on *your* terms. For example, the timing of your promotion can weaken competitors by making them use additional resources after they have completed a major sales promotion effort.

To identify communications strategies and initiate action:

1. List those forms of advertising and sales promotion that represent the best opportunities to build your brand and secure a positive company and product image. Then integrate them into a total communications plan.
2. Indicate what action is to take place and who is assigned the task of implementing specific parts of the strategy.
3. Relate feedback to the objective(s) desired and the strategies selected.
4. List immediate plans and future courses of action.

9 The Strategic Marketing Plan: How to Develop Business-Building Strategies and Action Plans

INTRODUCTION

This is the point where you put it all together into a plan: the foundation concepts and practices related to marketing management, customer relationship management, and market intelligence. Here is where you combine the overall attributes associated with operating a market-driven organization, discussed in the preceding chapters, into one organized document that drives your business decisions. Above all, here is the document that highlights your strategies and tactics.

The document permits an organized and rational look as you:

- Appraise customer needs.
- Decide on new product development projects.
- Analyze the business environment in which you operate.
- Identify your organization's core competencies.
- Evaluate current and potential market segments.
- Assess the impact of competition on your company's market position.

How important is it to add a planning structure to those diverse issues? What are the tangible outcomes of the labor-intensive planning process? In part, the answers are given in PricewaterhouseCoopers' 1998 Trendsetter Barometer Survey, which points out that two thirds of rapid-growth firms have written business plans. Further, the survey reveals that over a two-year period, firms with written plans grow faster, achieve a higher proportion of revenues from new products and services, and enable CEOs to manage more critical business functions than those firms whose plans are unwritten. Additionally, growth firms with a written business plan have increased their revenues 69% faster over a 5-year period than those without a written plan.

The planning format discussed here is the *Strategic Marketing Plan (SMP)*. It evolved into its present format in the 1990s by combining the best elements of the long-term strategic plan with the traditional one-year marketing plan that has served marketing managers for over four decades.

There are several reasons for joining the two previously separate planning formats into an integrated SMP:

1. While strategic planning permitted managers to create a long-term vision of how the organization could grow, for the most part the process lacked implementation. A survey conducted by Deloitte Consulting, the large accounting and management consulting firm, indicated that while 97% of the Fortune 500 companies wrote strategic plans, only 15% of that group ever implemented anything that came out of the plan.
2. Traditionally, marketing planning incorporated the various activities associated with the marketing function into a short-term, action-oriented plan. No formalized planning process existed to link the longer-term strategic plan that needed an implementation phase with the shorter-term marketing plan that required a strategic-vision phase.
3. Typically, each plan developed independently within the organization. No procedure unified planning efforts consistent with the marketing definition of "a total system of interacting activities designed to plan, price, promote, and distribute want-satisfying products and services to organizational and household users in a competitive environment at a profit."
4. The turbulent economic and market upheavals of the 1980s created a driving need to totally revamp the organization and create a crystal-clear vision, supported by immediate action plans. For instance, the staggering market problems included slow growth, changing demographics, changing life styles, fragmented markets, deregulation of major industries, intense global competition, rapid technological change, and shortened product life cycles.

Under those mind-boggling conditions, the SMP evolved to create a linkage of the strategic plan with the marketing plan. It joined the internal functions of the organization with the external and volatile changes of a competitive global environment.

To fully internalize these ideas, review the following case. Act as if you are participating in a strategy session where there is a need to identify long-term opportunities, yet there is also the practical urgency to manage day-to-day operations.

CASE EXAMPLE: EMERSON ELECTRIC

Emerson Electric makes basic products essential to a variety of industries, such as refrigerator compressors, pressure gauges, and garbage disposals. What distinguishes this well-run company from the herd is its dazzling record of 36 uninterrupted years of increased earnings, without any significant price increases since the mid-1980s. During the highly competitive 1980s, Emerson staunchly endured the challenges of low-cost Brazilian, Korean, and Japanese competitors.

Several explicit factors contributed to Emerson's superlative success:

1. Management recognized early on that low-cost, aggressive competitors would remain a permanent part of the global scene and would intensify into the next decade.
2. Management exerted the resolute discipline to secure cost-efficient operations at every level of the organization.
3. Management demonstrated its flexibility to focus on growth markets and exit those segments with little chance of turning a profit, such as defense and construction, and various niche businesses such as gardening tools.
4. It realized that cost cutting was only one part of the success equation to sustain growth; the other, that strategic marketing planning should function as an ongoing operating system for managing both long-term objectives and day-to-day operations.

A single example sums up Emerson's conspicuous accomplishments: 10 years ago a Japanese plant could offer temperature sensors for washing machines for 20% below Emerson's prices. Today, Emerson's costs are below the Japanese prices, and the company has regained market share. Rigorous planning, then, is at the heart of Emerson's system for managing growth.

Thus, you can see how the diverse business (and nonmarketing) activities intermingle to identify long-term opportunities while staying alert to managing day-to-day operations.

CRITICAL ISSUES IMPACTING THE STRATEGIC MARKETING PLAN

> **Key point:** Three noteworthy issues influence the outcome of a Strategic Marketing Plan: market-related problems, a company's orientation, and amount of managerial participation.

There are particular issues that should rouse you to intensify efforts to bring planning to the top of your operating agenda: market- and competitor-related problems, your company's orientation, and the extent of managerial participation.

MARKET-RELATED PROBLEMS

Here is where to get actively involved with identifying which issues affect your business, both temporarily or long-lasting. Your assessment of even seemingly insignificant market-related problems can influence the outcome of your company's plan. The problem categories include the following.

Sales Decline

A sales decline may be temporary due to local market conditions, or due to seasonal factors that could be remedied by short-term sales promotion incentives such as coupons or cash rebates. However, if a sales decline is inconsistent with industry trends and the sales performance of competitors, then there is a possibility of more serious problems. For instance, these problems could be as far-reaching as a faulty distribution network, deteriorating management/labor relations, poor-quality products, or even incompetent management. The possibilities are extensive and can influence the final outcome of your plan.

Slow Growth

Slow growth typically results from one of the following:

- Mature *products* identified by a flattening in sales growth due to the introduction of similar, undifferentiated products by competitors; or the use of a lower price as the dominant factor in influencing a sale. For example, the personal computer industry reached maturity in the 1990s, characterized by clones attacking the market at bargain-basement prices along with a leveling of consumer demand.
- Mature *markets* identified by total industry sales leveling off. The total computer industry during the mid-1990s — not just individual product categories — reported that sales increases were at single-digit levels compared with historical sales patterns measured in double digits.

Either one of these conditions should drive long-term objectives and strategies as well as short-term objectives and tactics. For example, the planning implications for a mature product should focus your attention on objectives and strategies to differentiate products based on such areas as quality, reliability, durability, or performance. The plan might even include such value-added services as post-sales technical support and just-in-time delivery to deal with market and competitive conditions.

On the other hand, for a mature industry the planning objectives and strategies would focus on market segmentation, with an emphasis on identifying emerging, neglected, and poorly served niches. Based on corporate objectives and the culture of the organization, the planning approach could even permit taking aggressive action to the point of assuming a combative attitude toward competitors. Such an attitude would result in pushing for sales or market share through competitive displacement.

Changing Buying Behavior

This category concerns management's responsiveness (or unresponsiveness) to a change in customer buying behavior. To what extent is management willing to acknowledge changing consumer buying patterns vs. continuing practices of the past regardless of changing market conditions? The prime example is the influence of e-commerce and all the aspects of using the Internet in influencing buyer behavior. Numerous examples are cited in previous chapters.

Increasing Competition

A market-related problem of immense impact on the SMP is competition. For example, consider these factors:

- More and more, hawkish companies may be competing with your firm for the purpose of gaining a foothold (measured by increasing sales and gains in market share) while your firm languishes with flat or declining performance. What could be wrong?
- What could you have neglected in product quality, customer service, or distributor relationships that might have created opportunities for competitors to enter against you?
- While attention is focused on traditional competitors, what attention do you give to the surprise intrusion of emerging competitors? Which firms are entering against you through acquisition, joint venture, licensing, or other forms of strategic alliances?
- What are your management's attitudes toward competition? Are they passive in their sensitivities to the urgency of potentially aggressive moves by competitors? Do they think the problem will dissolve or the competitors will not have an adverse effect on your market position because of customer loyalty? Or, conversely, are they active in tracking competitors' penetration of the market, assessing their strengths and weaknesses, and evaluating their future strategies? Also, what defensive and offensive strategies are planned to sustain your market position and grow in alternative markets?
- Overall, is there a defeatist attitude of relinquishing control of market segments against the threat of competitor attack? Or is there a militant feeling of assuming an aggressive stance of protecting a market position?

COMPANY ORIENTATION

> **Key point:** Marketing research provides the documentation to help management put the pieces together and clarify its position on short-term gains as well as long-term growth.

Another critical issue to consider before you begin creating the SMP is your company's orientation. The issues are fairly similar to the market-related problems. But the outcome of your assessment will be expressed in such areas as the aggressiveness or conservativeness of your plan; the level of risk your management will assume; and the caliber of innovative strategies related to market selection, product modification, promotion, distribution, and pricing. Further, your company's orientation should encompass attitudes toward both competitors and customers. Consider the following factors while assessing your company's orientation.

Focus on Products vs. Customers

"Give them any color they want, as long as it's black," declared Henry Ford. This now-famous comment reflects a company orientation that brought the Ford Motor Co. to the brink of bankruptcy in the 1930s. Compare that orientation to the declaration of a senior IBM executive decades later who said, "This is the year of the customer."

Each comment reflects an attitude that permeated throughout their respective organizations, and each influenced the entire business strategy, including the range of product offerings. Tangible measurements of the attitudes are reflected in sales volume, share of market, pricing, profitability, level of customer satisfaction, and degree of distributor loyalty.

Marketing Research: Insignificant vs. Extensive

Company orientation is exhibited by the thoroughness of marketing research used in making key decisions. Evidence of thoroughness is demonstrated by the amount of expenditures in dollars and number of people it takes to:

- Evaluate the long-term sales potential of market segments.
- Track changing consumer needs.
- Assess competitors' activities.
- Determine what would add value to existing products.
- Identify new products and technologies.
- Evaluate the competitive advantage of offering additional services.
- Participate in the vast potential of e-business and e-commerce.

A small company may not be able to afford much formal research, but it should take advantage of its size to maintain close relationships with customers, markets, industry movements, and technology advances and gather such insightful information informally. The implications for the SMP are that marketing research provides the documentation that helps management put the pieces together and clarify its position on short-term gains and long-term growth.

Product and Service Development: Self-Guided vs. Guided by Marketing

The Henry Ford statement previously cited reflects the self-guided engineering or production orientation toward product development. The IBM attitude, on the other hand, expresses a more desirable market-driven orientation. What is the focus of your organization? The this-is-what-we-make, this-is-what-we-sell mentality can impact negatively on a SMP. First, it defies the full intent of the strategic marketing definition presented earlier. Second, it implies a lack of organizational sensitivity toward markets and customers. (More on this point under the following topic, Managerial Participation.)

Primary Interest in Production Economies vs. Providing Need Satisfaction

If the criterion for deciding on new products is anchored primarily to the production department's self-interests of maintaining production economies, then a myopic, inside-out orientation dominates the decision-making process. This orientation reduces the strategic alternatives and has a profound effect on the scope and quality of the SMP.

In contrast, the outside-in approach of providing need satisfactions produces the more desirable orientation by permitting the industry, customer, and environmental and competitive factors to dominate the planning process. Therefore, it is important to determine where the organizational power is located within your organization.

MANAGERIAL PARTICIPATION

The third critical issue impacting the SMP consists of the amount and type of senior managerial participation. A delicate balance must be struck between too much or too little participation. Managerial participation can be positive or negative, based on the amount of authority given to mid-level managers and the degree of risk they are permitted to take.

All these factors impact on your approach to planning. Forming a cross-functional team creates an effective balance of participation. (See the duties and responsibilities of a cross-functional team in Chapter 1.)

Further, throughout the planning process, a manager cannot underestimate the importance of the culture of the organization. The culture includes the basic value systems as identified by the company's orientation, employees' backgrounds, decision-making authority at various organizational levels, the amount of risk tolerated, and the level of resources committed.

OUTCOMES OF THE STRATEGIC MARKETING PLAN

A critical issue related to planning is to fully internalize that the central outcome of a SMP is to develop strategies. Broadly defined for the purposes of the plan, strategies are actions to achieve objectives.

To reinforce this noteworthy claim about planning, Dwight D. Eisenhower, the much-heralded U.S. general and former U.S. president stated, "The plan is nothing; planning is everything." Meaning that strategizing, thinking, conceptualizing, and above all, implementing, represent the underpinnings of planning and thereby become the key outcomes of the SMP.

Therefore, as you initiate (or monitor) the development of a SMP keep in mind that strategies form the pivotal planning outcomes. In doing so, use the following guidelines to assess the value of your SMP:

- *Are there strategies for enlarging current markets?* Assuming that you plan to remain in your present markets, can you pinpoint strategies to enlarge and penetrate the markets by attracting new users, increasing sales to current users, or increasing customers' frequency of product usage (as measured by such criteria as sales, profits, unit volume, and share of market).
- *Are there strategies for developing new markets?* New markets are those that are emerging for your products and services because of:
  - Changing buyer demands.
  - Neglected segments available through new channels or distribution.
  - New technologies creating fresh opportunities in such areas as e-commerce and customer relationship management.
  - Poorly served markets surfacing due to new organizational capabilities that can provide superior service.

- *Are there clearly defined positioning strategies for your product or service?* Positioning is defined in two ways. First, how your company or product is perceived by your prospects and customers; for example, what image does your product project in terms of quality, delivery, application, or reliability? Second, how your product is positioned against competitors; is it positioned against a dominant competitor through differentiation using superior quality, just-in-time delivery, or improved post-sales service? Or, if you are the market leader, have you developed a positioning strategy strong enough to deter a competitor by canceling out any product advantage and thereby neutralizing the competitor's innovation? (See additional information on positioning in Chapter 5.)
- *Are there strategies to protect your existing sales volume or share of market?* This guideline suggests that while looking for new markets and pursuing other enticing opportunities, it is important not to neglect existing customers.
- *Are there strategies to launch new products?* Assuming that new products, line extensions, or modifications of existing products are included in your plan, have you identified appropriate strategies to develop and launch or relaunch those products?

DEVELOPING YOUR STRATEGIC MARKETING PLAN (SMP)

> **Key point:** Following the SMP process will add an organized and structured approach to your thinking that will result in numerous opportunities expressed through markets, products, and services.

A SMP is best developed by following a defined process, which is diagrammed in Figure 9.1. As you examine the flowchart, notice that the top row of boxes represents the strategic portion of the plan, covering a period of three to five years. The next row of boxes represents the tactical one-year marketing plan. It is the merging of the strategic plan and the marketing plan into one unified plan that makes it the multidirectional SMP.

Also, you will find that following the SMP process will add an organized, structured approach to your thinking, but not in a confining way. Rather, your thinking will take on far-reaching strategy vision that will elevate the creative process. Ultimately that vision will translate into dynamic opportunities expressed through markets, products, and services.

FIGURE 9.1 Strategic marketing plan.

STRATEGIC DIRECTION

Let's begin with the first box in Figure 9.1, Section I, *Strategic Direction*. Developing a strategic direction (also known as a mission statement) provides a long-term vision for a company, business unit, or product line. To construct a vision, or oversee its development, use the following guideline questions:

1. *What are your distinctive areas of expertise?* This question refers to your organization's (or business unit's) competencies. Answer the question by evaluating the relative strengths of your product or service, relationships with distributors and/or end-use customers, production capabilities, size of your sales force, financial strength, R&D expenditures, and quality of customer service. Measures of competitive strength would consist of customer satisfaction, profitability, and market share.

2. *What business should you be in over the next three to five years?* Are you in the railroad business or transportation business? Harvard Professor Theodore Levitt, in his classic article "Marketing Myopia," used a well-known analogy. Levitt cited how the railroads declined in use as technology advanced because managers defined their product too narrowly. He explained that to continue growing managers must determine customers' needs and wants and not simply rely on the longevity of their existing products. For instance, consider the following contrasting examples of

how businesses are categorized as myopic vs. expansive: oil vs. energy, baby foods vs. child care, computer vs. information processing, electrical wire vs. energy transfer, or valves vs. fluid control. You can strike a comfortable balance by defining the scope of your business on two dimensions. First, examine the culture, skills, and resources of your organization; second, identify customers needs, functions, and technologies. A usable strategic direction will emerge through the question and answer process suggested in this section.

3. *Which customers are to be served?* Customers exist at various levels in the distribution channel and in different segments of the market. At the end of the channel are the end-use consumers. The customers in-between serve as intermediaries with several functions. Examining the existing and future needs at each level of distribution helps project the types of customers you want to target for the in three- to five-year period covered by your SMP.

4. *What customer functions are to be satisfied?* As competitive intensity increases worldwide, each intermediary customer from distributor to dealer is increasingly pressured to maintain a competitive advantage. This guideline question asks you to determine what functions each level of customer must perform. In effect, you are looking beyond your immediate customer and reaching out further into the distribution channel to identify those functions that would solve your customers' *customers'* problems.

5. *What technologies are to be used to satisfy future customer or market needs?* Within the framework of the previous question and the practices of your industry, examine the impact of satisfying your customers' needs through your current technology, or doing so with such emerging technologies as expert diagnostic systems and the integration of the Internet into e-business and e-commerce.

6. *What changes are taking place in customer, competitor, industry, and environmental spheres?* This form of external analysis permits you to examine the critical issues related to customer behavior, competitive strategies, industry structure, and environmental factors. The critical issues can range from local economic conditions to broad governmental regulations.

The quality of answers you give to these six questions result in a long-term situation analysis that permits you to develop a credible strategic direction. Where time and resources permit, you can answer the questions comprehensively by conducting a total strength/weakness analysis that serves as a marketing audit (see Table 9.3).

Example of an SMP

To illustrate how a strategic direction is written, let's look at an actual statement developed for an auto parts manufacture:

Provide high-quality products and services to meet the existing and evolving needs of original equipment manufacturers and after-market customers by offering a full-line of mechanical and electronic vehicular parts. Our leadership position will be maintained through internal research and development and by acquisitions to ensure the total satisfaction of customers at all usage levels.

Guided by such a statement, managers could expand their vision and direct the company's product line into innovative product systems and technologies, and ultimately expand their hold on existing markets throughout the distribution chain. Note, too, that products are not defined as auto parts (myopic) but to the broader interpretation of *vehicular*, which magnifies the product and market possibilities.

OBJECTIVES AND GOALS

> **Key point:** The combination of both quantitative and nonquantitative objectives allows for the most accurate and effective form of planning.

In Figure 9.1, Section II, objectives and goals are stated in both quantitative and nonquantitative terms.

Quantitative objectives — Indicate in precise statements, performance expectations such as sales growth ($/units), market share, return on investment, profit, and any other quantitative objectives required by your management.

Nonquantitative objectives — These objectives could range from organizational structure, to distribution networks, and to product development. For example, you can forge objectives from any of the following:

- Upgrading distribution channels
- Expanding secondary distribution into new market segments
- Solidifying leadership or penetrating selected markets
- Launching new products
- Establishing or improving market intelligence systems
- Activating training programs
- Launching new and repositioning old products
- Upgrading field services
- Improving marketing mix management

Example of Objectives and Goals Statement

Continuing with the actual example of a U.S. auto parts manufacturer, the following data illustrate specific ways to state quantitative and nonquantitative objectives and goals. (Numbers are altered for purposes of confidentiality.)

Quantitative objectives and goals

- Attain net sales of $37.0 million by the year 200x within the following categories:

Categories	Net Sales ($ mil)	Mix (%)
Distributor	13.0	35.1
Corporate brand (direct)	6.5	17.6
Generic	7.0	18.9
National accounts	5.5	14.8
Military	3.0	8.1
Export sales	2.0	5.5
Total	37.0	100.0

- Launch 200 new products on a quarterly basis over the next three years, including electrical, front end, brake, air conditioning, and power train.
- Maintain 60 or more dedicated distributors strategically located worldwide to achieve sales objectives.
- Improve customer satisfaction to 94.5%, as measured by the Customer Service Index base period of 1997-98.

Quantitative objectives and goals

- Utilize as a marketing mix element an effective supply and distribution system for the potential launch of existing products into new market segments and into new markets defined as "vehicular."
- Develop a prototype of an Internet catalog/inventory/information/ordering system for use with distributors by the fourth quarter of 2003.

While some managers resist the use of nonquantitative objectives, there are occasions where long-term market and internal obstacles need to be overcome. In those cases numbers cannot always be attached to objectives. Therefore, it is appropriate to use dates and reporting periods to show progress. In combination, the use of quantitative and nonquantitative objectives allow for the most accurate and comprehensive planning approach.

GROWTH STRATEGIES

> **Key point:** A *strategy* is a longer-term action to achieve a long-term objective. A *tactic* is a shorter-term action to achieve a short-term objective.

Objectives and goals indicate *what* you want to accomplish. Growth strategies deal with *how*, or what actions you are going to take, to achieve those objectives. A practical guideline is this: for each objective there must be a corresponding strategy. If you cannot come up with a strategy for a particular objective, perhaps the so-called objective is not one at all; rather, it is a strategy for some other objective. Growth Strategies (Section III in Figure 9.1) are divided into two categories: internal and external. For example:

Internal strategies — These strategies relate to marketing, manufacturing,

R&D, distribution, and pricing. They also cover existing and new products, market research, packaging, customer services, credit, finance, sales activities, and organizational changes.

External strategies — These refer to such possibilities as forming joint ventures, soliciting licensing agreements, identifying new distribution networks, reaching emerging market segments, and creating fresh opportunities for diversification — that is, if diversification fits the company's strategic direction. As a general planning guideline, however, try to develop multiple strategies for each objective. In cases where you have broader, longer-term objectives, generalized strategy statements may be of use, for example: "form a committee to investigate a market segment," or "hire an outside consultant to conduct a feasibility study about a new product technology."

Example of Growth Strategies

Continuing with the auto parts manufacturer case:

Internal Strategies

- Install a computerized ordering program that links the top 80 distributors' inventories with independent repair shops.
- Complete the upgrade of the Memphis depot and launch just-in-time delivery service to distribute within 325 miles of the facility.
- Execute a new warranty administration program that is equitable to the company, distributors, and end-user customers, with a timing of 15 days for claims disposition, compared with the current 21 days.
- Implement a quality improvement initiative consisting of continuing-education programs. Also establish indices of performance levels in accordance with new corporate objectives.

External Strategies

- Establish quality teams to review causes of errors and recommend corrective action.
- Form joint venture with (name of company) to increase total market share in selected fuel and cooling system components, resulting in sales of $17 million and 22% market share.
- Establish an image for high-performance parts in the after-market by establishing 125 new performance center dealers in key segments of the U.S., Canada, U.K., and Germany.
- Establish Internet and teleconferencing broadcasting sessions with field sales to maintain a competitive advantage.

It is also appropriate here to distinguish between a strategy and a tactic. A strategy is a longer-term action to achieve a long-term objective. A strategy usually affects the functional areas of the organization, such as manufacturing, product development, and finance. It concerns the broader aspects of new markets and distribution systems.

On the other hand, a tactic is a shorter-term action to achieve a short-term objective. It is a subset of a strategy and is usually concerned with local issues of more limited impact, such as a single product being launched in a target market segment with specific promotional activities. In practice, a single long-term objective could be accomplished through 4 or 5 strategies, along with 6 to 10 related tactics.

BUSINESS PORTFOLIO

> **Key point:** Your strategic direction has tangible meaning only if it translates into a viable business portfolio plan consisting of markets and products.

A business portfolio (Section IV of Figure 9.1) contains a listing of all existing markets and products, and all potential new markets and products that are feasible within the next three to five years, and matches your company's strategic direction.

It is based on the strategic direction, objectives and goals, and growth strategies. In particular, the broader the scope of the strategic direction, the broader the range of market and product possibilities; the narrower the scope, the more limited the portfolio of markets and products.

Figure 9.2 illustrates a format for a workable business portfolio where you can categorize markets and products that reflect your strategic direction.

	Existing Products	*New Products*
Existing Markets	1. Market Penetration	3. Product Development
New Markets	2. Market Development	4. Diversification

FIGURE 9.2 Business portfolio plan guidelines.

As you view the diagram, note the following structure of the portfolio.

Existing Products/Existing Markets (Market Penetration) — Prepare a catalog listing of the products you already offer along with the market segments you currently serve. This listing, coupled with appropriate analysis of sales, profits, and market share, will help determine if your level of penetration is adequate or if possibilities exist for further growth. For example, changing market and customer behavioral patterns may create new opportunities for increasing market penetration by improving product quality, instituting just-in-time delivery, increasing technical support, improving customer service, or installing computerized inventory control systems. After identifying new opportunities, you may find it worthwhile to revisit Figure 9.1, Section III, Growth Strategies, and list actions you would take to implement the opportunity.

New Products/Existing Markets (Product Development) — The portfolio format permits you to expand your thinking, as long as it stays within the boundaries of the strategic direction created for your business or product line. Your aim is to look for new products that you can sell to current customer segments. With new products defined as those that are perceived by the customer as new, your new product can include adding features to existing products, or providing value-added services, or designing new packaging, as well as pioneering new-to-the-world products. That is, as long as the "new" perception exists.

However, remember the guideline: the broader the dimension of your strategic direction, the broader the possibilities for the content of your portfolio. If the definition of your business is narrow you may be limited in what you can list in this part of your portfolio. You still have the opportunity at this point to go back to the strategic direction and recast it to give you more possibilities for expansion. Do so, if that is consistent with the overall mission of your organization and the aims of senior management.

Existing Products/New Markets (Market Development) — Another growth direction is to take your current products into new markets. Explore possibilities for market development by identifying emerging, neglected, or poorly served segments in which existing products can be utilized.

New Products/New Markets (Diversification) — This portion of the business portfolio is truly visionary, since it involves developing new products to meet the needs of those markets new to the business. Interpret your strategic direction in its broadest context. Don't seek diversification for its own sake. Rather, the purpose is to develop an organized framework for meaningful expansion. New technologies, global markets, and new strategic alliances dictate this section's development. Looking at these factors will prime your mind to think about participating in new markets, rather than riding existing businesses into maturity and even decline.

To use the grid, list products and markets in each of the quadrants. The listing will then serve as a guideline for product and market growth over 3 to 5 years.

DEVELOPING YOUR TACTICAL MARKETING PLAN

> **Key point:** Avoid the temptation of walking into the middle of the SMP by beginning with the tactical 1-year marketing plan. There are no shortcuts. Doing so escapes the realities of the long-term opportunities in a competitive environment.

Bear in mind that the tactical marketing plan, shown as the second row of boxes in Figure 9.1, is not a stand-alone plan. It is but a portion of the total SMP made up of the top row of boxes and the lower row of boxes. For each major market or product line identified in the Section IV Business Portfolio, you must prepare a tactical marketing plan.

Where commonalities exist among products and markets, a single marketing plan can be used with the appropriate changes in such areas as the communications mix. However, substantial differences in the character of the markets would require separate plans.

As a precautionary measure, avoid the temptation indulged in by some managers who attempt to walk into the middle of the SMP by beginning with the tactical 1-year marketing plan. There are no shortcuts. Such an approach avoids the realities of the volatile competitive environment.

There are five sections that make up the tactical marketing plan: situation analysis, market opportunities, marketing objectives, strategies and action plans, and financial controls and budgets.

SITUATION ANALYSIS

> **Key point:** The situation analysis serves as foundation material for developing opportunities, objectives, and strategies/tactics.

The tactical marketing plan begins with a situation analysis for a specific product or market. Whereas the strategic plan looks *forward* three to five years, the situation analysis requires that you look *back* three to five years to obtain an historical perspective of your business.

This information is important because it serves as foundation material for developing the opportunities, objectives, and strategies/tactics that follow. This information also highlights any gaps in knowledge that exist about markets and customers and suggests types of marketing research needed to make more precise decisions.

Overall, as a nonmarketing manager, the analysis should give more valuable insights into your markets, and help assess the capabilities of your firm to maintain a viable position. The situation analysis is divided into three parts.

Marketing mix — Here you objectively describe your product by the following characteristics:

- Product's sales history, profitability, share of market; position in the industry related to market leadership, reputation, and stage in the product life cycle.
- History of pricing policies by market segment and distribution channel.
- Current distribution channels, effectiveness of market coverage, and key activities performed at each point of the distribution chain.
- Advertising and sales promotion directed at each segment of the market or distribution channel, including e-commerce, based on such elements as advertising dollar expenditures, creative strategy, media used, trade promotions, and consumer promotions.

Market background — The focus here is on the demographic and behavioral factors that characterize market size and customer preferences (both trade and consumer). Carefully assess the characteristics of your market by the following criteria:

- Customer profiles: define your present and potential end-use customers that you (or your intermediaries) serve. Also look further down the distribution channel and profile your end-use consumers by demographic and psychographic (life style) characteristics.

- Frequency and magnitude of product's use: define customer purchases by frequency, volume, and seasonality of purchase.
- Geographic aspects of product use: determine the geographic boundaries of customer purchases (both trade and consumer). Segment buyers by specific regional area or by other factors relevant to your industry.
- Decision makers: define who makes the buying decisions and when and where they are made. Identify the various individuals or departments that may influence the decision.
- Customer motivations: pinpoint the key motivations that indicate why customers buy your product. Why do they select one manufacturer (or service provider) over another?
- Customer awareness: define the level of consumer awareness of your products. To what extent do they recognize a need for your type of product; identify your product or company as a possible supplier and associate your product or company with desirable features?
- Segment trends: describe the trends in the size and character of the various segments or niches.

Competitor analysis — Examine your competitors' strengths and weaknesses. Specifically, look at the following criteria:

- Competitors' pricing strategies: identify competitive pricing strategies, price lines, and discounts.
- Product features and benefits: compare the specific features and benefits of your products with those of competitive products. Look, too, at product quality, design factors, and performance.
- Advertising effectiveness: identify competitive spending levels and their productiveness.
- Distribution methods: compare competitors' distribution strengths and weaknesses. Address differences in market penetration, market coverage, delivery time, and physical movement of the product by regions or sales territories.
- Packaging: compare package performance, innovation, and preference. Also review size, share, function, convenience of handling, ease of storage and shipping.
- Trade and consumer attitudes: review both trade and consumer attitudes toward product quality, customer and technical service, company image, and company performance.
- Competitive share of market: identify where each competitor is making a major commitment and where it may be relinquishing control by product and segment.
- Sales force performance and market coverage: review competence as it relates to sales, service, frequency of contact, and problem-solving capabilities by competitor and by market segment.

MARKET OPPORTUNITIES

> **Key point:** Consider opportunities as gaps in a product line, market, segment, or service that can be filled to satisfy customer needs and wants.

In Figure 9.1, Section VI, examine business strengths, weaknesses, and options. You'll find that enticing opportunities will begin to emerge from this examination as you consider the variety of alternatives open. To obtain the best results, however, avoid restrictive thinking. Rather, take the time to brainstorm with other members of a cross-functional team.

Look at all possibilities for expanding existing markets, as well as laying the groundwork for entering new markets. Also, think about opportunities related to your competition. Offensively, which of your competitors can be displaced from which market segments; defensively, which competitors can be denied entry into your market.

As you go through this section, once again revisit your strategic portion of the SMP (top row of boxes in Figure 9.1). While that portion represents a 3- to 5-year period, work must now begin to activate the strategic direction, objectives, growth strategies, and in particular the products and markets identified in the business portfolio plan. Do so by using the following screening process to identify your major opportunities and challenges. Once you identify and prioritize the opportunities, convert them into action-oriented objectives and strategies — the topics of the next two sections of the SMP.

Present Markets

Identify the best opportunities for expanding present markets by:

- Cultivating new businesses and new users.
- Displacing competition.
- Increasing product usage or programs by present customers.
- Redefining market segments.
- Identifying new uses or applications of the product.
- Repositioning the product to create a more favorable perception by consumers and to develop a viable competitive advantage over rival products.
- Expanding into new or unserved market niches.

Customers

Organize the best opportunities for expanding your customer base by:

- Improving or expanding distribution channels.
- Examining pricing discounts, rebates, and other purchase allowances.
- Reviewing advertising, sales promotion, Internet, publicity, and the sale force activities.
- Enhancing customer service, including technical service.

- Identifying changing trade buying practices where the buying power is focused or has shifted from manufacturer to distributor or to the end user.
- Locating attractive niches left vacant by competition.

Growth Markets

Name the major product growth markets in key geographic areas and specify which markets represent the greatest long-term potential.

Product and Service Development and Innovation

Describe the immediate and long-range opportunities for product development and innovation by:

- Adding new products to the line.
- Diversifying into new or related products or product lines.
- Modifying and altering products.
- Improving packaging.
- Establishing new value-added services.

Targets of Opportunity

List any areas outside your current market segment or product line not included in the above categories that you would like to explore. Attempt to be innovative and entrepreneurial in your thinking. Due to their innovative and risky characteristics, they should be set apart from the other opportunities and treated for special attention and funding by senior management.

MARKETING OBJECTIVES

> **Key point:** The marketing mix helps you identify sources of competitive problems and, in turn, suggests possible objectives.

Thus far, you have accounted for pertinent facts in the Situation Analysis section (Figure 9.1, Section V) and examined their possible outcomes to your product line in the Marketing Opportunities section (SectionVI). Now, you want to nail down specific objectives that you want to achieve during the current planning period — generally defined as a 12-month period.

At this point, you will find it useful once again to review Sections V and VI. Also, it is beneficial to scan the strategic portion of the plan to be sure that actions relate to your long-range strategic direction, objectives, and strategies are incorporated into your tactical plan.

Section VII in Figure 9.1 consists of three parts:

- *Assumptions*, which are realistic projections about future conditions and trends as you and others in your organization view the environment. They include economic, technology, political/legislative, and competitive assumptions that could positively or negatively affect your business and industry.

- Primary objectives, which relate to the quantitative areas of your responsibility, such as projected sales, profits, market share, return on investment, and other data required by your management. Also included here are any high-impact opportunities identified in the opportunities section of the tactical marketing plan.
- *Functional objectives*, which cover the operational parts of the business. These objectives cover an extensive list of possibilities, as shown in Table 9.1.

TABLE 9.1
Categories of Functional Objectives

Functional Objectives	Definition
Product quality	Perceptions held by your customers or accepted as an industry standard.
Product development	Carried on through internal R&D or acquisition of new technology through purchase or joint venture.
Product modification	Reformulating or redesigning a product to create a major or minor product change.
Product differentiation	Using function, performance, quality, value-added services, or any other meaningful changes related to enhancing a competitive position.
Diversification	Applying the technology or the actual product to new applications, or diversifying into new geographic areas.
Deletion	Removing a product from the line due to unsatisfactory performance. It would remain in the line only if it serves some strategic purpose, such as presenting your company to the market as a full-line supplier.
Segmentation	Creating line extensions (adding product varieties) to reach new market niches or to defend against an incoming competitor to an existing market segment.
Pricing	Determining list prices, volume discounts, and promotional rebates.
Promotion	Coordinating Internet, field sales, sales promotion, advertising, and publicity into a total marketing effort.
Supply chain management	Solidifying relationships from contract manufacturer through distributors to end users.
	Adding new services from product design to inventory management, delivery, and after-sales services.
Packaging	Using functional design and/or decorative considerations for brand identification.
Service	Offering the broad range of services, from providing customers access to key executives in your firm to providing on-site technical assistance.
Other	Testing entrepreneurial ideas suggested in Targets of Opportunities in Section VI (Figure 9.1).

You also have free reign to pinpoint other meaningful objectives that legitimately will contribute to the success of your SMP. These relate to manufacturing, market research, credit, technical sales activities, and human resource development.

STRATEGIES AND ACTION PLANS

> **Key point:** Objectives are no more than good intentions until you develop the strategies and tactics that will convert them into action.

On the basis of defining your marketing objectives, you can now develop the strategies and action plans that translate those objectives into action. Unless you support your objectives with firm action plans, they are useless. They are no more than good intentions until you develop the strategies and tactics that will make them happen.

Thus, for each and every objective, develop a relevant strategy and tactical actions to achieve the desired end result. Further, each strategy should include details about what is going to happen, when it is going to happen, and who is assigned responsibility for carrying out the actions.

FINANCIAL CONTROLS AND BUDGETS

> **Key point:** To monitor the SMP, develop procedures for comparing actual and planned figures, so that corrective measures can be taken where needed.

This step in the SMP involves the financial controls, budgets, and variance reports that translate into numbers those actions that you have stated in the previous planning steps. Most often, the types of controls and reports usually come from the financial department.

Specifically, however, for tracking marketing and sales performance, you can use these common measurements to monitor progress toward achieving your objectives:

- *Current to past-sales comparisons.* To measure the performance of sales reps and sales territories, you can generate periodic reports on the quantities of products sold by product line, the profitability of territories, and any quantitative data specific to measuring the overall marketing and selling effort.
- Customer satisfaction evaluation. This measure is vitally important when long-term relationship marketing is the strategy of choice. Although a sales representative's likability remains a factor, a more meaningful evaluation should assess outcomes and interests that are important to the customer. These may include being attentive to problems, solving complaints, overcoming technical obstacles, and meeting production and delivery schedules.
- *Qualitative evaluation of sales reps.* Use this measure to determine the sales representative's knowledge of your products, customers, competitors, and territory. And look at the state of the economy and any other issues that would impact the successful outcome of a sale. Also consider evaluating individual characteristics such as dress, speech, and personality as they relate to the image you are trying to expose to the marketplace.

With financial controls and budgets as an integral part of your SMP, the following discussion on sales forecasting should add greater accuracy to your plan.

SALES FORECASTING

> **Key point:** Sales forecasting is an organized effort to predict the future level of sales, given specific marketing strategies and assumptions about market conditions.

Forecasting provides a set of sales potentials based on assessing your market opportunities, objectives, and strategies. In turn, these sales estimates aid in developing budgets and controls to monitor performance and make mid-course corrections resulting from market, competitive, and organizational changes.

Thus, sales forecasting is an organized effort to predict the future level of sales given specific marketing strategies and particular assumptions about market conditions. You begin by examining past events and developments, as well as by making use of your present knowledge and experience to project future sales possibilities.

But merely projecting past figures into the future as if they were isolated from events is not sales forecasting. You need to combine objective, factual inputs with subjective judgment. Judgment is essential for meaningful sales forecasts. In fact, forecasts are typically generated in cycles. That is, they are made, refined, and then revised. These cycles are repeatedly run through until, in the opinion of the forecaster, the optimum combination of marketing strategy and sales results occurs.

A well-managed forecasting program will make projections in time to allow for corrective measures, not wait until developments are too advanced. Such a program can also provide you with frequent comparisons of actual-to-forecast figures so you can revise your pricing tactics during the forecast period.

No forecast should ever be allowed to go unmonitored or become outdated. Instead, it should be used as a powerful tool to develop meaningful pricing strategies for both new and established products.

SALES FORECASTING TECHNIQUES

It is advisable to use multiple approaches for arriving at estimated sales. If they all yield similar results, you can place great confidence in your figures. If, however, they diverge widely, find out why and reconcile them before a commitment is made. Using a multiple-method procedure acts as a system of checks and balances, assuring you of meaningful composite predictions.

Although various computer models are available to do sales forecasts, time and budget restrictions often bar their use. Rather, many executives rely on a set of relatively simple, quick, do-it-yourself techniques that substantially reduce the time and money required in forecasting.

There are a number of such forecasting techniques that, along with subjective judgment, add precision to sales estimates. These consist of nonmathematical forecasting techniques that are subdivided into: (1) judgmental methods, involving the opinions of various kinds of experts such as executives, salespeople, and informed outsiders, and (2) market surveys using buyer surveys and market tests.

Judgmental Methods

Judgment from the extremes

Judgment from the extremes entails asking for an expert's opinion as to whether future sales are likely to be at an extremely high or extremely low level. If the expert's reaction is that neither seems probable, the range between the extremes is successively reduced until an approximate level of expected sales is reached. Resulting in a range rather than a single figure estimate, this approach is appropriate in situations where experts feel incapable of giving one-level forecasts.

Group discussion method

The accuracy of a forecast hinges heavily on the ability of the expert(s) to produce realistic estimates. As a quick check on figures, the judgment-from-the-extremes approach proves very useful. But the forecaster often feels that a team of knowledgeable individuals should be invited to participate in forecasting. Most often, such a team meets as a committee and comes up with a group estimate through consensus. This group discussion method has the advantage of merging divergent viewpoints and moderating individual biases.

However, guard against the potential disadvantage of one or more individuals dominating the discussion. Also, be alert to superficial responses by those who lack individual responsibility for pricing and are unwilling to participate actively in the process.

Pooled individual estimates method

While the pooled individual estimates method avoids the potential pitfalls of group discussions, it also lacks the benefits of group dynamics. A project leader simply merges separately supplied estimates into a single estimate, without any interplay with or between the participants.

Delphi technique

A popular method for forecasting is the Delphi technique, which overcomes the drawbacks of both group discussion and pooled individual estimates methods. In this approach, group members are asked to submit individual estimates and assumptions. These are reviewed by the project leader, revised, and fed back to the participants for a second round. Participants also are informed of the median forecast level that emerged from the previous round.

Domination, undue conservatism, and argument are eliminated because of the written, rather than oral, procedure. And the group members benefit from one another's input. After successive rounds of estimating and feedback, the process ends when a consensus emerges.

Jury of executive opinion

The experts consulted in one or more of these methods typically are recruited from one of three pools: executives, salespeople, and informed outsiders. A jury of executive opinion is often composed of top-level personnel from various key functions such as sales, production, and finance. The major advantage is that forecasts can be arrived at quickly.

However, this advantage is easily outweighed by the disadvantage inherent in involving people in the estimating process who, in spite of their high rank, are relatively unfamiliar with the grass-roots forces that shape market success.

Composite of sales force opinion

The composite of sales force opinion approach collects product, customer, and/or territorial estimates from individual salespeople in the field. Since they are in constant contact with customers, salespeople should be in a position to predict buying plans and needs. They may even be able to take into account probable competitive activity.

Salespeople who call on relatively few industrial accounts and work very closely with them are likely to produce the best forecasts. Conversely, salespeople who call on many accounts in visits that are widely spaced will be of relatively little help in predicting sales.

Few companies simply add up their sales force's estimates to compute the sales forecast. Since sales quotas are frequently based on these estimates, a salesperson will tend to be conservative or pessimistic in estimating sales. This tendency is partially corrected by rewarding accuracy and distributing records showing the accuracy of past forecasts. Or management can allocate promotional support to a territory in line with the sales estimate (in which case it may, of course, become a self-fulfilling prophecy).

To counter the additional problem that many salespeople are unfamiliar with broad economic trends, many firms supply their salespeople with basic assumptions to guide their estimates. In spite of its drawbacks, the effort may well be worth it. For one thing, morale is likely to be higher if salespeople have had a hand in their own forecasts and quotas.

Outside experts

When it comes to outside experts, any knowledgeable source should be consulted — for example, trade associations or economists. Marketing researchers are another valuable resource, as are dealers and distributors. However, it is generally difficult to assess the degree of familiarity with industry conditions and trends of such outsiders. Thus, they should be used with caution and only in a supplementary capacity.

Market Survey

> **Key point:** Use surveys of consumer buying intentions where past trends are unlikely to continue or historical data do not exist.

Consumer surveys

The judgmental methods just described involve estimates by people who are not themselves the ultimate buyers. Some observers consider this fact a weakness and suggest getting the word directly from "the horse's mouth."

Surveys of consumer buying intentions are particularly appropriate when past trends (such as energy consumption) are unlikely to continue or historical data (as for a new product or market) do not exist. This technique works best for major consumer durables and industrial capital expenditures, since these types of buying decisions require a considerable amount of planning and lead time, and the respondents are able to predict their own behavior with reasonable accuracy.

However, where some types of consumer purchases are not planned sufficiently in advance, these estimates end up as guesses. Also, a substantial bias may be involved because interviewees might want to please the interviewer, or might give an arbitrary answer because they cannot predict their own behavior in an unfamiliar situation.

In addition to the possible drawback that prospective purchasers might be unwilling to disclose their intentions, it should be remembered that answers given refer to future, and thus hypothetical, behavior rather than actual behavior.

Test marketing

The problem of accuracy can be remedied by using the test-marketing approach whereby a new product, or a variation in the marketing mix for an established one, is introduced in a limited number of test locations. That is, the entire marketing program that is scheduled on a national basis is put into effect, but scaled down to the local level. Otherwise it is identical in every detail, including advertising, pricing, packaging, and so forth.

The new marketing effort now has to compete in a real sales environment. Purchases, if any, are actual, not hypothetical. If carefully chosen and monitored, test markets can provide a significant minipicture of the full-scale reaction to the planned change. On the basis of actual sales results in the test markets, sales forecasts are simply scaled up by appropriate factors. Table 9.2 summarizes the methods discussed.

TO SUM UP

As a nonmarketing executive, you may not be immersed in all the intensive aspects of writing the SMP. However, it is presented here in detail so that you can see how the various sections of the SMP impact virtually every function of the business. In whatever role you may have in managing a company, division, or product line, you will now be able to assess the quality and breadth of the SMP that may be submitted to you for approval — or advice.

BEST PRACTICES

Use the following checklist to zero in on viable prospects for growth. Once identified and prioritized, you can monitor the progress of your Strategic Marketing Plan based on long- and short-term marketing objectives, strategies, and tactics.

Present markets — To identify the best opportunities for expanding present markets:

- Look for feasible approaches to increase product usage among your current customers.
- Redefine market segments where there are changes in customers' buying patterns, which will further result in greater product usage.

TABLE 9.2
Comparison of Forecasting Methods

Technique Judgmental	Characteristics	Advantages	Disadvantages
Judgment from the extremes	Successive narrowing of high- low range	Range instead of single figure	Depends on individual estimating
Group discussion	Group consensus estimate	Merges divergent views, moderate biases	Domination by one individual, superficiality
Pooled and individual estimates	Averaging of individual estimates	Avoids group discussion pitfalls	Lacks group dynamics
Delphi technique	Successive written rounds of estimating with feedback from other participants	Eliminates domination, conservatism, superficial response	Lacks group dynamics
Jury of executive opinion	Top-level committee	Rapid response	Unfamiliar with market conditions
Composite of sales force opinion	Adjusted estimates from individual salespeople	Front-line expertise, Motivational tool	Bias due to impact on compensation, Unfamiliar with economic trends
Outside experts	Merging of outside opinions	No bias due to personal interests	Difficult to assess degree of expertise
Market Surveys			
Consumer surveys	Consumer interviews about buying intentions	Directly from users	Hypothetical behavior
Test marketing	Sale in limited number of locations	Actual sales results	Costly, time-consuming, Exposes strategy to competitors

- Work jointly with customers on innovative ideas to reformulate or repackage the product or service according to their specific needs.
- Identify new uses (applications) for your product.
- Reposition the product to create a more favorable perception over rival products.
- Investigate where to expand into new or unserved market niches.
- Give maximum attention to every conceivable opportunity to displace competition; this is a particularly significant action in flat, no-growth markets.

Customers — To identify the best opportunities for expanding your customer base:

- Improve or expand communications everywhere in your distribution channel, as well as with those connected within your supply chain.
- Enrich your market communications, including the Internet, advertising, sales promotion, and publicity.
- Deploy the sales force to target new customers with high potential.
- Enhance customer service, including technical service and complaint handling.

- Identify changes in trade buying practices, where the buying power may have shifted from manufacturer to distributor or to the end user.

Growth markets — To identify the major growth markets:

- Target key geographic locations, specifying which markets or user groups represent the greatest long-term potential.
- Investigate emerging businesses and pinpoint new users for your product.

New product development — To prioritize new product and service projects that will impact on immediate as well as long-range opportunities:

- Focus on differentiating any new product that has the potential for an extended life cycle.
- Search for ways to diversify into new or related products, product lines, and/or new items or features — providing they match the intent of your SMP's strategic direction and the content of the business portfolio.
- Examine techniques to modify products by customer groups, distribution outlets, or individual customer applications.
- Work on improving packaging to conform to customers' specifications and to distinguish your product from its rivals.
- Establish new value-added services.

Targets of Opportunity — To focus on any areas outside your current market segment or product line not included in the other categories:

- Be innovative and entrepreneurial in your thinking.
- Be somewhat prudent, and determine how far your company can realistically diversify from its core business and still retain its vitality.

TABLE 9.3
Strength/Weakness Analysis

Part I: Surveying Your Firm's Market Environment

Consumers
1. Who are our end-use buyers?
2. Who or what influences them in their buying decisions?
3. What are our consumers' demographic and psychographic profiles?
4. How do prospective buyers perceive our product?
5. Are our consumers' cultural attitudes, values, or habits changing?

Customers
6. Who are our customers, e.g., distributors, wholesalers, retailers?
7. Who or what influences their buying decisions?
8. What are their sizes and what percentage of our total revenue does each group represent?

9. How much support do they give our product?
10. How can we motivate them to work harder for us?
11. Do we need them?
12. Would we be better off setting up our own distribution system?

Competitors

13. Who are our competitors?
14. Where are they located?
15. What is their size and product mix?
16. Is their participation in this field growing or declining?
17. What new domestic and international competitors may be on the horizon?
18. Which competitive strategies and tactics appear particularly successful or unsuccessful?

Other Relevant Environmental Components

19. What are the legal constraints affecting our marketing effort?
20. To what extent does government regulation restrict our flexibility in making marketing decisions?
21. What threats or opportunities does technological progress hold in store for us?
22. What broad cultural shifts are occurring that may affect our business?
23. What consequences will demographic and geographic shifts have for our business?

Part II: Surveying Management Procedures and Policies

24. Do we conduct regular, systematic market analyses?
25. Do we subscribe to any regular market data service?
26. Do we test and retest carefully before we introduce a new product?

Planning

27. How carefully do we examine and how aggressively do we cope with opportunities and threats to our business?
28. Do we develop clearly stated and prioritized short-term and long-term marketing objectives?
29. Are our marketing objectives achievable and measurable?
30. Do we have a formalized strategic marketing plan procedure?
31. What are our core strategies for achieving our marketing objectives?
32. How effectively are we segmenting our target market?
33. Are we allocating sufficient resources to take advantage of e-commerce breakthroughs?
34. How well do we tie in our SMP with the other functional plans of our organization?

Implementation and Control

35. Do we continuously monitor our environment to determine the adequacy of our plan?
36. Do we compare planned and actual figures periodically and take appropriate measures if they differ significantly?
37. Do we systematically study the contribution and effectiveness of various marketing and nonmarketing activities?

Organization

38. Is there a need for more training, incentives, supervision, or evaluation?
39. Are our marketing responsibilities structured to best serve the needs of different marketing activities, products, target markets, and sales territories?
40. Does our entire organization embrace and practice the marketing concept?

Part III: Surveying Strategy Aspects of the Marketing Mix

Product Policy

41. What is the makeup of our product mix and how well are its components selling?

42. Do we carefully evaluate any negative ripple effects on the remaining product mix before we make a decision to phase out a product?
43. Have we considered modification, repositioning, and/or extension of sagging products?
44. What additions, if any, should be made to our product mix?
45. Which products are we best equipped to make ourselves and which items should we buy and resell under our own name?

Pricing
46. To what degree are our prices based on cost, demand, and/or competitive considerations?
47. Do we use temporary price promotions and, if so, how effective are they?
48. How do our wholesale or retail margins and discounts compare with those of the competition?

Promotion
49. Do we state our advertising objectives clearly?
50. How is the Internet integrated into our promotion strategy?
51. Are our advertising themes effective?
52. Do we make aggressive use of sales promotion techniques?

Personal Selling and Distribution
53. Is our sales force the right size to accomplish our marketing objectives?
54. What is the role of the sales force in an e-commerce environment?
55. Is it adequately trained and motivated, and characterized by high morale, ability, and effectiveness?
56. Are we taking advantages of opportunities in supply chain management for streamlining our distribution network?
57. Is our customer service up to par?

10 Wrap-Up

> **Key point:** The prudent application of technology blended with sound strategy principles makes for marketing success.

INTRODUCTION

The much-touted new economy is now clearly a reality. As a nonmarketing executive or business owner, it is quite likely you are involved to a greater or lesser extent in deciding how your organization or group can develop a workable business strategy for an Internet technology-driven economy.

As the old- and new-economy companies maneuver with innovative applications for e-business and e-commerce, no one knows for sure what precise model will work and will profit. One outcome appears to be consistent among those companies that are prospering: the time-tested principles, concepts, and techniques of marketing that have evolved over the last four decades, known as the period of modern marketing, can serve you well as the groundwork for devising business-building strategies. While the scrappy dot-com companies appear on the scene with tremendous rapidity, the stalwart old-economy companies are not backing down. They are changing swiftly to survive, fight back, and grow.

They are finding that the Internet in and of itself is not the primary answer to prosperity. Rather, it is the judicious application of technology blended with sound strategy principles that makes for success. This is evidenced by the rapid rise and fall of those dot-com start-ups that didn't put into place the planning systems to analyze customers' needs and problems. In many situations, they didn't examine the structure and inner workings of the industry they targeted; nor did they reckon with the impact of varied customer buying behavior and ethnic diversity; nor did they set up contingency plans to restrain the driving power of aggressive competition through well-developed marketing strategies and tactics.

Exactly what are the sound strategy principles and how do they compare with the so-called current business practices? And what are the similarities of the marketing techniques that have evolved in marketing practice over the past 40 years (many of which are covered in this book) with the so-called new wave approaches? Consider the following:

- The current emphasis on customer-relationship management is in fact anchored to the most fundamental marketing concept of maintaining a customer-driven orientation. This singular point is the foundation of market-ing theory that has evolved over the past four decades — and certainly one that has existed in various formats, verbiage, and slogans since the dawn of commerce.

• Segmentation, targeting, and positioning are firmly established concepts within the marketing lexicon and have been practiced by savvy marketers for decades — and historically for centuries, as well.

• And consider communications within the organization. Insightful execu-tives continue to organize and reorganize to adapt to speed of communi-cations. While the downsizing of organizations so prevalent in the 1980s and 1990s was used as an opportunistic approach to cut cost, the optimum benefit resulted in streamlining heavily layered operations and speeding communications from senior management to those in the field. Internet and related technologies enhance those communications capabilities.

• As for markets, the traditional demographic, geographic, and psycho-graphic (behavioral) classifications for understanding the nature of mar-kets are now supplemented by still another category: the fertile contributions of cultural anthropology that result in adding greater preci-sion to market selection. With the explosive growth of Web markets (per-haps, an electronic portrayal of marketplaces in days of yore), the methods for profiling the characteristics of markets still work by using those time-tested marketing principles cited in this book, particularly in Chapter 2, The World of Markets.

• Lastly, let's look at the rules of strategy.

RULES OF STRATEGY

> **Key point:** The strategy principles derived from 2000 years of recorded military history still survive as the foundation maxims of business and marketing strategy.

Strategy, as defined in this book, is action to achieve objectives. The term is com-monly used in practically every facet of business. Yet its roots are not in business at all. The word comes from the Greek *Strategia* or *Strategos*, meaning to lead an army or generalship. The unrivaled principles derived from 2000 years of recorded mili-tary history still survive as the foundation maxims of business and marketing strat-egy. They are synthesized into five propositions, expounded in Chapter 3, that are inextricably woven into virtually all marketing methods, namely:

1. *Speed.* Swift implementation is as essential to the success of a marketing campaign as it is to the military. Extended deliberation, procrastination, cumbersome committees, and long chains of command from home office to regional sales office are all detriments to success. The gaps of time cre-ated through lack of action give competitors a greater chance to react and blunt your efforts. Today's dazzling communication technologies associ-

ated with e-business and e-commerce and the assorted palm-size gadgetry permit the activation of this principle.

2. *Indirect approach.* The purpose of the indirect approach is to avoid a direct frontal confrontation with competitors. Instead the object is to concentrate in those markets that promise long-term growth. The intent is to use a competitive advantage built around product, price, promotion, and distribution — known as the marketing mix that is so deep-rooted in marketing practice.

3. *Concentration.* This classic principle derived from the military has two uses in business terms. First, it means deploying human and financial assets toward a market without draining valuable company resources. Concentration translates to targeting and segmenting markets to maximize the impact of your resources. Second, concentration means focusing your strengths against the weaknesses of your competitor.

4. *Alternative objectives.* By designing a number of alternative objectives, any of which can be used depending on the circumstances, you hold viable options for achieving one objective when others fail. And, most importantly, alternative objectives keep your competitors in an untenable situation as they attempt to detect your real intentions. By displaying a number of possible threats, you force a competing manager to spread his/her resources and attention to match your action.

5. *Unbalancing competition.* One of the central aims of strategy is to reduce the level of competitive resistance against your movements by creating situations that unbalance the competition. You create an unbalancing effect on the opposing manager through speed, indirect approach, concentration, and alternative objectives.

There is a final procedure that you should initiate to round out your commitment to develop — and, most importantly, monitor — a market-driven organization: Benchmarking.

BENCHMARKING FOR SUCCESS

> **Key point:** Benchmarking consists of systematic and continuous assessments that compare and measure a firm's business processes against those of business leaders anywhere in the world.

Implicit in previous chapters is the exceptional value of ongoing market research and competitor intelligence as vital cornerstones in the development of your market and product strategies. Yet, there is still one more procedure needed to assure your success: establishing a procedure for continuous tracking by benchmarking. Still fairly new to many organizations, benchmarking consists of systematic and continuous assessments that compare and measure a firm's business processes against those of business leaders anywhere in the world.

One key outcome of benchmarking is information that would permit you to re-examine your operations, reassess traditional methods, and learn how and why some companies perform with greater success than do others inside and outside their industries. Such information helps initiate actions to improve performance in areas critical to success.

Conducting a competitive benchmarking study provides the following benefits for a business group or product line:

- Improves your understanding of customer needs and sensitizes you to the underlying dynamics operating within your industry.
- Helps document why other organizations can perform similar processes at a higher performance level than at your organization.
- Creates a sense of urgency to develop long-term improvement and performance objectives.
- Encourages a spirit of competitiveness as managers at all levels recognize that performance levels in best-in-class organizations may exceed their own perceptions of what constitutes exceptional performance.
- Motivates individuals to strive to new heights of innovative thinking and achievement.

Xerox Corporation is an outstanding example of successful benchmarking. Hit hard during the early 1980s by intense Japanese competitors, it made a successful turnaround and regained substantial market share. Many factors contributed to the about-face. Among them was a process of using 12 success factors for conducting a competitive benchmarking study. Table 10.1 outlines those factors, which are broad enough to apply to most organizations.

TABLE 10.1
Competitive Benchmarking Actions

Planning	Analysis	Implementation
1. Identify benchmark outputs	4. Determine current competitive "gap"	7. Establish functional goals
2. Identify best competitor		8. Implement specific actions
3. Determine data collection method	5. Project future performance levels	9. Monitor results and report progress
	6. Develop functional action plans	10. Recalibrate benchmarks
		11. Obtain leadership position
		12. Integrate processes fully in business practice

Benchmarking is not a stand-alone activity. Objectives, statistical quality control, and total quality management intrinsically link to the hallmarks of solid management practice. In turn, this linkage translates into three pragmatic guidelines essential in any competitive encounter:

- Develop quality beyond that of competitors.
- Harness technology before competitors.
- Keep costs below those of competitors.

Benchmarking seeks to transform those guidelines into a set of procedures leading to customer satisfaction. In turn, they serve as the strategies to capture and maintain market share.

How do you get started? Implementing benchmarking requires three basic ingredients: (1) a supportive management group, (2) access to prospective benchmarking partners who have previously addressed a competitive problem you are facing, and (3) a benchmarking team with the ability to use reliable research practices to investigate the root cause of your problem.

Keep in mind, however, that the benchmarking process is more than just conducting a competitive analysis — a practice that has been emphasized throughout this book. Rather, benchmarking aims to assist an organization such as yours in achieving market leadership and improving overall performance. If benchmarking is already underway in your group, the next step is to further refine measurements that result in a deeper understanding of competitors' cultures, attitudes, and business practices.

A FINAL WORD

As a nonmarketing manager or business owner functioning in a 21st-century business, the dominant principle is that the more you know about marketing practices and the better you understand how to apply their techniques within the framework of the Internet Age, the greater your chance for success.

This new era promises to be an exciting and exhilarating time for commerce, even with its pitfalls and uncertainties. While pursuing its remarkable opportunities, you can lessen the interminable risks by adhering to the marketing principles that have survived in the old-economy, brick-and-mortar companies and still seem to be working for those budding new-economy organizations that are making it.

Good luck and good marketing.

Index

A

Administrative cost, 180
Adopter groups, 138
Adoption, 135, 136, 137
Advertising, 167
  campaign development, 171
  decisions, 172
  print, 159
  spending, 173
  support, 105
  techniques, 170
Affordable method, of advertising spending, 173
After-sales service, 107, 156
AIDS, anxiety about, 128
Alta Vista, 183
Amazon.com, 3, 57, 66, 67, 147, 161
America Online Inc., 140, 161
A&P, 166
Arthur D. Little, Inc., 35, 39
A. Schulman Inc., 97
Abbott Laboratories, 59
AT&T, 26, 68
Aucnet, 181
Automated radioimmunoassay, 41
Awareness, 136

B

Baldor Electric Co., 133
Bank of America, 169
BASF, 97
B2C approach, *see* Business-to-consumer
    approach
BCG, *see* Boston Consulting Group
Behavioral purchase patterns, 50
Behavior model, 132
Bell Atlantic-Vodafone, 4
Benchmarking, 217–219
  actions, competitive, 218
  performance, 95
  team, 219
Bertelsmann-American Online, 4
Blood collection system products, 41
BMT, *see* Business Management Team

Body language, 34, 76
Book-of-the-Month Club, 57
Booz Allen & Hamilton, 93
Borders, Louis H., 66
Boreham, Roland, 133
Boston Consulting Group (BCG), 35, 36, 37, 122
BP Amoco, 4
Brand
  names, on-line, 161
  personality, 174
  -recognition surveys, 161
Braun appliances, 60
Business
  analysis, 93
  Management Team (BMT), 12, 13
  model
    pull, 120
    push, 119
  partners, information technology and, 1
  portfolio, 198
  practice, key to successful, 54
  strength, 38, 39
Business-to-business demands, 13
Business-to-consumer (B2C) approach, 51
Buyer behavior, 25
Buying
  behavior, changing, 188
  patterns, 160

C

California State Auto Association, 124
CarParts.com, 59
CarPoint Web site, Microsoft, 120
Cash cows, 36
Catalogs, on-line, 145
Caterpillar Inc., 14
CDnow Inc., 124
Cell phones, Net-ready, 152
Chain of command, 56
Chambers, John T., 2
Channel control, 153
Charles Schwab & Co., 3
Chinese population, San Francisco, 33
Chrysler Corporation, 166